Praise for *Lead Like Ike*

"Novel, intriguing—and more importantly—a highly-instructive approach to enabling us to truly grasp fundamental management principles. In the person of Dwight Eisenhower planning and executing the D-Day landings and the subsequent liberation of Europe, these basic concepts are vividly brought to life. As Loftus rightly observes, no CEO ever faced a more daunting, pressure-filled, obstacle-laden mission than did Ike. Perfect reading for these turbulent times."

— STEVE FORBES,
Chairman & CEO, Forbes Media

"Geoff Loftus has written an intriguing, and highly useful book on Dwight Eisenhower's extraordinary ability as a leader. If you liked Ike before, you'll like him even more now. And you'll be grateful to Geoff Loftus."

— CHRISTOPHER BUCKLEY,
author of *Boomsday* and
Thank You for Smoking

"In *Lead Like Ike*, Geoff Loftus provides keen insights on management lessons that can be drawn from one of the greatest battlefields in military history. The lessons may appear simple, but it's the simplest management principles that we often forget. Listen to your people. Set your vision. Be consistent about your message. Let your managers manage."

— SALVATORE J. VITALE,
Senior Vice President,
The Conference Board

LEAD LIKE IKE

LEAD LIKE IKE

Ten Business Strategies
from the CEO of D-Day

GEOFF LOFTUS

THOMAS NELSON
Since 1798

NASHVILLE   DALLAS   MEXICO CITY   RIO DE JANEIRO

Published in Nashville, Tennessee, by Thomas Nelson. Thomas Nelson is a registered trademark of Thomas Nelson, Inc.

Thomas Nelson, Inc., titles may be purchased in bulk for educational, business, fund-raising, or sales promotional use. For information, please e-mail SpecialMarkets@ThomasNelson.com.

Library of Congress Cataloging-in-Publication Data

Loftus, Geoff, 1954–
    Lead like Ike : ten business strategies from the CEO of D-Day / Geoff Loftus.
        p. cm.
    ISBN 978-1-59555-085-9
    1. Strategic planning. 2. Business planning. 3. Industrial management.
    4. Competition. 5. Strategic planning—Case studies. I. Title.
    HD30.28.L634 2010
    658.4'012—dc22   2010004815

Printed in the United States of America

10 11 12 13 14 WC 5 4 3 2 1

To Dwight D. Eisenhower and the men and women of D-Day

for saving the world from horror and insanity.

And to Margy and Greg

for making everything worthwhile.

CONTENTS

Good Luck! And let us all beseech the blessing of Almighty God upon this great and noble undertaking.

— Dwight D. Eisenhower
Order of the Day:
June 6, 1944—D-Day

The most difficult and complicated operation ever to take place.

— Winston S. Churchill

The history of warfare knows no other like undertaking from the point of view of its scale, its vast conception, and its masterly execution. . . . History will record this deed as an achievement of the highest order.

— Josef Stalin

Nothing like it had ever been seen before, or would again.

— Stephen E. Ambrose
Eisenhower: Soldier and President

INTRODUCTION

The World's Most Daunting Business Initiative

In the early hours of the morning of June 5, 1944, more than 150,000 men in more than 5,000 ships and 11,000 airplanes waited. Around the world, the president of the United States, Franklin D. Roosevelt; the prime minister of the United Kingdom, Winston Churchill; and the absolute leader of the Soviet Union, Josef Stalin, also waited. In Berlin, Adolf Hitler watched and wondered; and along the northern shores of France, the German army was ready with miles of barbed wire, machine-gun nests, and artillery emplacements. The occupied nations of Europe and millions of Jews imprisoned in death camps waited, desperately hoping.

The fate of the world hinged on the decision of one man—living in a small trailer, drinking too much coffee, smoking too many cigarettes, sleeping too little.

He had already decided to postpone the project, called Operation Overlord, from May to June. Only twenty-four hours earlier, he had decided to postpone again, for a day. And he had already decided that it was necessary to send some of his very best young men into what one of his commanders described as "futile slaughter."

Now, at about 4:00 a.m. local time in England, surrounded by his senior commanders of the American and British armies, navies, and air forces, Dwight D. "Ike" Eisenhower had to make one last decision. Gamble on the weather and the English Channel tides and hurl those thousands of young men at the Germans on the far side of the Normandy beaches. Or delay again—forcing a wait of two weeks for the next operational window, condemning the victims of Nazi tyranny to more oppression and slaughter, and postponing the eventual defeat of Adolf Hitler.

Eisenhower expressed his decision quietly and clearly. "Okay, let's go."

With those three words, Eisenhower set into motion what author Cornelius Ryan called "The Longest Day." Ike's staff moved into action immediately, and Eisenhower visited some of the troops who would be leaving for France within a matter of hours.

He met with the press and casually announced that the invasion was on—confident the press was on his side and would not leak the news until given the okay. After talking with the reporters, Eisenhower performed an astounding feat of leadership in the face of extraordinary stress: he wrote the following "just in case" press release *before* the troops had landed, *before* the results were known:

> Our landings . . . have failed to gain a satisfactory foothold and I have withdrawn the troops. . . . The troops, the air and the Navy did all that Bravery and devotion to duty could do. If any blame or fault attaches to the attempt it is mine alone.[1]

"It is mine alone." That's leadership. On June 5, Eisenhower stared into the abyss of complete catastrophe and did not blink.

His career as D-Day's CEO has much to teach us.

★ ★ ★

Decades after that cataclysmic D-Day, it is easy to take Operation Overload's success for granted. We know the Allied forces were able to gain a beachhead and eventually push their way through France, over the Rhine, and into Germany itself. We know that Hitler, faced by his own moment of defeat, was incapable of taking responsibility and instead escaped through suicide. But on June 5, 1944, those events were still in the future, the results of Overlord were unknown.

As I write this, in the midst of the "Great Recession," we live in a different world. While we are not engaged in a world war, the global economy is, to put it mildly, a mess. Everywhere you look, top management is operating under the most extreme pressure. Corporations' stock values have been shredded, balance sheets seem to come only in the color red, it seems to have been forever since the credit markets functioned properly, and jobs are disappearing at the fastest rate in decades. Again and again, economists, businesspeople, politicians, and the average American all say the only time in our history that was worse was during the Great Depression. And many people think that even after the current recession finally ends, we will find ourselves mired in an economic environment radically different from the prerecession economy. It will be a long time before the future looks bright again.

Why write a book treating General Dwight D. Eisenhower as a CEO? How is that supposed to help Corporate America's executives do their jobs? Eisenhower's record is unique. Eisenhower was the chief executive of the organization that pulled off the most daunting "business" project in history: Operation Overlord, the Allied invasion of Normandy on June 6, 1944. He was the chief executive of the company that operated under the greatest pressure any executive has ever seen. *Ever*.

Overlord required years of strategic and tactical planning. The manufacturing and inventory of the necessary supplies consumed the majority of Corporate America's industrial capacity. The supply chain stretched across an ocean. The workforce was multinational, trained in many countries and several languages, transported to England, where training continued, then transported to work in its destination market.

Like any well-run company, Ike's had a mission statement: force the unconditional surrender of its competitor, Nazi Germany. Eisenhower's success wasn't measured by achieving a certain predefined portion of market share—it was defined by seizing complete control of the market and eliminating the competition. The first phase of that mission involved the successful penetration of the competitor's territory. The second phase meant that Ike had to stretch the supply chain even farther, build or acquire local infrastructure, and increase the workforce on the ground. Continued strategic and tactical planning were necessities, along with the ability to improvise when conditions suddenly shifted.

All of this planning, training, and execution of plans had to occur in the toughest competitive environment on earth—not a battle of market share and bottom lines but a battle for human lives. Talk about "skin in the game"!

★ ★ ★

Lead Like Ike takes the military-metaphor-for-business model a large step forward and analyzes military operations as business operations, and the commanding general as CEO.

It examines Eisenhower's relationship with

- his *board of directors* (Franklin D. Roosevelt, Winston Churchill, Josef Stalin, and the chiefs of staff of the American and British armies and navies),
- his *C-level staff* (the senior commanders, like Generals Omar Bradley and George Patton and Field Marshal Bernard "Monty" Montgomery),
- *affiliated organizations* (the Free French and Polish forces in exile in England), and
- *stakeholders* (the soldiers, sailors, and airmen of the Allied forces in Europe; the citizens and taxpayers of the United States and Great Britain; and the millions of victims of Hitler's insanity).

Lead Like Ike draws analogies to contemporary business enter-prises and delineates the strategic lessons we can learn from Ike. *Strategy* comes from the Greek word *stratēgia*, meaning "generalship" and is defined in Merriam-Webster as "the science and art of military command exercised to meet the enemy in combat under advanta-geous conditions." Secondary definitions include "a careful plan or method; the art of devising or employing plans toward a goal." The primary definition sounds very high level and potentially long-term—the kind of "science and art" that is exercised at a lofty executive level. The secondary definitions—a careful plan or method; the devising or employing of plans toward a goal—seem closer to frontline manag-ers, the folks who actually make things happen. In fact, strategy in this sense seems awfully close to the word *tactics*.

Tactics, again as defined by Merriam-Webster, is originally derived from the Greek word *tassein*, meaning "to arrange, to place in battle formation." The definitions are: "the science and art of disposing and maneuvering forces in combat; the art or skill of employing available means to accomplish an end; a system or mode of procedure." Strategy's "employing a plan toward a goal" is almost the same as tactics' "employ-ing available means to accomplish an end."

The paragraphs above aren't just a semantic exercise for my personal amusement, although I find the blurry overlap of the defi-nitions pretty interesting. The real point is that defining the word *strategy* can be a dicey affair. So can defining *organizational* strategy. And once a company has a strategy in place, implementing it can be even tougher.

Fortunately, Eisenhower's career as D-Day's CEO provides an encyclopedic case study for designing and implementing organiza-tional strategies. *Lead Like Ike* is that case study, with ten strategic lessons:

1. *Determine Your Mission.* This is the ultimate goal of your
   organization—the purpose, the very reason it exists.

2. *Plan for Success*. How you are going to achieve your mission. High-level, overarching planning.

3. *Stay Focused*. Know and get what you need to succeed at your mission. Don't wander into interesting but non–mission-critical territory.

4. *Prioritize*. Do what you need to do for the success of your mission. Nothing else, no matter how productive, matters and will waste your resources.

5. *Plan to Implement*. Train your people, equip your people, and arrange your support logistics.

6. *Communicate*. To your people and to your markets. If you can't communicate, you can't implement.

7. *Motivate Your People*. This is where leadership comes into play—getting your people to commit to your organization's mission as completely as you do. You need to model the behavior you want and expect from your executives and frontline workforce.

8. *Manage Your People*. Discovering and developing talent, rewarding your solid performers, and handling the prima donnas. (Unfortunately, everyone has prima donnas.)

9. *Avoid Project Creep*. Closely connected to staying focused and prioritizing. Project Creep is insidious. During an operation, things develop that relate closely to the mission, so closely that you can easily confuse them with mission necessities.

10. *Be Honest*. With yourself, with your bosses, executive team, employees, shareholders, and the markets at large. It's one of the oldest and most exhausted of clichés but true nonetheless: honesty is the best policy.

We'll analyze these strategic lessons in a summary chapter at the end of the book. Don't worry; you won't be quizzed on the material.

At least not by me. I can't make any promises concerning the business environment and how it will test you.

★ ★ ★

By analyzing Eisenhower's D-Day strategy and tactics from a business perspective, we in no way mean to diminish the sacrifice of the men and women who were part of that titanic effort. In this book we are simply focusing on Ike's extraordinary management of a gigantic organization operating at the absolute extreme. We honor the supreme sacrifices of each person who fought and supported the mission during World War II.

They gave their all and saved the world.

ONE

THE PRESSURE COOKER— START-UP

Forging a New Business to Face Staggering Competition

Let's start with a hypothetical case. Your company, Hypothetical Inc., has been plugging along in the good ole U.S.A. for decades. Most of your shareholders have been holding their stock quietly for years and seem to be perfectly content with the steady, if small, dividends. Since you have no substantial domestic competition, all is bliss—until a fearsome competitor looms over the Atlantic from Europe. A German-based company has emerged with global designs, a super-aggressive business plan, and almost complete control of the European market. This German company hasn't jumped the ocean yet to go after your market, but it's pretty clear it will as soon as it has consolidated its gains in Europe. Remember, the German company has global ambitions.

Hypothetical Inc.'s board of directors decides that the only way to counter the German company's plans is to form an alliance with companies in Britain and Russia and create a jointly owned subsidiary, based in England, to compete directly with the Germans for control of the European market. Hypothetical's board names you as the CEO of this subsidiary and sends you to London with these goals:

1

- Build an organization from scratch that will compete
  successfully with the extremely successful German
  company that has almost absolute control of its market.
- Create a management structure for your brand-new
  organization.
- Oversee the hiring and training of a massive multicultural
  and multilingual workforce—eventually numbering more
  than three million.
- Do all of the above in twelve months—if it takes longer,
  Hypothetical Inc. may not survive.

This is a daunting set of challenges, but you head off to England fully committed to delivering on them because you, like your board, are absolutely convinced that the very survival of your company is dependent on your success. Urgent as these problems are, they are not the worst aspects of your job as CEO. If you succeed in building this subsidiary in the severely limited time frame, you will be rewarded with a demotion. Before leaving the United States, it was made clear to you that a star executive from the parent company in the United States will replace you once the organization is ready. He will lead the effort against the German company—he will reap the fame and glory.

The prospect of getting to watch someone else succeed—thanks to all your hard work under extreme pressure—is not the worst of your problems. Your competition is incredibly well organized, is highly innovative, and has years of successful experience in executing its often daring strategies. And formidable as your competition is, your board of directors is a collection of overpowering personalities, is in complete disagreement about strategy, and has not empowered you to decide where and how to implement Hypothetical's plan of direct competition with the Germans.

If you are a normal human being, at this point in your career as CEO of Hypothetical's European subsidiary, you are well on your way to an ulcer or a drinking problem. Remember, you believe (as does your board) that if you fail, Hypothetical will go out of business. The value of company stock will disappear, devastating your large body of shareholders. There will be massive job losses, not only for your employees but also for those of your alliance partners in England and Russia. The ripple effect in the economies of your country and your alliance partners could be disastrous. No wonder that, as you head to London to take your post as the European subsidiary's CEO, you are feeling more than a little anxiety.

This hypothetical case more or less describes what Dwight D. Eisenhower faced as he became the CEO of an organization that, for simplicity's sake, we'll call D-Day Inc. No executive in history has ever had more skin in the game than Eisenhower.

If he failed in planning and building D-Day Inc., the failure would not be measured in devalued stock and unemployment. Failure would result in hundreds of thousands, possibly millions, of deaths.

★ ★ ★

On June 24, 1942, Dwight D. Eisenhower, CEO of D-Day Inc., arrived in England to start his new job.

It's hard to imagine any executive taking over a company with more pressure. His assignment was much more of a concept than an operational reality, but that didn't stop Ike's board from giving him a twelve-month deadline for launching the most ambitious business project ever: the cross-Channel invasion of the competition's territory. No organization had ever attempted such a large-scale project. No organization had ever faced tougher competition. The Germans had complete control of their European territory, short supply lines, and a robust industrial base supplying their operations. They had a large, well-trained, well-equipped, experienced workforce already in the field.

Ike also had to forge success despite amazingly low expectations for his personal success. A few months shy of his fifty-second birthday, when he became CEO for the first time, his entire thirty-year career with his company (the U.S. Army) had been spent in middle management. As you might expect from a career middle manager, Ike was seen as the perfect staff man—not true top-executive material—despite decades of experience and rave reviews from all of his superiors.

Now that he had reached the top spot, he was expected to build the organization and then hand over the job to the organization's next CEO—someone higher up in the parent company—who would take over D-Day Inc. once it was ready to launch operations. Someone more suited to the glories of successfully completing the most daunting business project ever.

Eisenhower was aware of all this and went into the job knowing that the accolades would go to someone else. He didn't care. His focus—his only focus—was to build an organization capable of penetrating the competition's territory and then taking every bit of it away, to free Europe from the clutches of the Germans. This invasion came to be known as Operation Overlord. After Overlord, D-Day Inc. would push through France, Belgium, and Holland into Germany itself.[*]

D-Day Inc.'s board, however, wasn't unanimous about the best path to success. Some of the Brits, including Winston Churchill (who, from Ike's viewpoint, functioned as the lead director of the board), thought going into northern France was the wrong way to compete with the Germans. Churchill didn't completely buy into Operation Overlord until the final weeks before D-Day. Many of the senior British commanders agreed with Churchill. They felt that a gigantic cross-Channel project was out of the question. Better to launch smaller projects as soon as D-Day Inc.'s workforce could handle them. These smaller projects would be followed up cautiously, and Germany would be beaten through a course of slow and steady progress. Eisenhower,

---

[*] There were smaller projects—D-Days for the invasions of North Africa, Sicily, and Italy—in advance of the French invasion, but all were part of the organization's buildup to the final D-Day. That's why, instead of worrying about the military's terminology and organizational names, we'll call Eisenhower's organization D-Day Inc.

however, felt that doing smaller projects was a distraction and would delay the organization's completion of its true mission—seizing Europe from the Germans, which was only doable, in Ike's mind, by going through northern France.

PLAN FOR SUCCESS

- **Attack the competition's core**. Maybe it's possible to nibble your competition to death. But if you compete with them straight up, delivering better value, you'll win bigger.

The Germans, Ike reasoned, could afford to lose territory in North Africa or Italy or even in southern France. He considered Churchill's oft-mentioned plans of going through the Balkans to be a waste of time. Ike and the Americans on his board of directors believed that if you want to take down the competition, you have to attack the core of the business, not take out satellite operations that are not essential to the competition's survival. That meant D-Day Inc. had to go through northern France—the shortest route—into the industrial heartland of its German competitor.

When Eisenhower arrived to take charge of D-Day Inc., his board had given him a mixed set of directions. Prepare to go through northern France in a year (1943), but also get ready to launch a suicide initiative almost immediately (September 1942). Why the suicide project? FDR, Churchill, and the senior American and British commanders had one overriding fear: their alliance with the Soviet Union would collapse at any moment.

Since June 1941, only the Soviets had been competing directly with the Germans for territory in Europe. A massive share of America's industrial output, and that of Britain's as well, was going to support the Soviet effort. Everyone at D-Day Inc., from FDR on down, believed the Germans would get stronger if the Russians ceased to compete—and the Americans and Brits were aware the Russians had signed a noncompete agreement with the Germans before the war (the Molotov-Ribbentrop Pact in August 1939) and that at the rate the Soviets were suffering now, if the Germans offered a new noncompete agreement, there was a high likelihood of Soviet acceptance.

This fear of a Soviet collapse is what drove the creation of the suicide project, delicately named Operation Sledgehammer. If the Soviets suffered too many setbacks between Eisenhower's arrival in England in June and September, Ike was supposed to launch Sledgehammer to divert pressure from the Soviets and keep their massive workforce in direct competition with the Germans.

The only problem with Sledgehammer was that almost no one believed in it. It was almost impossible that Ike could launch anything three months after taking the CEO's job. The Americans and Brits didn't have sufficient resources—in personnel or supplies. Even if Sledgehammer was launched, there was no guarantee the Soviets wouldn't sign a noncompete anyway. And Sledgehammer, if activated, would cause unforeseeable delay in the main mission—the invasion of France.

Like many executives, Eisenhower found himself saddled with a directive that he had to accept and at least create a semblance of complying with. His only hope was that the competitive situation in Europe would never reach the point that it required him to launch Sledgehammer. (It didn't.)

STAY FOCUSED

- **Fight distractions**. In other words, avoid "mission creep" like the plague. It's just as deadly as the dreaded disease, even when it's forced on you by senior management or your board.

MANAGE YOUR PEOPLE (BOTH UP AND DOWN)

- **Give in gracefully**. If it becomes apparent that mission creep is unavoidable, give in. You may get lucky and factors outside your control may keep you on track—as they did for Ike with Sledgehammer. (Making sacrifices to pagan gods might not be a bad idea . . .)

Eisenhower arrived in England in late June 1942 with his mixed set of directives (go into France, but get ready to launch Sledgehammer too!); without the actual, in-place resources to accomplish his mission; and with an aggressively ambitious timeline for launching the project.

On his first day on the job, Ike set the tone he wanted for the organization. He met with the American staff he was inheriting and immediately stated their mission: build D-Day Inc. to be ready to go into France in a year's time.

MOTIVATE YOUR PEOPLE

- **Start the way you mean to finish**. If you believe that optimism and enthusiasm are necessary to achieve success—you need to model those attitudes, constantly and consistently.

BE HONEST

- **Take responsibility**. You help no one by shoving problems off to others. And there is absolutely no better way to push for success than taking on responsibility.

He explained to his fellow Americans that they had to present an attitude of "determined enthusiasm and optimism."[1] Ike made it clear that pessimism was out—any officer who couldn't handle the challenges without talking of defeat should leave. Ike also changed a fundamental way of doing business. From that moment on, the staff would take complete responsibility for solving its own problems instead of referring them to Washington. As he reported to his boss, General George C. Marshall, "No alibis or excuses will be acceptable."[2]

As a young officer, Eisenhower had spent a great deal of time coaching football teams on army posts, and he emphasized the most important lesson of his football experience once he became the top executive: team first. He wanted a coordinated effort, not dazzling solo performances. In his experience, successful teams were the ones who pulled together with the players selflessly supporting each other. Stars and prima donnas were often successful through sheer brilliance, but brilliant performances are about as predictable, and as dependable, as the weather.

Despite his clarity on the themes of optimism and team first, Ike found that the staff in London was not particularly adaptive. The staff members were entrenched middle management—they heard what Eisenhower said, but like lots of middle managers who have survived a change in executive management, they were not particularly impressed. And Eisenhower—perceived by everyone (including himself) as an interim executive in charge of setting up the project and then handing it over to the "real" boss—didn't have the pull to fire and hire the people he wanted. He couldn't build the staff he needed. When officers left or were added to his staff, it was due to the normal course of rotation within the organization. Personnel decisions were being made for Ike thousands of miles away in Washington.

Historian and biographer Stephen Ambrose wrote, "Eisenhower forcibly impressed his presence on the staff," but Ike wasn't sure that wasn't part of the problem, saying, "Too many staff officers are merely pushing paper"[3] and were coming to him for decisions. Eisenhower couldn't get the staff to stop pushing paper and decisions toward him, but he could take steps to make sure that his time was spent focused on the invasion project. He dumped almost all of the administration duties onto the extremely able Major General John C. H. Lee and freed himself to focus on strategy. There would be plenty of tiny details Ike needed to consider as he strived to meet his project's daunting one-year deadline, but he wanted to be sure they were the crucial details involved in executing the project, not the adminis-trivia of it.

In his first months on the job, Ike fought the perception of himself as a weak interim CEO and struggled mightily to get the British and the Americans back home to take his position seriously. Sure there was ego involved, but mostly Eisenhower was convinced he couldn't do the job properly if no one respected him. He even told off superiors in Washington when he felt they were being dismissive. When Washington approved the transfer of a man from one part of Ike's command to another without telling Ike, he fired off a letter to the general responsible, a man of higher rank and senior to Ike. Eisenhower firmly told the general that "'such a move involves only the authority of the theater commander,' and told him in the future to see to it that such assignments were made only to the theater commander."[4] It took time, but with consistent and rational arguments, Ike began to convince one and all that the CEO of D-Day Inc. was a dead-earnest, serious position.

Of course, arriving with a one-year deadline, Ike couldn't just focus on his own position and his staff. The British Isles were about to be inundated with American servicemen, who would require housing and training facilities and a massive supply chain. With a twelve-month time frame, there was no time to waste.

One area—public relations—presented Eisenhower with an opportunity for quick success, and that success would have immense impact on almost all the other phases of his work. If Ike could generate favorable publicity, he would increase his credibility with his allies and with the folks back home, and that would help with the perception of his job and with the strategic decisions that were coming, and it would help American and British morale as the Yank workforce "invaded" England.

STAY FOCUSED

- **Keep your focus**. Everything you do should further your mission, whether it's employee morale or press relations. *Everything*.

Ike didn't waste any time before leaping into the public relations arena. On June 25, 1942, his second day in England, he held a press conference. Before the conference he was an anonymous staff man; in Stephen Ambrose's words, "His role was more that of an administrator than a commander." After the conference, the spotlight remained intensely trained on him. His appointment as CEO was front-page news in Britain—the English did not need to be convinced that no organization was more important than D-Day Inc. for successful competition with the Germans. And the man himself was a natural. He was blunt about the difficulties facing the organization but always optimistic. He let his passion for the project show—no one was in any doubt that he meant to beat the Germans completely and totally. And, hard as it is to believe in our modern era of "gotcha journalism," Ike trusted the press, referring to them as "quasi members of my staff."[5]

There was one more important ingredient in Eisenhower's successful public relations plan—there was no ego in it. He spent no time on self-aggrandizing. Ike was committed to beating his competition, and he believed that the only way to do that was with an Allied organization. He knew that when D-Day itself came, Americans wouldn't be the only ones going into German territory. Success was utterly dependent on the Allies, and Ike used the press to push Allied unity constantly. The press couldn't get enough stories on him, and almost every single story had a positive angle on the Allies because that's the drum Eisenhower beat.

Just as Ike's commitment to the Allies was more than savvy press relations, his optimism was something that went to the core of his being. Whether he was dealing with the press, speaking at a public function, or managing his staff, he exuded confidence about the ultimate success of D-Day Inc. When he complained—and he had an astounding number of reasons to do so—it was focused and constructive, usually coupled with proposed solutions. He avoided sounding defeatist or depressed to everyone but a very small circle of close friends and family. Given the massive pressure, meager resources, and tight deadlines Eisenhower was dealing with, it would have been understandable if he occasionally showed his worried side. But—except for the tiny group noted above—he was calm and confident. And he urged everyone who worked for him to show the same kind of attitude to the world. Success would be driven in large part by attitude, and Ike knew that attitude had to radiate out from his position.

MANAGE AND MOTIVATE YOUR PEOPLE

- **Talk isn't enough—take action**. If you don't like something, change it. Don't wait for someone else to do it. If you want something done, or want your executive team to behave a particular way—show them what you mean.

During the first few months of Eisenhower's tenure, his attitude and energy took hold, and the organization began moving his way. In August, after months of trying, Ike finally secured the most crucial appointment to his staff: Brigadier General Walter Bedell Smith, known to almost everyone as "Beetle" (a play on his middle name).

Beetle Smith had been serving as secretary to the general staff at the War Department in Washington, but Ike knew he was the perfect man to become chief of staff for D-Day Inc. Beetle could be Ike's "No" man; and he had a thorough grasp of details as well as the major issues confronting the organization. Possibly his most important attribute was his toughness (which became legendary throughout the Allied organization in Europe). Ike characterized him as "strong in character and abrupt by instinct."[6]

MANAGE YOUR PEOPLE

- **Get the right person to work for you.** Does this really need an explanation?

Once Beetle Smith became chief of staff, Ike was freed up to run the organization on a strategic level. Their teamwork was so good that Beetle remained chief of staff throughout the war.

As problematic as some of Ike's early staffing issues were, they paled in comparison to the larger human resources problem. When he arrived in June 1942, his workforce numbered fewer than fifty thousand. But D-Day Inc.'s plans called for a massive buildup of personnel—by the time the Allies launched Overlord, scheduled to take place twelve months later, the workforce would be three million. Slightly more than half were American; most of the remainder were British or Canadian. But there were also Australians and sizable, non-English-speaking contingents from Belgium, Czechoslovakia, France, Norway, and Poland.[7] The entire workforce had to be maintained in the field, forcing the Allies to confront massive housing needs, feeding and medical issues, and equipment challenges. The supply chain and inventory control necessary to feed, clothe, and equip this multimillion-man force was a gigantic challenge in and of itself.

But the key personnel issue was training.

MOTIVATE YOUR PEOPLE

- **Stay positive**. Be honest, but *stay* positive. If you need to vent, do it in private.

Ike's American workforce had basic training when they arrived in England. The multicultural, multilingual Allies had to learn to work together, however, and the mission called for many specialized functions that this mostly new workforce didn't have as it assembled in England.

Ike pushed for training and practice and more training and more practice and large-scale rehearsals. He was well aware that improper training would result in massive loss of life—something a lot more daunting than loss of sales. Ike recognized that the only way his personnel were going to be able to meet the almost overwhelming challenge that faced them was if they were properly trained. There was no substitute for on-the-job experience, but intense training was the next best thing.

HOW IMPORTANT IS TRAINING?

In 2000, Best Buy's managers realized they were losing customers because their sales force couldn't do their jobs properly; they were unable to explain the products for sale.

According to a December 12, 2005, story on *Forbes.com*, the solution to increasing sales was training for new sales employees. By the time the article appeared on the *Forbes* Web site, Best Buy was spending more on employee training relative to sales than any other retailer.

Best Buy set up classroom work and Web-based training, and the sales force had to pass exams. But, just as Ike knew that training was no substitute for combat, Best Buy realized the only way to give a person sales experience was to get him or her out on the retail floor. Rookie salespeople shadowed experienced colleagues until the rookies were ready to be let loose on customers. Afterward, there were monthly product-training sessions to keep everyone up-to-date.

From 2000 to 2005, Best Buy's sales averaged 17 percent growth. In 2005, it generated $897,000 in sales per employee versus $235,000 for competitor Circuit City. During 2000–2005, shares of Best Buy were up 215 percent versus 122 percent for Circuit City and a decrease of 11 percent for the S&P 500.

Challenging as the day-to-day issues of starting up D-Day Inc. were, they were not Eisenhower's only large-scale problem. From the moment he started as CEO, he was entangled in a strategic debate at the highest levels of his parent organization. About the only thing FDR, Churchill, Stalin, and the senior military chiefs of the Allies agreed on was their determination to beat Germany.

And there was the rub. Ike's board of directors argued bitterly over what strategy would accomplish that. With a twelve-month deadline looming, it's hard to imagine that Eisenhower didn't want a strategic road map to follow—guidelines that he could use to shape D-Day Inc. to fulfill its purpose within the larger strategies his board was debating.

Churchill functioned on Ike's board as the lead independent director. Winston Churchill was the prime minister of England and had a long and impressive history: a combat soldier in the Boer War in South Africa at the end of the nineteenth century, a cabinet minister in Britain's World War I government, a member of Parliament for decades, and a successful writer and public speaker. There are no parallels to Churchill in modern Corporate America—it would be as if someone had been a success at the highest levels of several corporations while writing a dozen or so best-selling, award-winning histories, writing large numbers of magazine and newspaper articles, and being in constant demand as a highly paid and sought-after speaker, à la a former U.S. president. While a member of the World War I cabinet, Churchill had been one of the men responsible for the tragic Gallipoli invasion (he probably took considerably more than his fair share of the blame), and as prime minister in 1940, he oversaw the retreat from Dunkirk—a reverse of D-Day. He was much better acquainted with the difficulties facing Eisenhower and D-Day Inc. than any other World War II leader.

Since Churchill was in London, he was able to collar Ike for face-to-face discussions, and he was a passionate force to be reckoned with. He absolutely believed that an invasion of northern France— direct, head-to-head competition with the Germans on territory they controlled completely—was a plan for failure. "When I think of the beaches of Normandy choked with the flower of American and British youth, and when, in my mind's eye, I see the tides running red with their blood," Churchill said directly to Ike, "I have my doubts . . . I have my doubts."[8]

Josef Stalin, another formidable presence on Ike's board, wanted direct confrontation with Germany, and he wanted it immediately. The Germans and Russians were enveloped in a gargantuan struggle in the Soviet heartland, competing along thousands of miles of territory, with combined workforces of eight million fighting for control. Stalin wanted his American and British allies to relieve the pressure as soon as possible. He also knew that Churchill disliked the northern France idea and wanted to go into the Balkans—probably to establish a more competitive position with the Soviets after Germany was beaten. (Stalin was correct in this assessment—Churchill was focused on beating the Germans in the short term, but he believed that the Soviet Union would be his next opponent and was convinced that the Germans could be defeated in a way that would maximize England and America's competitive position versus the Soviet Union after the war. Kind of like a pool player who sinks one ball with an eye for setting up his next shot.)

Stalin was every bit as difficult as Churchill. After all, Soviet

Inc. was the only one in direct competition for territory with the Germans. His workforce was suffering massive losses, and Stalin had an ugly history of dealing with senior subordinates. Prior to the outbreak of the war, he had had many senior officers of the Red Army killed, securing his position as the CEO and chairman of Soviet Inc., but also wiping out huge resources of well-trained, highly educated, experienced personnel. (Note to modern CEOs: slaughtering your C-level officers, no matter how much you disagree with them or are threatened by them, is never a good idea.)

Most of the other members of Eisenhower's board were senior commanders in the American and British armed services—all of whom were senior to Ike, many of whom had combat experience from World War I. Combat experience was the sine qua non of military organizations, and Ike didn't have it. Even with the promotion he had received upon taking over D-Day Inc., he was still seen as a senior staff man—not a true CEO. This collection of experienced, powerful men formed a daunting obstacle for Ike as he sought strategic direction from his board. As everyone else did, he turned to the chairman of the board, the one man who would ultimately decide the mission of D-Day Inc. The last major player on Ike's board was the most powerful and simultaneously the most difficult to figure out—Franklin D. Roosevelt. To call him complex would be an understatement. Churchill once said of Russia: "It is a riddle wrapped in a mystery inside an enigma"—he could have been describing Roosevelt.

FDR was a living contradiction in terms. In charge of the most potent organization on the planet, the U.S.A., he was extremely reluctant to enter the competition, even though he acknowledged to his intimates that U.S. entry into the war was inevitable. America was one organization no one wanted to compete with in the early 1940s. Many historical documents show that both the German and Japanese high commands knew that once the United States entered into direct competition with them, there was no way to overcome its massive advantages of resources, manpower, and manufacturing prowess.

Churchill and Stalin were also aware that the United States' industrial muscle was crucial. Churchill admitted in his memoirs that the moment he knew the Allies would beat the Germans was the moment he heard about the attack on Pearl Harbor.

Yet, despite all this power, FDR did not choose his time and place of entering the global competition—he allowed events to dictate the terms of entry. Why? Because he was the master marketer. He understood the mind-set of his constituency, and knew they would have to be pulled into the competition. He had the patience to wait for events to come to him. He also had the deviousness to create the necessary waiting period. FDR made many comments and campaign promises that the United States would not become embroiled in direct competition with Germany, even though he knew full well that, sooner or later, the competition would begin.

Roosevelt had astounding reserves of strength—he was crippled by polio when he was thirty-nine years old, yet he never stopped trying to walk, became governor of New York and then president of the U.S. He is the only handicapped person ever to sit in the White House. Through the last decades of his life, this fantastic triumph over the adversity of polio was kept a secret.[9]

FDR was the ultimate communicator. And the ultimate non-communicator. He was the first executive to understand modern communications technology, skillfully exploiting the possibilities of radio to bypass the traditional media and Congress and speak directly to his constituency, the equivalent of his shareholders. And he was superb in dealing with people face-to-face. Journalist John Gunther described one of Roosevelt's earliest press conferences:

> Mr. Roosevelt's features expressed amazement, curiosity, sympathy, decision, playfulness, dignity and surpassing charm. Yet he said almost nothing. Questions were deflected, diverted, diluted. Answers—when they did come—were concise and clear. But I never met anyone who showed greater capacity for avoiding a direct

answer while giving the questioner a feeling that his question had
been answered.[10]

FDR avoided direct answers and left people satisfied, employing
this talent with everyone—politicians, statesmen, admirals, and generals. Many who spoke with the president left his presence believing
they had received the answer or permission they needed, only to figure out later that Roosevelt had made no such commitment.

This contradictory man held the key to the dispute over D-Day
Inc.'s mission. Churchill was frightened by the consequences of failure—he had already lived through it at Gallipoli and Dunkirk. Stalin
was desperate for relief that only the United States could supply.
FDR's was the final, deciding vote because America would supply the
majority of the workforce for D-Day Inc., as well as the vast majority
of logistical support (manufacture and distribution of ships, airplanes,
trucks, tanks, and jeeps), and the overwhelming majority of the supplies (everything from ammo and uniforms to food and cigarettes).

Roosevelt was sensitive to the concerns his lead directors had:
Churchill and the British had been competing with the Germans and
absorbing losses for longer than anyone else. But by 1942 the Russians
were doing most of the heavy lifting involved in the competition, deplet-
ing the German resources and workforce on an unimaginable scale. In
addition to these competing concerns, Roosevelt had two of his own.
(1) D-Day Inc. had almost no experience in this kind of competition.
The executive team Ike was building hadn't actually handled a project
of this scale, and the workforce (the American majority of it, anyway)
had not gone head-to-head with an organization like their German
competitor. (2) In addition, the two men who were most important
to D-Day Inc.'s operations, Eisenhower and George C. Marshall, the
army's CEO and a member of D-Day Inc.'s board, were convinced
that the only way to beat the Germans was by Operation Overlord—
any other operations would prolong the competition and increase the
Allies' losses. It was difficult to ignore their shared opinion.

Roosevelt's solution was as simple and brilliant as Alexander the Great's in cutting the Gordian Knot. He satisfied no one. His compromise:

- D-Day Inc. would invade Northern Africa, giving the organization a chance to cut its teeth against a lesser opponent. (The Americans would compete with Italians in Africa before they faced the Germans.) This project was called Operation Torch.
- If the Russians' competition with the Germans took a seriously negative turn, the Americans would launch a "suicide" mission in France to alleviate the pressure.
- D-Day Inc. would continue to prepare for the northern France project.

FDR felt that by going into North Africa, he lessened the possibility of failure (assuaging Churchill's concerns), gave D-Day Inc. a chance to gain experience (alleviating his own concerns), created the opportunity to link up with British operations in North Africa (a bone to Churchill), and, most importantly, FDR could claim to be opening a second theater of competition to relieve pressure on the Russians (a concession to Stalin). Roosevelt's compromise worked. The major players weren't completely satisfied, but they weren't completely frustrated either.

Ike, the man who had to make this all happen, hated the compromise. He thought the day of the decision, July 22, 1942, could go down as the "blackest day in history."[11] He absolutely believed that competing in North Africa—Operation Torch—created a longer, more draining mission for D-Day Inc. and also that the losses would be measured in a higher total of deaths.

But the board had made its decision.

TWO

LIGHTING THE "TORCH"

Prioritizing to Deal with the Pressure

Ike quickly pulled himself together. His board's vision for Torch required an extraordinarily short timeline—Ike was expected to launch Torch in two months, by September 1942. Torch was a smaller-scale project than Overlord, but still the largest of its kind in world history. It would call for a new process because much of his workforce would be coming directly across the Atlantic, reporting at the moment the project kicked off.

The twelve-month timeline for Overlord was *not* being extended. While Ike was running Torch, he was also expected to continue planning the launch of Overlord. The pressure on Eisenhower had increased gigantically. He was now in charge of two projects whose scale exceeded anything ever done, with shortened deadlines, and utilizing a process never attempted before.

But that's what the D-Day Inc. board had ordered. Ike would succeed. Or else.

Almost immediately, Eisenhower's British allies pushed for a larger operation (almost doubling the manpower involved) and an increase in the scope of the project with three separate landing points instead of one. Talk about mission creep: instead of taking over French North Africa, the British wanted Torch to clear their German competition completely out of Africa, which meant a clean sweep from the Atlantic coast in the west to Egypt in the east. Ike's American bosses quickly agreed to the British proposals. Michael Korda wrote,

> Nobody else in the U.S. armed forces . . . had a command anything like as ambitious and far-reaching as this, or as independent—or one with as many thorny diplomatic and political problems. . . . Not since Foch,* at the supreme moment of crisis in World War I, had so much power been handed by allied nations to one man.[1]

Stephen Ambrose put it a little more simply: "This increase in scope made Eisenhower's responsibilities far too broad for one man to handle."[2] Ike's solution was simple—delegate.

Eisenhower appointed Major General Russell P. Hartle as his deputy commander for Europe and Major General Mark W. Clark as his deputy for Torch. Each man assumed primary responsibility for planning in his area. Ike trusted them completely, and both moved their projects forward.

It's easy to say that all Ike had to do was delegate, but remember the pressure under which he did so. The cost of failure was an increased death toll. Once he assessed his responsibilities, he realized he could not meet them on his own and delegated, which required an astounding lack of ego on Ike's part. Many of the senior commanders in the American and British military had more seniority in service, higher rank, and more combat experience than Eisenhower.** Mark Clark, his deputy for Torch, achieved the rank of major general before Ike did. George Patton, who would become one of his frontline executives for

---

* Marshal Ferdinand Foch was placed in supreme command of all Allied armies in 1918, late in World War I.

** Eisenhower had spent World War I in command of training units in the United States. The war ended as Ike's sole combat-destined command was about to sail for Europe. Many senior British commanders had combat experience in both World War I and World War II, since the Brits had been fighting for almost three years when Ike became D-Day's CEO.

Torch (and for operations in Sicily and France later), was older, had more time in the service, and, until 1942, had a higher rank than Eisenhower. Charles W. Ryder, another one of Ike's American commanders in the Torch operation, was a decorated World War I combat hero. But as Korda wrote, "Ike was the least rank-conscious of generals. This made his task easier. . . . His sincerity, his grasp of detail, and his lack of ceremony made it difficult, even impossible to refuse him, and enabled him to assemble very rapidly a team whose members might quarrel and try to pull rank between themselves, but rarely, if ever, with Ike."[3]

Eisenhower didn't allow himself to be overwhelmed by another man's record of success, and he trusted that the men on his team were as dedicated to D-Day Inc.'s mission as he was, that they would put aside their own egos and get to the job at hand. For the most part, Ike's approach worked quite well, and he followed it throughout D-Day Inc.'s existence.

Along with assembling a high-level team, Eisenhower had to build the staff for Allied Force Headquarters (AFHQ—the military has always been as fond of acronyms as any corporation). Ike decided to use the American military staff system with staff sections designated as G-1 (Personnel), G-2 (Intelligence), G-3 (Operations and Training), G-4 (Logistics), and G-5 (Civil Affairs). Because Ike was convinced that the only way to succeed was through an Allied organization, he balanced the staff, making sure that each section head was a different nationality from the section's deputy. And below the level of section head and deputy, the sections were equally balanced between American and British personnel.

Torch was supposed to launch in a hurry, only two months after the decision date of July 22, 1942. Eisenhower had to move quickly and name the executives who would be leading the frontline workforces. This was the equivalent of appointing regional managers to run your business—within their regions, each executive has a great deal of power and autonomy, each man or woman can make or break your success in that region.

MANAGE AND MOTIVATE YOUR PEOPLE

- **Don't reinvent the wheel**. The U.S. Army's staff system had been effective for a long time, and Ike knew how to make it work.
- **Match workforce to mission**. Ike was convinced that only a truly allied force could succeed at displacing the German competition. His organization reflected that from the top down.
- **Delegate**. Micromanagement does not work. No matter how much you may want to believe that you are the only person who can do the job—you aren't.
- **Keep your ego out of it**. Sure it's a cliché, but if you expect to lead a team, you need to be a team player yourself. If you model that kind of behavior, your teammates will follow your lead.

Ike needed ground commanders for Torch. He picked George S. Patton Jr. to lead the American forces. Ambrose said, "Patton was widely regarded as an officer who caused more headaches than he was worth."[4] But Ike saw through Patton's theatrical persona: "Many men who believed they knew him well never penetrated past the shell of showmanship in which he constantly and carefully clothed himself. But he was essentially a shrewd battle commander."[5]

Sir Kenneth A. N. Anderson would head up the British forces. Ike, in describing Anderson later, said: "General Anderson was a gallant Scot, devoted to duty and absolutely selfless. Honest and straightforward, he was blunt, at times to the point of rudeness. . . . He was not a popular type, but I had real respect for his fighting heart."[6]

Ike's naval and air force executives continued the Allied balance. The leader of the naval forces was Sir Andrew B. Cunningham, a man who so impressed Eisenhower that as D-Day Inc. evolved, Ike would compliment someone else by describing him as "almost as good as Cunningham."[7] The air forces were split east and west, with the eastern "regional director" being British Sir William L. Welsh and the western director being American James H. Doolittle, winner of the Medal of Honor for planning and leading the daring air raid on Tokyo in April 1942.

At the same time the organizational structure was being created and the senior-management team put in place, Eisenhower and his executives focused on operational plans for Torch. Stateside logistics pushed the kickoff date for Torch to November 7, 1942. It was the soonest the U.S. Navy could get enough ships across the Atlantic to handle the landings at Casablanca. The extra time was to be used for more training of the workforce, which, until very recently, had been civilians who were completely untrained in the ways of combat and amphibious assaults—essential skills for employees of D-Day Inc. The added time also allowed U.S. industry to provide more landing craft—oddly shaped boats and "swimming" trucks and tanks—which would allow more personnel and supplies to get to the competition's territory faster.

The early November date also gave Ike's team more time to refine the plans for Torch. It's important to remember that Torch was, up until that time, the largest-ever project of its type, and it was the first ever to be produced by an Allied organization. D-Day Inc.'s executive team literally made it up as they went along because no one had experience at this kind of operation.

There were a number of intangibles that left D-Day Inc.'s planners with no choice but to guesstimate:

- *The quality of the American workforce, which had no experience in the field.* While history argued that civilians successfully adjusted when they joined the military workforce, there were no guarantees about the quality of their performance in Torch.
- *How the French in North Africa would react.* The territory that Torch was set to compete in was actually held by the French, not the Germans. And the French were not of

one mind. Some Frenchmen were in an uneasy alliance
with the Germans, and others devoutly wished to
compete with the Germans themselves. No one,
including the French, knew how they would react as the
Allies came into their territory.

- *The Germans' reaction.* If the French opened their territory
  to the Allies or resisted and were overwhelmed, would the
  Germans in Africa move west to take control of the
  territory in direct competition with the Allies? If so, how
  forcefully? What kind of forces would the Allies need to
  ensure their continuing in the region and competing
  successfully?

Given that failure would be measured in increased fatalities and
that Ike and most of his American executives believed Torch was a
wrongheaded diversion from D-Day Inc.'s mission, it wouldn't have
been surprising if Eisenhower and his team had stalled for time in
hopes that the situation would change enough to allow them to
bypass Torch. After all, that was what happened with Sledgehammer
(the "suicide" mission to relieve pressure on the Russians), and many
Allied executives—consciously or not—did stall for time throughout
the course of the war. (Note: Corporate America doesn't have this
problem—we all know there is no such thing as an executive who
stalls for time.)

But Eisenhower was convinced that Torch was a go, and he went
at it with every bit of energy and care he could.* Ironically, while he

---

* This kind of commitment wasn't unique to the Allies. Germany's legendary Desert Fox,
Erwin Rommel, was the executive in charge of defending Normandy against D-Day Inc.
Rommel had his doubts about his mission, convinced that he wasn't given enough time or
the proper resources. He did everything he could, however, and the Americans who came
ashore at Omaha Beach could attest to the quality of Rommel's work. In the Pacific, Isokoru
Yamamoto desperately did not want Japan to go into direct competition with the United
States, but when his board of directors, Japan's Imperial War Cabinet, said to compete, he
came up with the Pearl Harbor attack, which almost beat America in one stroke.

and his team worked on the operational plans, the Allies' most senior executives continued arguing about Torch's shape and purpose. (Think of these as the C-level officers of D-Day Inc.'s parent company.) Ike was pulled into the debate—which he called the "transatlantic essay contest"[8] with memos flying back and forth between Washington and London. But Eisenhower and his team had to continue planning, even if their superiors kept changing the nature and goals of the operation.

A final challenge for Ike regarding Torch will be familiar to any CEO who has ever felt as if his board were hovering over his shoulder, watching his every move. Winston Churchill made it very clear to Eisenhower that he wanted Torch to happen as soon as possible, and to be as big an operation as possible. Why? Because Churchill and FDR agreed that Churchill would go to another member of Ike's board, Josef Stalin, and attempt to soft-soap Stalin with the news of Torch. Remember, keeping Stalin and the Soviets competing with the Germans in Eastern Europe was so urgent for the Allies that they had agreed to mount a suicide project, Sledgehammer, if necessary. Now Churchill was offering Stalin the gift of Torch, and the British prime minister wanted it to seem like a truly imposing gift.

With all of the intangibles, ever-changing purposes, and pressure from the board, Ike and his team still had to make plans or the operation, when it finally crystallized, wouldn't come off. How did they manage this tactical piece of sleight of hand?

They established goals and figured out how to achieve them accordingly. If changes were mandated by the parent company and/or the board, the team established new goals and revised or created new methodology to achieve the new goals. As frustrating as the transatlantic essay contest was, Ike and his team stayed engaged in the debate even as they continued the process with its stream of almost continual changes. When considering the intangibles, they made the most informed "guess" they could and tried to create a safety margin in case the intangible went a different and negative way. And, Eisenhower and his team accepted that there were gigantic risks involved. They understood that no matter how careful they were and no matter how well they anticipated the course of Torch, it was possible the project would still fail. One of the realities of competition is that you can lose as easily as you can win. But to avoid paralysis, D-Day Inc.'s executives accepted the risks. The only other option, inaction, was the same thing as failure and was unacceptable.

DETERMINE YOUR MISSION

- **Set goals**. Just not in cement.

PLAN FOR SUCCESS

- **Change is inevitable**. You might as well go with it.
- **Accept risk**. It's also inevitable. Accept it, and plan for it.

Closely related to the problem of the hovering board of directors is the reality that boards aren't always of a single mind. CEOs frequently receive mixed messages from their directors. The same is true for executives below the C-level who find themselves searching for meaning in conflicting instructions from different corporate officers and sometimes board members. The U.S. Navy, represented on D-Day Inc.'s board by Admiral Ernest King, resented the Europe-first strategy of the Allies and wanted to concentrate its efforts on the Pacific. George Marshall, the U.S. Army's top man, was a Europe-firster, who was convinced that the only route to success lay through northern France.

Churchill and most of the British officers were Europe-firsters but hated the idea of direct competition going into France. They wanted to fight in Africa or Greece or the Balkans or to compete in the air over Germany itself, almost anything other than matching up against the Wehrmacht, the German army, an experienced, well-trained, well-equipped workforce that was responsible for most of Germany's success.

Stalin disagreed with the British and agreed with Marshall—he needed relief in his competition with Germany and felt the only way that could be achieved would be direct engagement of German forces in northern France.

Roosevelt, being Roosevelt, bided his time and waited to push in the direction he wanted (and the direction he thought would be acceptable to most of the players involved) when he felt he could achieve his vision.

Ike's solution to the problem of mixed messages from above is useful for any executive in the same situation. He used the "prevailing wind" solution.

In the movie *Casablanca*, Captain Renault is a self-described "poor corrupt official," played by Claude Rains. Ostensibly in charge of law enforcement in the city of Casablanca, Captain Renault receives orders from the Vichy French government, is leaned on heavily by the local Nazis, is badgered by the nearby Italians (who occupied Libya), is troubled by the Free French (the anti-Nazi resistance), and is swarmed over by refugees begging for a way to escape the Nazis. Renault is in the middle of a constant and overwhelming flow of conflicting messages. And yet, he always seems calm and unruffled. When asked about his own personal political convictions, Renault responds, "I have no convictions . . . I blow with the wind, and the prevailing wind happens to be from Vichy."[9] The captain lets his voice trail off, indicating he has no convictions whatsoever.

Unlike Renault, Ike had very strong convictions. Like the fictional Frenchman, however, forces more powerful than Eisenhower wanted different things from him. Ike stayed calm and waited to detect the prevailing wind. Fortunately, it became clear early on that the wind did not blow from the war or navy departments or 10 Downing Street or the

Kremlin. Throughout Ike's time as the CEO of D-Day Inc., the prevailing wind was from the White House and only the White House.

Again and again through the course of his career at D-Day Inc., Ike would discern what "that man in the White House"[10] wanted and move toward that goal. When he was uncertain as to FDR's vision, Eisenhower argued firmly for what he believed but always allowed those who disagreed with him to have their say. He kept the dialogue open until Roosevelt made it clear what he wanted.

PLAN FOR SUCCESS

- **Find the dominant vision**. There is always one opinion that is more important than all the others. Find it.
- **What if the dominant vision is wrong?** Do what you can to change it. But if you are unable to persuade your seniors to change, follow their vision with everything you've got.
- **What if you can't find the dominant vision?** Engage others in an open process while you keep looking for it.

Torch came to pass because from the board's standpoint, at a certain point in time, it became clear that of all the options that was the one FDR wanted. Later, the Allies would not launch any kind of Balkans initiative because FDR wouldn't sign off on such a thing. And Overlord, the massive competitive movement into northern France, occurred because Roosevelt finally agreed with Marshall, Ike, and Stalin—it was the only way to seize the entirety of Europe from the Germans.

★ ★ ★

Another issue for the Torch planners bears close scrutiny in today's world of global competition—the political environments that corporations operate within. As mentioned in the list of intangibles above, the Allies were about to compete in French territory in North Africa, specifically Morocco and Algeria. They were stepping into an uncertain situation. The territory was considered Unoccupied France, a semi-independent entity that largely did what the Vichy government in Paris told it to do. And Vichy did what it was told to do by its German masters. But there was also a large group of Free French who wanted the African territories to operate independent of the Germans.

To make matters more complicated, the Free French broke into two groups: (1) those who loved Charles de Gaulle (first and foremost, de Gaulle himself and most of the British) and (2) those who wanted anyone but de Gaulle (many of his fellow French and Franklin Roosevelt). Assuming (and fervently hoping) that most of the French in Africa would drop Vichy like a hot potato the minute the Allies arrived, D-Day Inc. needed a French leader to act as a cooperative figurehead and to bring his countrymen into the Allied effort.

Since FDR didn't want to deal with de Gaulle, Ike and his team attempted to find someone suitable for the post of cooperative leader. The most likely candidate was General Henri Giraud. But Giraud, every bit as arrogant as de Gaulle, demanded to be named supreme commander once the Allies had finished the hard work of launching Torch. He sincerely believed that he was the right man to take complete operational control of the Allied project since it would be happening on French soil. He ignored the fact that the entire workforce and logistical support of the project was Anglo-American.

Eisenhower tried to negotiate with Giraud, but the French general was adamant that he must be given overall command of the Allied forces. That was a nonstarter, so Ike began looking around for someone else. He settled on Admiral Jean Darlan, who was the best of a bad lot in Ike's estimation. Darlan was a Vichy man, but he made it quite clear that he would be happy to become the nominal leader of the French in Morocco and Algeria. Eisenhower didn't feel he had any reasonable alternatives, and even though he suspected

many of the French would never forgive Darlan for his involvement
with Vichy, Ike made him the French commander. It turned out Ike
was right. Many French, and quite a few of the Allies' senior executives, were very unhappy with the choice of Darlan.

Fortunately, Ike was not the kind of executive who indulged in
self-recrimination and second-guessing. Early on in the process of
finding a French leader, he knew that he was going to have to choose
the lesser of evils—and having done that, he moved on. When faced
with criticism, he patiently explained the reasons behind his decision, and in private he vented his anger at those who found it easy
to criticize without all the relevant information or having to take
responsibility for the decision.

PRIORITIZE

- **Make your choices and live with them**. This is a corollary to the "accept
  risk" lesson—sometimes none of your choices are good. Make the best one
  you can under the circumstances, and then move on.
- **Compromise**. You don't have to like all aspects of your business. Plans don't
  have to be pretty. They just need to do the job.

MANAGE YOUR PEOPLE

- **Friends vs. allies**. You don't need to like the people you're doing business
  with. They're not your friends or your playmates or your lovers. Nothing
  personal, just business.

Other political realities muddied the waters for Torch. Abutting
the French territory was Spanish Morocco in the west and south and

Italian Libya to the east. Spain was officially neutral but as a fascist dictatorship, not a source of comfort to the Allies. Italy was one of the Axis powers, a junior partner in Germany's operations. It was difficult to project how active Italy would be in Africa other than to protect its own interests in Libya. And, of course, a large German workforce was already deployed in Africa, and the Allies couldn't be sure it wouldn't charge west to prop up the Vichy regime and push out the Allies. No matter how much planning and how much intelligence gathering Ike and his executives did, sooner or later D-Day Inc. would have to discover the realities on the ground—literally.

Just as D-Day Inc. struggled to find sure footing in the political swamp of French North Africa, modern corporations may discover that going into new markets is difficult at best. Assessing the situation and the inherent risks in entering foreign markets can be as tough as picking the right French leader was for Ike. For instance, for most of the last one hundred years, the specter of nationalization has hung over countries all over the globe. It's easy to dismiss this as a problem for communist nations like the Soviet Union after 1918 or a variety of Third World countries that claimed it was necessary to nationalize corporations (usually American) to stabilize their economies.

Democracies, however, have not been immune to the lure of nationalization. The United Kingdom and France of the late 1940s nationalized coal, electricity, gas, and transport industries. (Yes, they were both socialist-leaning at the time, but they were democracies.) Corporations need to watch for a reverse in the trend as well. Margaret Thatcher set the UK on a course of denationalization in the 1980s, which created growth opportunities and simultaneously some market disruptions. Communism struck again and was the driver of Cuba's nationalizing foreign businesses in 1960. Good old-fashioned xenophobia seemed to be the major motive in the nationalizing of the oil industries in Mexico (late 1930s) and Iran (under the Shah in 1951).

Nationalization is a very old policy—King Henry VIII of England employed it in 1532 to nationalize the Roman Catholic Church in England and create the Church of England with himself its head. This was not merely a theological dispute—as head of the Church, Henry acquired all of her money and real estate, vastly increasing his power in England.

And nationalization is alive and well today—one of the ongoing debates about the U.S. federal government's intervention in the "Great Recession" is whether the government is nationalizing financial institutions by receiving stock in those companies in exchange for federal bailout funds. By the most literal definition—"federal ownership of any portion of a company"—yes, some institutions are being nationalized.

There are other concerns for U.S. companies looking to operate overseas. If America gets into an international spat with the country you are operating in, and if America freezes the other country's assets, will your corporation get paid? Might the other country throw you out, in effect, as revenge for America's actions?

And what about companies that have contracts with foreign governments, especially technology, defense, and energy industries? What if America's elected officials (and their regulatory buddies) decide to cut off your foreign business as a way of sending a message to those governments?

Like Ike and the executives at D-Day Inc., you may well find yourself in a situation with no good options. There are times when every choice seems ugly—haven't you ever felt that way walking into a voting booth? But as ugly as your options may be, there's usually one that's less ugly than the others.

For Eisenhower, finding a French leader for Africa was definitely the preferred route and lesser of evils for Torch. Designating a pro-Allied French leader in Africa meant that Torch had overcome whatever level of resistance it met upon entering the territory. If Ike couldn't name a French leader, it meant the competition from the French in the territory was too strong to gain traction in Africa. D-Day Inc.'s intelligence regarding French support of the Allies could have turned out to be mistaken. The losses to the Allied workforce were potentially staggering, not to mention the loss in equipment and the money spent in support of Torch. As terrible as the options for a French leader in Africa were, they beat the other option: defeat.

When Eisenhower chose Jean Darlan, he knew the choice would produce mixed results, and he prepared to deal with the fallout both with the local French and with D-Day Inc.'s board.

Ike also prepared for defeat. It was the ultimate ugly option, but it was a possibility. The Allied forces might be beaten as they moved into French North Africa. It was even possible the Allies would be sent reeling backward, desperately looking for a way out. Eisenhower said, "Plans are worthless, but planning is everything."[11] He knew that the reality of battle dictated the course of events and that all the pre-battle planning in the world cannot cover every conceivable option. The same is true of business projects—and the larger, more complicated and expensive the project, the more likely that as the project unfolds, its reality will be different from what was planned. The more variables in the project, the more likely you are to have variations.

But how do you deal with the unexpected realities, when they are, after all, unexpected?

You need one last plan. In the movies, this is always referred to dramatically as the Doomsday Plan or the Doomsday Option. It often involves pressing buttons and large explosions. In the heat of a project as immense as Torch, pressing a button isn't going to do the trick, and the last thing you want to do is blow up your workforce. Considering the politics of the local environment and the never-before-attempted transatlantic delivery of workforce and equipment on a just-in-time basis—it was likely that Torch would deviate from the plan. The deviation was potentially catastrophic.

The if-all-else-fails plan for Torch was simple: evacuate the workforce along the train line that ran along the northern top of Africa and get the men out by ship at Casablanca. It was simple to describe, but it required a number of decisions to make it possible. The major points along the railway had to be held, and that meant that the Allies needed to jump-start Torch in three places at once: Algiers, Oran, and Casablanca. Having a triple-origin project wasn't easy, but if D-Day Inc. needed to evacuate, it had to have the railroad, and that meant it had to start in those three locations.

Sometimes in creating this if-all-else-fails plan, you need to ask yourself if the project is absolutely necessary to your organization's mission—because you may have to endure failure. In the late 1950s, Ford Motor Company decided to launch the Edsel. It was built for a market niche the company did not operate in; it required major reorganizing of the dealer network, not to mention the design, manu-facturing, and distribution expenses. The Edsel became a legendary failure, a corporate catastrophe on a previously unimagined level— and given how well Ford was doing immediately before and then after the Edsel, it's impossible to argue that it was a necessary project for the company's mission. But the Ford family's control of the company meant the executive in charge—Henry Ford II—was safe in his job.

★ ★ ★

D-Day Inc.'s board had decided Torch was necessary, and fortunately for Ike and his execs, they never needed the doomsday plan. After Torch, eventually everyone from the board to Ike to all of D-Day Inc.'s executives came to understand that Overlord was absolutely essential to the mission—seizing complete control of European terri-tory from the Germans. And Overlord's if-all-else-fails plan was very simple—evacuate the workforce back over the beaches and into the ships that had brought them. It would represent a horrendous setback for D-Day Inc.'s ultimate mission, but it would allow the Allies to salvage some of their men and equipment, draw up new plans, rein-force the workforce, and try again. Overlord met the test of being absolutely necessary, and it had a workable doomsday plan.

When the Allies launched the Market-Garden project (an airborne invasion of German-occupied Holland in September 1944, designed and commanded by Field Marshal Bernard Law Montgomery), the project did not allow for an effective if-all-else-fails plan. The project was an all-or-nothing-at-all deal. There was no easy way to evacuate the workforce in the event of failure. Market-Garden did fail, and the losses to the workforce were quite high. Worst of all, it failed to meet the "absolutely necessary" test. In the Edsel fiasco, Henry Ford was saved from the metaphorical axe because his surname graced the side of the company's building. Market-Garden's executive, Montgomery, was saved because he was the British darling of the Allies, a master of PR, and Ike felt there was no realistic way to demote or fire him. Ike also was guilty of okaying the project in the first place and was aware that he had ignored his own concerns about its not being absolutely necessary when he approved it.

There will be more on Market-Garden later, but the important thing to note is that in the midst of all-out competition, it is necessary to run big risks. The key word in that sentence is *necessary*. Any large-scale, risky project must meet the necessary test, *especially* if there is no way to execute an if-all-else-fails plan.

CASE STUDIES: IF ALL ELSE FAILS

Business failures are always unpleasant and undesired. Whether or not they become disasters is up to the executives running the business initiatives.

JOHNSON & JOHNSON

In the fall of 1982, seven people in the Chicago area died when they consumed Tylenol contaminated with cyanide. Tylenol had more than one-third of the over-the-counter pain relievers market at the time, which dropped rapidly as news of the poison pills spread. Conventional wisdom suggested that Johnson & Johnson withdraw the brand or, at the very least, not throw away advertising dollars on the tainted product. Instead, Johnson & Johnson immediately warned customers to avoid Tylenol and pulled all the potentially tainted products off the market. The executives at J&J understood that they needed to be straightforward and demonstrate that they were putting the consumer first. Within months, Tylenol, now in tamper-proof packaging, was selling extremely well again and, a quarter of a century later, remains a strong brand.[12]

COCA-COLA

In April 1985, the Coca-Cola Company launched New Coke and discontinued the ninety-nine-year-old Coke. Almost instantly, a firestorm of customer protest exploded on the company, and within three months, old Coke returned. The company may have lost as much as $34 million in the process and suffered tremendous embarrassment—but market awareness of Coke was at the highest level ever. Ten years later the company held a celebration in its Atlanta offices, with then chairman and chief executive of the company, Roberto C. Goizueta, saying, "Today we are in the best shape as a company in many decades, and our stock price and our earnings are at an all-time high."

Coca-Cola's if-all-else-fails plan was like that of Torch or Overlord: retreat to your original position. In the case of Coke, the company was able to snatch success out of the jaws of failure simply by retreating. (My father, William V. Loftus, was a longtime creative director for a couple of different ad agencies. He was also a lifelong cynic and claimed that the plan for New Coke was always a way to reignite interest in Coke. If he was correct, Coke's if-all-else-fails plan was, in fact, the main plan.)[13]

MCDONALD'S

Death and illness put fast-food giant McDonald's in the painful and unusual position of having three CEOs within the space of seven months during 2004. Many companies struggle with succession planning even when they are not coping with a crisis. According to a *Forbes* story:

At the 1,000 largest American companies (by revenue) in 2008, 80 new CEOs were appointed, and only 44 of them—55 percent—were promoted from within.

If you view a board's having to go outside to hire a CEO as a failure in succession planning, that represents a breakdown in the system. A failure rate of 45 percent means that far too many plans aren't working.[14]

Amazingly enough, McDonald's managed a smooth transition after James R. Cantalupo died after suffering a heart attack while at a McDonald's convention for franchisees in Orlando, Florida, in April. His successor was a longtime employee of McDonald's, Charles H. Bell. Bell's tenure was horribly short, as he was diagnosed with cancer soon after becoming CEO and resigned in November. His replacement was James A. Skinner. Despite the transitions at the top, McDonald's continued to perform well, with the stock rising 24 percent during the year. Why? Because McDonald's had a worst-case-scenario plan.

"It's one of the most basic questions: what happens if a CEO gets hit by a bus?" said Michael Mayo, then an analyst at Deutsche Bank who felt that many boards had fallen short in their succession plans. "Back in the old days," Mayo said, "a company would groom several successors, any of which could step in for the CEO on a day's notice." Fortunately for McDonald's stockholders, the company was still operating as if back in the old days. Cantalupo, Bell, and Skinner were all longtime executives with the company, and all were ready to step up to the big responsibility when the crisis hit.[15]

APPLE

In the summer of 2007, Apple introduced one of the most heavily hyped products in its history—this from a company that knows how to hype—the iPhone. Customers literally lined up on the streets outside stores to buy one. The iPhone became a massive success—and two months after its introduction, Apple cut the price by $200. The price cut followed a general pattern of falling prices for consumer electronics due to intense competition and the steady decrease of the cost of electronic parts. The initial iPhone buyers inundated the company with angry e-mails, blogs, and phone calls. It was a rare marketing misstep for Apple.

"Our early customers trusted us, and we must live up to that trust with our actions in moments like these," said Steven P. Jobs in a letter on the Apple Web site. Apple gave $100 credit to all iPhone customers who had paid the higher price. Almost two years later, the iPhone still dominated the "smart phone" category.[16]

While none of these companies anticipated these worst cases, they all reacted very well and continued to succeed. Whether it was a specific plan, such as McDonald's development of a talented pool of executives capable of moving into the top responsibility, or a more general policy of keeping the customer first (as seems to have been the case with J&J, Coca-Cola, and Apple), these companies never lost sight of their missions or their commitments to succeeding at those missions. Effective if-all-else-fails plans are born from that kind of commitment.

★ ★ ★

Operation Torch also proved the value of just-in-time delivery. In the case of Torch, just-in-time wasn't about simplifying logistics by eliminating warehousing and cutting inventory costs—it was essential to the project's success. If just-in-time delivery didn't work, Torch would fail. And there was no fall-back plan, because there was no place to fall back to.

Much of Torch's equipment and a large percentage of the workforce would not be ready until very late in the schedule and therefore had to be shipped directly to North Africa. Thousands of tanks, jeeps, and half-tracks rolled off American assembly lines, were immediately transported overland in the United States, and then packed onto ships. And most of the American workforce involved in Torch was still in training in August 1942 when the November 7 date was set.* Training would not be complete until it was time for the workforce to board the ships—the same vessels that were being packed with the equipment corresponding

---

* November 7 was chosen because of another just-in-time issue—it was the earliest date that the U.S. Navy could provide the necessary ships for the project.

to the troop units going aboard. It was a fantastically intricate jigsaw puzzle that had to come together at exactly the right time and place.

Transatlantic just-in-time delivery was a big enough challenge, but D-Day Inc. had to manage a second just-in-time delivery. Substantial portions of equipment, as well as American and British personnel, were coming by sea from England. The organizing challenges were very different depending on the country. In the United States the equipment and the troops would largely be fresh and new, flowing directly into ships for oceanic transport. In England, the veteran British troops and the untested Americans had been in place for a while. They had to be sent to the correct ports and then boarded on the correct ships at exactly the right moment.

Equipment stockpiles in England had been building up during 1942, largely for the purpose of invading France. It had to be resorted (weapons and vehicles not designed for desert fighting were left behind for Overlord) and then packed into ships in the reverse order of its deployment once Torch began. Figuring out the order of packing took considerable planning all by itself.

And as if having two huge streams of equipment and personnel being delivered on a just-in-time basis weren't tricky enough, it all had to arrive at three different locations at precisely the right time to kick off Torch.

PLAN FOR SUCCESS

- **Risk is inevitable**. Yes, I said it before, but it bears repeating. Competition involves risk. Sometimes the only route to success is tremendously risky. If it is the *only* way, and it is *necessary* to your mission—go for it.

It was the largest attempted just-in-time delivery in history. It may well have been the first international, industrial-scale attempt of its kind. Completely innovative, untested, and absolutely essential to the success of Torch. If it worked, it would become the model of operations in Sicily, Italy, and France. If it failed, people would die.

It worked.

CASE STUDY: DOING IT NEW

When Eisenhower first took the D-Day CEO job in June 1942, he had to build an organization to do something no one had ever done before: invade a competitor's territory on a gargantuan scale using an Allied workforce. The size of the project was so large it created challenges without precedent, the organization had to build an integrated workforce out of multinational and multilingual employees, and the executive team had to be formed out of men with very different philosophies of how to compete. The solution to doing something never done before was to build an organization like none that had existed before—D-Day Inc.

In 1990, General Motors was facing a similar problem. GM had to compete with Japanese manufacturers who built cars very differently in terms of design and marketing, in a different and advantageous labor environment, and sold cars perceived to be of higher quality than their American counterparts.

The solution: Create an entirely new car company within GM. Build a new factory from the ground up, in a location that wasn't part of the Detroit environment, with a cooperative labor agreement with the autoworkers union. Build the car out of plastic, so it would be lighter and much easier to maintain scratch- and nick-free. Sell it at one price—never any haggling. The new company was called Saturn, and its original motto trumpeted its uniqueness: "A different kind of car. A different kind of company."

Jerry Flint, writing in *Forbes,* said, "Saturn had excellent managers and was successful in winning hearts and minds of new customers. The dealers, few and far enough apart so they weren't competing with each other, won a reputation for treating people squarely. The one-price-for-all strategy seemed extra-honest, too."

Unfortunately, most of the executives at GM didn't want to do something new. They wanted more of the old way—never mind that it wasn't effective in combating the Japanese automakers. Flint, writing in 2005, fifteen years after Saturn was created, said:

> A few years ago GM began dismantling Saturn, taking away its ability to design, engineer and build its own cars. Today Saturn is a separate company in name only. . . . The old Saturn had its own management, its own engineers, its own plant. The idea was to get away from the old GM way of doing things. But now Saturn has been beaten down and squeezed into the GM mold. The new cars won't have that plastic body—too much trouble. That special union contract is gone.[17]

June 2009: GM, plunging into bankruptcy, sold Saturn to Roger Penske.[18] Three months later, the Penske deal fell apart, and GM announced it was shuttering the brand. It is jumping to galaxy-sized conclusions to say that Saturn could have saved GM, but given that by 2008 GM was having a hard time selling versus the Japanese and found its traditional union contracts onerous in the extreme, maybe Saturn was a model for doing things differently and successfully.

Eisenhower ran into all kinds of entrenched, old-line thinking as he built D-Day Inc. He believed that the new organization with its Allied structure was the only way to succeed, and he refused to give up. Turns out, he was right.

Torch's massive just-in-time delivery wasn't the only part of the project that Ike and the D-Day executives went to school on. In fact, the entire project was an organization-wide training exercise. Once completed, the payoffs for Torch were significant:

- An integrated Allied executive team. Nothing pulls people together into a team like the combination of hard work and success.
- A flexible, tested planning process.

- New techniques that proved to be effective. Before Torch, no one knew if such a massive, transoceanic, just-in-time operation could be done. After Torch, they knew.
- An experienced workforce.

There's an old saying that experience takes experience. Until Torch, no one had experience in executing this kind of massive business project. After Torch, D-Day Inc. was the industry leader.

It never surrendered that leadership position.

DEBRIEFING NOTES

STRATEGIES: MANAGE AND MOTIVATE YOUR PEOPLE

- **Match Your Workforce to Mission**. Be sure you have the right people in the right departmental and geographic structures to be successful.
- **Delegate**. Micromanagement does not work.
- **Keep Your Ego Out of It**. If you expect to lead a team, be a team player yourself. Model that kind of behavior and your teammates will follow your lead.

STRATEGIES: DETERMINE YOUR MISSION, PLAN FOR SUCCESS, AND PRIORITIZE

- **Set Goals**. But not in cement.
- **Change Is Inevitable**. Go with it.
- **Find the Dominant Vision**. Find the one opinion that's more important than all others. If it's wrong, change it—if it's unchangeable, follow it with everything you've got.
- **Risk Is Inevitable**: Accept it and plan for it. Competition involves risk.

THREE

FIRST OP

Leading When You're a Rookie Manager

On November 5, 1942, after intensive planning (and changing plans) the D-Day executives moved to Gibraltar, the only Allied military base that was close to Torch's location and had sufficient communications.

No one would have confused Gibraltar with the executive suite in any modern corporate headquarters. D-Day Inc.'s executives were going to direct the largest operation of its type from "subterranean passages under the Rock," wrote Ike.

> Damp, cold air in block-long passages was heavy with stagnation. . . . Through the arched ceilings came a constant drip, drip, drip of water that faithfully but drearily ticked off the seconds of the interminable, almost unendurable, wait which occurs between completion of a military plan and the moment action begins.[1]

Despite describing the interval between planning and executing as "interminable, almost unendurable," Eisenhower never demonstrated any anger or impatience. Ike had an explosive temper, which only his closest confidantes ever saw, and he was as impatient as any other Allied executive, civilian or military. But he projected calmness

45

because he was confident that he and his staff had done what was necessary in the planning phase, and equally confident that they could meet any contingencies that developed. Eisenhower described the mood within the dank and dripping headquarters: "Yet in spite . . . of dreary surroundings, and of all the thousand and one things that could easily go wrong in the great adventure about to be launched, within the headquarters there was a definite buoyancy."[2]

Their internal debates over what actions to pursue or not to pursue had been completed, and Eisenhower had made final decisions. There was nothing left to do but watch the operation unfold and adjust to developing realities as quickly as possible.

Torch launched on November 8 with more than one hundred thousand men coming off of four hundred ships protected by more than three hundred naval vessels. Awaiting them were almost one hundred thousand French troops and their five hundred aircraft—potentially tough opposition for the incoming Allies. The Americans landed at Casablanca on the western end of the operation; American and British troops came ashore at Oran and at Algiers in Algeria. It was about six hundred miles from Casablanca to Algiers. This is a little bit like launching a rookie sales team into a virgin territory of customers spanning the distance from Washington DC to Boston, Massachusetts.

The vast majority of the workforce arrived on time and made it ashore, mostly against light opposition. But the political complications mentioned in the last chapter took hold almost immediately. The Germans leaned on Vichy France to make a better show of competing with the Allies. Remember, Germany had complete control of all northern France. Vichy ordered French troops in Africa to fight, and they did. Jean Darlan managed to parlay his Vichy connections and quell the opposition to the Allies by convincing his compatriots in Africa to stand down, but not before there had been substantial casualties on both sides.

It took the Allies three days to settle the French opposition, but the three days were an eternity. Eisenhower wrote, "Always in the back of our minds was the need for haste in getting on to the Tunis area. On the night of the eighth I scrawled a penciled memorandum . . . in it appears the notation, 'We are slowed up in the eastern sector when we should be getting toward Bône-Bizerte at once.'"[3] Bône was almost on the Algerian-Tunisian border, approximately three hundred miles away from the nearest Allied landings in Algiers, and Bizerte was a major port almost one hundred miles deeper inside of Tunisia—and Ike was writing about moving on them as of November 8, the first day of Torch.

PLAN TO IMPLEMENT

- **Adjust, adjust, adjust**. No matter how much planning you do, you will have to improvise as you go. Accept that as part of your planning, and give yourself contingency plans. This is another way of saying *you must manage risk*.

MANAGE YOUR PEOPLE

- **Support and move on**. When your subordinates—whether they be CEOs or department managers—tell you they are doing the best they can with a bad situation, you need to trust them or get them out of there. If you trust them, give them all the support you can and let them move on. FDR was desperate to keep his fingerprints off the Darlan deal, and that bogged down Ike terribly.

Unfortunately, the Germans moved into Tunisia on the ninth, and they were determined to make the Allies struggle for every bit of territory in North Africa. Having stretched themselves as thinly as they dared to make the initial landings, the Allies couldn't move on Bône until November 12.

Torch's political fallout continued—Darlan left a bad taste in almost everyone's mouth—and Ike was forced to explain over and over to FDR, to Churchill, and to George Marshall why he had made a deal with Darlan and how he had seen no viable alternative. Almost everyone hoped Admiral Darlan would be able to bring the French fleet over to the Allies. Instead, on November 25, the Germans looked as if they were about to take over. The French decided to sink their own fleet and sent 3 battleships, 7 cruisers, and 167 other ships to the bottom. Darlan had accomplished almost nothing—he was unable to secure the French fleet for the Allies, and his cease-fire order to the French troops arrived when they "were ready to quit anyway."[4]

The two-plus weeks of haggling over Darlan did produce a serious, negative result. Eisenhower spent so much time working on the Darlan deal with French officials and the American and British governments that he was unable to give combat operations the intense focus they required. At the end of November, Ike moved out of Gibraltar and to Algiers, to assume operational control of the Allies in North Africa.

Being on the ground with his workforce provided Ike with a rude awakening. The coastal areas of Africa along the Mediterranean Sea were muddy beyond belief. Airfield operations were difficult in the extreme since airplanes had to be moved off the paved runways onto boards so the planes wouldn't sink in the mud. The railroad line that the Allies had taken such pains to control was nowhere near sufficient to move large portions of the workforce, along with their equipment, to their designated locations. The roads were only passable by half-track (half a truck on wheels and half an armored-track vehicle, similar to tank tracks), but the half-tracks were being held in reserve because the tracks' useful life would be exhausted in the slippery terrain. Ike's workforce was literally stuck in the mud. The Allies were having a hard time moving anywhere, and the Germans were busily reinforcing their grip on Tunisia.

Eisenhower wasted no time releasing the half-tracks, allowing his workforce to move much more freely. What's the point of having equipment capable of helping you accomplish your goals if you won't use it? Ike knew that he was in Africa to take away German territory, not to preserve his organization's vehicles in mint condition. (I worked at a magazine publisher once upon a time, and the building manager seemed to think we were in the business of operating a building that just happened to have tenants who published magazines. He never seemed to realize that the point of our company was to dispense information, not maintain his building in pristine condition.)

If Ike hadn't been stuck in the political mud about who was the correct Frenchman, he might have been on hand to send the half-tracks into action two weeks earlier. It's hard to say how much Eisenhower's inexperience hurt the situation. The simple facts were that the French were in place when Torch was launched and it made sense to attempt to negotiate with them instead of competing directly and suffering losses. After all, the French were not the true opposition—every second wasted resolving the situation with the French was a second that delayed the Allies from taking on their German opposition head-on. But would a different CEO have had any more luck discovering who was the correct French leader? Unlikely.

A more experienced CEO might have realized he needed to get on the ground as soon as possible to bring his decision making into play. Only the top executive can cut through his subordinates' competing priorities—the troops needing an effective mode of transport versus the logistical team's desire to preserve their equipment. But Ike wanted to assume control in Algiers sooner than he did, while his superiors in Washington and London continued to hold him up for more discussion of the political problem. It's possible that a more experienced CEO than Ike would have been believed sooner when he said, "This is the best I can do; we need to move on."

As November slowly ground into December, there was very little progress to report. Eisenhower's board of directors began chafing at the lack of forward motion and what they perceived to be too much caution on Ike's part. Since the Allies seemed unable to move east-ward with any success against the Germans (and the winter mud), the chiefs suggested that Eisenhower expand the scope of operations and tackle Sardinia. They recognized that Ike would not be able to pull many troops from Torch, but they also felt Sardinia was weakly controlled by the Italians and represented low-hanging fruit, ripe for the plucking.

Eisenhower was stunned. According to Stephen Ambrose, "He had no maps, no plans, no intelligence, no preparations" for an oper-ation outside Africa. Ambrose quoted Ike's reaction to his board's Sardinian suggestion: "For God's sake, let's get one job [Torch] done at a time. . . . I am not crying wolf nor am I growing fearful of shadows. . . . Don't let anybody get screwy ideas that we've got the job done already."[5] If Sardinia was out, the chiefs wanted aggres-sive action toward Tunis, hoping that the Allies could swiftly beat the Germans there. They nudged Eisenhower with the observation that "large initial losses in a determined assault were much preferable to the wastage inherent in a war of attrition."[6]

Despite all the pushing from his board of directors, Eisenhower avoided aggressive action by consolidating his troops' current posi-tions and moving only when he felt that he held territory securely. Late in December, believing that his workforce was unprepared for a final aggressive push into Tunis, he halted the effort. As a result, the Germans arrived first, unopposed, and the Allies were stuck with a long, grinding struggle to push them out. It would take four months and thousands of casualties to accomplish this.

Given Eisenhower's final World War II record, it's hard to argue with the way he led D-Day Inc. He was a rookie CEO when he managed Torch, however, and his lack of experience showed. Even sympathetic biographers like Stephen Ambrose and Michael Korda felt compelled to mention that things might have turned out much differently if an aggressive executive such as George Patton had been in charge. Ike's board was displeased, according to Korda: "Churchill grumbled that Ike's army was all tail and no teeth." Roosevelt "refused to promote Ike to the rank of general until he had produced some kind of victory." British general Alan Brooke said, "I am afraid that Eisenhower as a general is hopeless!"[7]

MANAGE AND MOTIVATE YOUR PEOPLE

- **Back up your people.** As unhappy as Ike's bosses were with his African campaign, they remained confident he was the man for the job. They didn't have blind faith, but after careful assessment, they decided to stick with it. Remember, if you replace a manager, the new person will be a rookie in that particular spot, and your organization will have to absorb the costs—in money, people, and resources—of the new person's learning curve.

Fortunately, Ike's board was willing to hear him out. In January 1943, FDR, Churchill, and the combined chiefs of the Allied military services arrived in Casablanca to hold a conference. Eisenhower, sick with the flu, flew through awful weather to get there. The first impression he gave was that he was "jittery." But he stayed confident in his abilities and focused on his job as he saw it and made a report on the North African situation that was "satisfactory and upbeat." Among other things, Eisenhower was able to report that Torch had achieved the minimum objective considered necessary for success: control of all the main ports between Casablanca and Algiers. "The successful action of the first few days assured attainment of the minimum object," Ike wrote.[8] Roosevelt and Churchill were impressed enough to keep him as D-Day's CEO.

Part of the reason they were willing to do so was that Churchill and Brooke realigned the executive structure under Ike so that he had three British deputies immediately under him. Churchill and Brooke left Casablanca thinking Ike would make a suitable and necessarily American figurehead for D-Day Inc., while the three Brits would handle all the real work. American board member George Marshall liked the new arrangement because it left the ultimate command—at least nominally—in the hands of an American.

DETERMINE YOUR MISSION

- **It's a balancing act**. Figuring out your personal Risk Appetite is no easy matter. You have to juggle your tolerance for risk with the organization's tolerance for it, and then figure how much risk you *must* take if you're going to achieve your goals. The balancing is necessary for building an organization that can absorb the hit when the risk goes bad. But the very tendencies that help build such an organization—proper anticipation and planning—may lead to risk aversion. Being too cautious can be as bad as failure itself. Ike didn't fail in North Africa, but his cautiousness made success much more costly.

As it turned out, Eisenhower disappointed everyone who thought he would be an empty suit at the top. Ike had two qualities going for him that left him in real control of D-Day Inc. He was so competent and friendly to his three British deputies that they were happy to work with him instead of controlling things from behind the throne. And Ike's volcanic temper worked to his advantage in this case. He quickly realized the Brits on his board thought they had seized the real responsibilities from him, and he was having none of it. If he was *named* the commander, he would *be* the commander. He fired off a furious memo to the military chiefs on his board, explaining how he was going to be in charge, no ifs, ands, or buts about it. The memo was so scathing that Ike's chief of staff, Beetle Smith, a man notorious for his own rough edges, pleaded with Ike to tone it down. Ike relented to a softening of the language but not the meaning. This was not about ego; it was about having one man who had ultimate responsibility—a true, unified command. If Ike was that man, he wanted everyone to understand that he was, in fact, in charge.

PLAN FOR SUCCESS

- **Stick to your guns**. If you absolutely believe something is necessary for success—as Ike believed in a unified, Allied command—fight for it.

PRIORITIZE

- **It's principles, not personalities**. Eisenhower's willingness to take the second spot in the executive structure, under a British general, demonstrated that he really believed in the need for a single Allied CEO, whether he was the man in the job or not.

Almost simultaneously, Eisenhower offered to serve as the deputy commander to British general Sir Harold Alexander, the top deputy assigned to Ike in the structure described above. Ike made this selfless gesture because once the Allied forces in Morocco and Algeria met up with the British forces in Egypt, the vast majority of the workforce would be English. Ike felt that if his board wanted a Brit in charge of a predominantly British force, they should have one, and he would gladly support that man.

The one-two punch of anger regarding who was really in charge and Eisenhower's selfless gesture of offering to take the No. 2 spot worked. Ike's board was forced to resolve the situation and recognize him as the true leader.

This recognition did not mean the job was Eisenhower's forever. Just because Ike was the CEO of D-Day Inc. while it operated in North Africa did not mean that anyone expected Ike to be in charge when the main show—Operation Overlord—launched in France. Everyone on D-Day Inc.'s board fully expected that one of their own members, George Marshall, would become CEO when it was time to go head-to-head with the Germans in Europe. Ike operated under no delusions about his career status. He was well aware that he continued to be a seat warmer for the ultimate choice. But he felt he had a job to do while he kept the seat warm, and he was going to do it as well as possible.

★ ★ ★

The challenges in the winter of 1943 were twofold:

- The Allies had to push east through Tunisia and link up with the British forces moving westward from Egypt, seizing complete control of the territory from the Germans, which would severely limit Germany's ability to operate in the Mediterranean, and at the same time create opportunities for the Allies to go after Germany's European ally, Italy, intensifying the competitive squeeze on the Germans.
- With the idea of seizing those opportunities, Ike was directed by his board to plan Operation Husky—the invasion of Sicily—scheduled to take place in late spring of 1943 only a few months away. This meant Ike would need to plan an entirely new operation at the same time as he was completing the North African operation begun in Torch. (As often happens in the corporate world, reality intruded on D-Day Inc.'s schedule and pushed the actual date of Husky to July 10.)

The pressure never let up—the same old problem for Eisenhower. Ike had to finish one project, Torch, and simultaneously do all of the planning and start-up work for the next project, Husky.

That's the plight of most modern senior executives. In the entertainment business, this week's hit movie or hit song probably buys you all of thirty seconds of comfort before you need to worry about where the next hit is coming from. And where are the hits going to be coming from in twelve months? The same is true if you manufacture toys or pharmaceuticals. This year's top-selling toy will probably be in a discount bin by next year. This year's most prescribed drug will need an added ingredient so that it can be patented again and continue selling in a nongeneric form.

No one is exempt from this. This year's killer app in software will need a new version pretty soon, not to mention a couple of "bug fixes" in the intervening months to make sure the application continues to work properly. If you happen to be in one of the service industries, whether it is express delivery or food services or anything else, every day comes to you with a complete set of challenges that must be met. All the packages have to go where they're going and arrive on time. Every meal has to be prepared and served. And all the while you are handling the daily load of challenges, as Ike was doing while the Allies finished up in North Africa, you are dealing with longer-term problems, such as planning for growth, handling inventory, manufacturing, distribution, whatever—all the things D-Day Inc. had to get ready for operations in Sicily.

Unfortunately for D-Day Inc., its competition was moving rapidly with practiced skill in North Africa. The German executive in charge of operations in North Africa, Erwin Rommel, was already a legend for his successes. He burnished his reputation as he tackled the Allies in Tunisia, dealing them an especially bruising setback at Kasserine Pass. Just prior to Rommel's moves at Kasserine, Ike had come to the front lines to form his own estimate of the situation and take stock of his executive team in the field, led by Lloyd Fredendall.* Ike's assessment was that the American workforce wasn't yet properly toughened up, that Fredendall's entire operation had a slack feeling to it. Ike considered replacing all of Fredendall's second-level executives but dismissed it as unrealistic. His other option was to replace Fredendall and put someone in charge who would get the Americans fired up.

The man who had previously dismissed American executives for minor infractions such as making anti-British remarks decided to do nothing. Eisenhower was still cautious regarding the overall conduct of his operation, still lacking combat-command experience. He left Fredendall alone. The results were terrible as D-Day Inc.'s forces continued to move exceedingly slowly into Tunisia, and the casualties mounted.

At approximately the same time as the debacle at Kasserine, Ike was in the early stages of setting up his team for Husky. His board had directed him to make his deputy, British general Alexander, the overall commander for operations in Sicily. The British members of D-Day Inc.'s board thought they had successfully booted Eisenhower upstairs to an ineffective executive position in charge of D-Day Inc., leaving the important job to Alexander. The Americans on the board had acceded to this because they felt it was important to have an American in the CEO position of D-Day Inc. It was the reason they had already declined Ike's offer to serve as Alexander's deputy.

Ike's cautious approach, demonstrated by his slow, systematic movements against his competition and his unwillingness to fire an executive he deemed inadequate, meant that final success in North Africa took longer, costing more lives along the way. But Eisenhower kept his twin focus. He did succeed in Africa by seizing Tunisia and

---

* At one point during his trip, Eisenhower heard the sound of gunfire, and according to Michael Korda, went toward the sound, with his pistol in hand. Ike may well have been the only executive of his rank to do that in the entire war—and it's hard to recommend this kind of gun-in-hand competitive behavior as a good technique for most CEOs. But the attitude, the willingness to commit all, is a good one.

crushing the competition throughout the entire area, and he did oversee all planning for Sicily. Despite the setbacks such as Kasserine and the ego blow of Alexander being made ground commander, Ike continued to do his job, venting his frustrations only in private and never allowing self-doubt to overwhelm him. Even more important, he never panicked.

As it turned out, the engagement at Kasserine Pass was the high point of the German campaign. Rommel was overextended and pulled back. In doing so, he allowed the Allies to consolidate their forces and inflict losses on the Germans almost equal to what they had suffered.

The operations immediately following Kasserine were also positive in that Eisenhower had a chance to know Alexander much better. Ike's willingness to shove ego out of the picture paid off; he and Alexander formed a solid working relationship. As Ike said, "I quickly formed a great respect and admiration for his soldierly qualities, an esteem that continued to grow throughout the remainder of the war."[9]

As the German casualties increased and their forces retreated into a small territorial pocket around Tunis from which they would evacuate, Eisenhower assessed the situation:

> These lessons [from the results of actions taken and not taken by the Allies] were dearly bought, but they were valuable. . . . Whenever the initiative is lost to the enemy there is bound to be tension and worry, because it is always possible for anything to happen. No one escapes; in spite of confidence in the overall situation and eventual outcome, there is always the possibility of local disasters.[10]

Beginning with the German pullback toward Tunis in mid-February, the Allies made slow-but-steady progress against them, while the all-British force from Egypt pressured the Germans and Italians from the other direction. In March 1943, George Patton won the first major American victory against the Germans at Gafsa, a huge milestone for the American part of Ike's Allied workforce.

The Americans had finally beaten the Germans head-on, just as their much-more-experienced British counterparts had done.[11]

Along with much-needed experience for the American cohort, the last months of operations in Africa also introduced some of the men who would have major executive roles later in the war: Erwin Rommel, Bernard Law Montgomery, George S. Patton, and Omar N. Bradley.

Erwin Rommel was the lead executive for the Germans until March, when he withdrew for health reasons. He would be the executive in charge of the competitive forces in France in June 1944. Highly competent, Rommel was one of the few Germans who thought the Allies would come into France at Normandy instead of Calais (which is much closer to England). He would make massive defensive preparations in Normandy that would result in considerable damage to Operation Overlord.

Bernard Law "Monty" Montgomery was commander of the British forces closing on the Germans from Egypt. Monty was a decorated veteran of World War I and the first man, British or American, to lead any force to victory against the Germans at El Alamein. He would become Ike's leading British commander in Europe and would stretch Ike's ability to get along with people to the breaking point. Even other Brits would urge Eisenhower to fire Monty, but Ike recognized the British hero's star power for the Allies and absolutely believed that a multinational Allied organization was the only way to succeed. If you are going to operate with an ally, you don't fire its biggest star, no matter what kind of a pain in the posterior he is.

George S. Patton was commander of the American forces at Casablanca and then in Tunisia. Like Montgomery, he was a decorated combat veteran of World War I and had graduated a few years ahead of Eisenhower at West Point. Ike and Patton had formed a friendship as junior executives before and after World War I because they both saw the opportunities in what was then an emerging technology: tanks. Both men embraced the possibilities of mobile, armored warfare.

Patton was in charge of the American forces at Casablanca and moved eastward across the rim of Africa, leading the Americans to their first major success. Soon after, he would be placed in charge of the Americans going into Sicily as part of Operation Husky. His track record throughout the rest of the war was astonishing. He was brilliant, aggressive, successful, and outrageous. Sooner or later almost everyone wanted Eisenhower to fire Patton, but Ike knew that a genius like Patton comes along very rarely and that no one else could produce the way Patton could. Like Monty, Patton would often stretch Ike's patience almost to the breaking point, but Eisenhower felt that Patton was absolutely the best executive for leading a combat workforce. For Ike, the ultimate measure of Patton as an executive was results, and Patton consistently produced the best results of any executive on either side of the competition.

Omar N. Bradley replaced Patton as the executive in charge of American forces in Tunisia. Like Eisenhower, he had been a lifelong staff man and had no combat experience prior to taking the job in North Africa. Being a staff man didn't stop him from capturing the major port of Bizerte on May 7, closing off one of the Germans' major supply and communication lines, and adding another victory to the American's total.

Like Monty, Bradley favored the slow-but-sure approach. However, while Monty would prove to be a little too slow on repeated occasions, Bradley was, as a war correspondent reported, "a tough, knotty fighter with the tremendous sledgehammer persistence of General Grant, the shrewdness of a New England horse trader and the personal dignity of character and integrity that can be compared only to the same spacious qualities shown always by Gen. Robert E. Lee." The men who served under Bradley loved him, dubbing him the "G.I. General."[12] Eisenhower would come to lean on him more and more, eventually placing him above Patton and on an equal level with Montgomery as operations in France unfolded after Overlord.

Ike's handling of Monty, Patton, and Bradley evidenced his ability to put aside his personal reactions to each and accurately value them for what they brought to the mission. Monty—with his grating personality and lack of results—would repeatedly frustrate Eisenhower, but Monty was the Brits' favorite general and cemented the Allied nature of D-Day Inc. in a way that no other executive could. Patton was a constant nightmare with the higher-ups in Washington and London, as well as with the press, but he was the best-producing executive in the organization. Both men remained on Ike's staff until control of Europe had been wrested from Germany.

Bradley, on the other hand, was a management dream. Ike described Bradley's "ability and reputation as a sound, painstaking and broadly educated soldier. . . . He . . . demonstrated real capacity for leadership. He was a keen judge of men and their capabilities and was absolutely fair and just in his dealings with them. Added to this, he was emotionally stable and possessed a grasp of larger issues that clearly marked him for high office."[13]

The management challenge with Bradley was that by late 1943 Eisenhower planned to promote him above Patton and equal to Montgomery, despite Bradley being junior in age, time in service, and combat experience to both men. Ike wasn't about to let some kind of seniority system dictate to him. When the time came to go into France, Eisenhower was convinced that Bradley was best suited to be in charge of all American forces, and so Ike put him in charge. Eisenhower and Bradley had been at West Point together in the same graduating class, which helped Ike know the quality of the man. But Ike's willingness to disregard the system and employ the best man for the job was what distinguished his use of Bradley.

★ ★ ★

The grinding competition in North Africa continued until mid-May 1943, when the Allies seized control of all Tunisia, putting the combined German and Italian workforce out of business, capturing more than 240,000 men (125,000 of them Germans, generally considered the more effective force).[14] When casualties (dead and wounded) were added to those captured, the Allies had succeeded in neutralizing almost 900,000 of their competitor's workforce.[15] Obviously, killing, wounding, or capturing your competitors' workers are not methods you can deploy in business. But these results demonstrate that even though Eisenhower was cautious in exploiting his opportunities, his refusal to panic, his avoidance of political battles, and his steady confidence and forward action produced results.

By May 13, the Allies controlled all territory in North Africa—the same result they intended to produce in Europe. The original mission for Operation Torch had been to eliminate the Germans and Italians as active competitors in North Africa. Torch had been slow, sloppy, and costly, but it was a complete success. D-Day Inc. had accomplished its mission and gained a great deal of valuable experience. Ike learned some important lessons about what he needed to do as a manager and which of his executives he could count on for the future.

But there was no time to enjoy the success. There was no letup in the pressure—competition with the Germans and Italians was a long way from finished. Operation Husky would begin in less than two months.

DEBRIEFING NOTES

STRATEGIES: DETERMINE YOUR MISSION, PLAN FOR SUCCESS, PLAN TO IMPLEMENT, AND MANAGE YOUR PEOPLE

- **Adjust, Adjust, Adjust.** You have to improvise.
- **You Must Manage Risk.** Figure how much risk you *must* take if you're going to achieve your goals. And plan how to handle things if the risk goes bad.
- **Managing Risk, Part 2.** Being too cautious can be as bad as failure itself.
- **Support and Move On.** Trust your people or get rid of them.

FOUR

GETTING HUSKY

Managing Difficult Personalities

Eisenhower faced pressure familiar to many senior executives as he began planning for Operation Husky, the invasion of Sicily   he was still finishing the follow-up to Operation Torch in North Africa, the largest project D-Day Inc. had ever attempted. Ike and his senior staff had to plan Husky and build a new team for it at the same time they continued to oversee the massive, intense competition centered in Tunisia. D-Day Inc.'s board of directors made it clear to Eisenhower that they wanted both the wrap-up of North Africa and the launching of operations in Sicily to happen swiftly and successfully. The fact that one operation competed against the other for D-Day Inc.'s resources was Ike's problem, not theirs.

Assembling the force to go into Sicily was a balancing act from top to bottom. Patton was pulled from his job in Africa almost immediately after he had won the Americans' first major victory over German forces at Gafsa. He would be the top American executive on the ground in Sicily. Moving Patton out proved fortuitous. His replacement, Omar Bradley, gained valuable experience leading troops in combat, which he had not previously had, and picked up a victory of his own along the way at Bizerte. Montgomery was in charge of the British forces in

Sicily even as he continued to lead the British who were moving west from Egypt.

The workforce was a combination of experienced American and British forces shifted out of Africa into Sicily, and new troops coming directly from America and Canada. The delicate bit of combining was necessary because Eisenhower didn't want to pull too many of his forces out of Africa too soon, and he needed to blend "rookies" with veterans to create yet another integrated workforce. Having done much the same thing with Operation Torch gave Ike a great deal of confidence that he could do it again, and since he was actively directing the continuing operations in Africa, he was well equipped to decide which troops should go and which should stay. Typically, Ike made the best of whatever the situation presented to him.

Taking whatever the situation presented and exploiting it might also have turned out to be quicksand for Eisenhower, especially on the strategic scale of competing with the Germans throughout Europe. The more involved D-Day Inc. became in operations in the Mediterranean, the more resources would be sucked into that conflict, and the harder it would be to mount Overlord.

STAY FOCUSED

- **Focus on your main purpose**. Always remember why you are in business. If your original purpose is still valid, stick to it. If it is not, adjust. But it is incredibly important to not lose sight of the original objective and to make absolutely certain that it is not still valid: Is there a market that still needs to be served by what you do? Do there continue to be customers for your products and/or services? Are you abandoning them if you change your objective for the sake of a new opportunity?

Much of the push for more operations in the Mediterranean came from the British. Churchill frequently spoke of going after the Germans by way of the "soft underbelly" of Europe, specifically Italy or southern France. Ike and his immediate superior, George Marshall, felt that Churchill and many of his senior officers wanted to go after the Germans in any way except over the beaches in northern France. The World War I disaster of Gallipoli and the desperate evacuation of British forces from Dunkirk in 1940 loomed large for them. But Eisenhower felt that Marshall and he "shared the belief that everything done in the Mediterranean should continue to be subsidiary to and in support of the main purpose of attacking across the Channel in early 1944." Ike continued in *Crusade in Europe*:

> Others held that, in war, opportunity should be exploited as it arises. . . . The doctrine of opportunism, so often applicable in tactics, is a dangerous one to pursue in strategy. Significant changes in the field of strategy have repercussions all the way back to the factory and the training center. . . . Moreover, in the specific case, all the original reasons for adopting the cross-Channel operation as our basic strategic aim were still valid.[1]

Eisenhower wrote *Crusade in Europe* in 1948, three years after the war was over and after the arguments regarding Overlord had long been settled. He acknowledged the conflicts at the board level and their effect on strategic discussions, but he was diplomatic about recognizing the conflicts. In reality, the back-and-forth at the D-Day Inc. board level continued almost to the moment the men hit the beaches in France. Ike was not the first executive—and will not be the last—forced to handle mixed messages from his board.

Stalin wanted a Second Front and wanted it as soon as possible. He needed the Allies to relieve the pressure he was facing from the Germans all along the entire western section of the Soviet Union.

Stalin was the only board member who was directly competing with the Germans, head-to-head and on his own territory. To Stalin, the only way to get the Germans to ease off was to have D-Day Inc. move into Germany's territory in Europe and move in close enough to Germany to be threatening. That meant operations in northern France. No substitution would do.

Churchill wanted to compete with the Germans anywhere but over the beaches in northern France, and he was constantly looking for any and every opportunity to have the Allies compete in another territory. Most of the British senior military men on Ike's board agreed with Churchill. (The ones who didn't were quiet about it.)

FDR was constantly playing the middle, biding his time, waiting for his American workforce to gather the size, training, experience, and matériel necessary to tackle something as huge as Overlord. He agreed to non-France operations to placate Churchill while attempting to mollify Stalin that he was serious about a Second Front by launching these other operations. Although operations in Africa, Sicily, and Italy did engage large numbers of Germans, the continued pressure on the Soviet Union was painful. Stalin remained unsatisfied until the Allies landed in Normandy.

The senior U.S. military men on the D-Day Inc. board were also split pro and con regarding Overlord. George Marshall (the U.S. Army's boss) was completely and absolutely committed to going into northern France. Like Eisenhower, he was convinced that this was the only way to beat the Germans and seize all of Europe. Admiral Ernest King (the U.S. Navy's top exec) realized that America was committed to working with the Brits and Russians in a "Europe First" policy. King had his hands full dealing with the Japanese, however, who were every bit as successful in their Pacific operations as the Germans were in Europe. The Japanese had started the war for the United States, and many Americans were more interested in beating them than worrying about the Germans. King frequently argued to the rest of the board that if the British weren't going to do things the American way, maybe the Americans should pick up their chips and go play exclusively in the Pacific.

It's unlikely that FDR would ever have let that happen. Being the cagey political operator that he was, Roosevelt probably allowed King to operate as his pit bull on the board, pushing and prodding the Brits while Marshall used persuasion instead of anger and bluster.

While all of this strategic back-and-forth over Overlord and Mediterranean operations made for fascinating debates at the board level, it created nothing but headaches for Eisenhower. Given that he spent a great deal of his time in London, Ike had to be ready to meet with Churchill almost every time the prime minister wanted to make another attempt at persuading him to expand Mediterranean operations, and yet Eisenhower always had to stay faithful to the pro-Overlord charge given him by FDR and Marshall. At the same time, Ike had to push forward, always moving D-Day Inc. in the direction he believed was necessary for successful completion of its mission.

How did Ike handle the pressures of ongoing operations against the competition in Africa, of planning for another large operation in Sicily, of holding to the long-term strategy of competing in France, and of the ever-shifting guidance of his board of directors?

BE HONEST

- **Be true to yourself.** If you believe in yourself and your vision of your organization's mission—don't be shy about it. When the time comes to execute the plan, go at it with everything you've got.

For starters, Eisenhower was confident in his abilities and intellect. Despite the powerful personalities on his board, he never appeared to be overwhelmed or to doubt himself. He knew that his experience and background were perfectly suited to the job he had; he knew that he understood the problems facing D-Day Inc. better than anyone else, with the possible exception of George Marshall.

Marshall's presence on the board was also reassuring, and not just because he was Overlord's ultimate champion. He was Eisenhower's immediate boss in the army, and Marshall and Ike agreed the vast majority of the time. Their agreements were not due to internal politicking by either man but were founded on mutual respect and a similar philosophical approach regarding D-Day Inc.'s operations.*

Thanks to his native self-confidence, Ike spoke honestly and directly to any question or in any debate about strategy. Eisenhower was constantly pointing out to the board what the ramifications of their decisions would be on the ultimate mission of D-Day Inc. At the same time, once the board made its decision, even if it went completely contrary to what Ike thought and believed, as it did with Operation Torch, he threw himself into it heart and soul. His board never had any doubts about whether he was following orders. They were concerned with the quality of his results, but never with the direction of his actions.

Ike's relationship to his board may not seem analogous to that of many modern executives. It's easy to dismiss Ike's behavior as a military man following orders. He had no choice.** But Corporate America isn't so rigidly hierarchical. As of 2008–2009, surveys by the Society of Corporate Secretaries & Governance Professionals showed that most CEOs are also chairmen of their boards.[2] Most CEOs do not have a direct reporting line to a single individual but rather to a board as a whole, a board of which the CEO is the most powerful

---

* Eisenhower was not the only one who had a high regard for Marshall. According to Stephen Ambrose in a blurb written for *General of the Army: George C. Marshall, Soldier and Statesman* by Ed Cray: "All the big men of the age—Ike, Roosevelt, Churchill, Truman, Stalin, Patton, Bradley—thought George C. Marshall was the greatest man they ever met." In the entire history of the United States, only Marshall has been the chief of one of the military services and then gone on to be secretary of state and later secretary of defense.

** By the by, military history is full of generals and admirals who did not follow orders in lockstep, with both good and awful results. Abraham Lincoln struggled through the first couple of years of the Civil War trying to find generals who would take direction from above.

player. However, as of this writing, it looks as if the SEC will be giving shareholders much easier access to the proxy—the annual statement and ballot for shareholders to vote at the company's annual meeting. Congress is poised to make sure the SEC has the legislative "right" to grant such proxy access. This means unhappy shareholders will be able to place their own initiatives in front of all shareholders to vote on. The power to run the corporation, held unchallenged for years by corporate management and boards, will now be more evenly shared with the shareholders, who, after all, own the company.

In addition, "Say on Pay" initiatives look to become common at all publicly held companies. Say on Pay is the term for advisory votes by the shareholders on the compensation of the top executives at a company. It is common in several European countries, including the United Kingdom. U.S. companies receiving federal TARP* funds also must have it. Proponents of Say on Pay argue that it will make management and boards more responsive if the shareholders have a simple and direct way of making their displeasure known. And, since the vote is advisory, the shareholders can't tie the hands of management and the board and prevent them from doing anything that is necessary even if it is unpopular with shareholders. Critics of Say on Pay say it amounts to corporate governance by referendum. Management and boards of directors will move very gingerly indeed if they feel the hot, heavy breath of shareholders from over their shoulders.

What proxy access and Say on Pay mean is that CEOs (whether they are chairmen or not) will need to be much more responsive to the wishes of the great mass of shareholders. This is not unlike the situation that Ike's ultimate boss, the chief executive of the United States and chairman of the D-Day Inc. board, Franklin Roosevelt, found himself in. He had millions of voters (shareholders) who could and did express themselves in such ways as political demonstrations,

---

* TARP: Troubled Asset Relief Program, enacted in October 2008, allows companies to sell equities to the federal government to build capital and increase liquidity. TARP was an early part of the federal bailout of companies during the economic fallout in 2008–2009.

labor protests, elections every two years, and editorials. While the voters couldn't knock him out of office except at four-year intervals, he needed their support every day of the war. He had to be responsive to their wishes, and FDR was a master at knowing what the people wanted. (Well, enough of the people at any given moment.)

PLAN TO IMPLEMENT

- **There are never too many plans**. D-Day Inc. was ready to go in any necessary direction because it already had plans to do so. Even the plans you don't use build your staff's abilities to analyze, plan, and forecast, which is always worthwhile. Effective advance planning for multiple scenarios is closely related to risk management, improving your chances of surviving a crisis.

- **Keep your options open—make one decision at a time**. Okay, this can get ridiculous—some people use "keeping their options open" as an excuse for not making decisions. But as D-Day Inc. discovered in 1943, it can also be a way of making one decision at a time and freeing your organization to move forward when it is impossible to anticipate every future eventuality.

The president, balancing what was necessary for the good of the country (the parent organization) with the needs and wants of his shareholders, would make final decisions. And since Eisenhower believed in the principle of civilian leadership of the military, no matter how much Ike disagreed with those decisions, he always respected them because the president, speaking for the people, had the absolute right to make them, even to be wrong about them.

With proxy access and Say on Pay in place, many more CEOs arc going to find themselves in Ike's shoes—having to execute decisions that may not be the most strategically sound choices, but are necessary in light of the board of directors' demands as influenced by shareholders.

★ ★ ★

PLAN FOR SUCCESS

- **When the boss has a good idea—jump on it**. Marshall solved the problem of what to do after Sicily by suggesting twin staffs to create two different sets of plans, giving Eisenhower more options. Ike adopted the suggestion immediately, allowing D-Day Inc. to move forward.

Eisenhower continued to be forthright about what he believed to be the most advantageous course for the Allies. He never just went along to be a good boy for the board. But his were not the final decisions to make, and he understood that his board members were in a difficult place as they attempted to plan for operations after Sicily. As Ike said, "It was completely normal that some differences in conviction should obtain—we were not yet far enough along in the process . . . to produce crystal-clear and unanimous conclusions as to the specific actions that would obviously produce victory."[3]

How was the post-Husky debate resolved? By going for Sicily and leaving decisions regarding future operations to the future. This might sound a little too "Que Sera, Sera" for many managers, and it would have been except for one detail: George Marshall suggested that Eisenhower create two staffs to plan two entirely different operations post-Sicily. The first was the invasion of Sardinia; the second was the invasion of the Italian mainland. Ike agreed and immediately established the two staffs. This way, no matter which way D-Day Inc. moved after Operation Husky, it would have the necessary plans.

★ ★ ★

The high-tension juggling act of planning for Operation Husky (Sicily) while also planning for post-Husky (Sardinia or Italy) and at the same time finishing up in Tunisia began in February 1943. In the middle of the month, Eisenhower felt that the situation in Tunisia required his personal attention, and he toured the front for several days. At almost the exact same time, his dual staffs began the planning work for Sicilian operations. Even as Ike was overseeing the final phase of the African campaign, he was in charge of planning for the gigantic Sicilian campaign. The African campaign that followed Torch was so large it would net the Allies the entire territory of North Africa, eliminate almost a million troops from the German and Italian forces (as compared to total losses for the Allies of approximately seventy-one thousand), and end competition with the Germans completely in that area. When it began the previous November, Operation Torch had been the largest amphibious invasion ever attempted. Operation Husky, in the works only months after Torch, would surpass it. The challenges for D-Day Inc. were continuous, and they increased in scope and difficulty.

Eisenhower's British board members had imposed its wishes for an executive staff structure on Ike at the Casablanca Conference in January 1943. The British had made General Sir Harold Alexander Ike's overall deputy at D-Day Inc. At the same time, Alexander was in command of the land forces involved in Husky. Air Chief Marshal Sir Arthur Tedder was in charge of D-Day Inc.'s air forces. And Admiral Sir Andrew Cunningham was in charge of naval forces for Operation Husky. This staff structure forced Eisenhower to delegate authority.

Ike could have steamed and schemed over this arrangement, but he didn't. He could have politicked behind the scenes to regain all power, but he didn't. He could have thrown up his hands in disgust and played the part of the figurehead that the British had designed for him. But he didn't.

Eisenhower embraced the staff structure he was handed and made it work—yes, he made lemonade out of lemons. The new structure called for Ike to make final decisions on the plans that others designed, in effect turning him into the ultimate yes/no man but with little influence over the direction of the plans or the implementation of strategy. Eisenhower delegated the planning work to his staff as his board had intended he should, but he did not sit idly at the top of the organization and wait to approve or disapprove the work of others. He engaged his three executives by "holding weekly meetings with the three British officers, by having frequent casual conversations with them individually, by acting as referee to settle their inter-service disputes, and most of all by the force of his personality."[4] Ike explained how his engaging the executive team worked: "The idea is to get people working together, not only because you tell them to do so and enforce your orders but because they instinctively want to do it for you. . . . You must be devoted to duty, sincere, fair and cheerful."[5]

MANAGE AND MOTIVATE YOUR PEOPLE (INCLUDING YOURSELF)

- **Embrace the madness**. When you are faced with an illogical organization structure—even with a nonfunctional job description for your own job—embrace it and move on. It's amazing what can be accomplished if you spend your energy on doing things rather than infighting or sulking.
- **Watch out for jackasses**. Literally and metaphorically. They can bite you in the rear, and they have one heck of a kick too.

The operation to seize control of Pantelleria—a small rocky island approximately halfway between Tunisia and Sicily—demonstrated how completely Eisenhower's theory of commanding his top executives worked. Pantelleria had a good airfield that could provide tactical support to the landings in southern Sicily—something that could not be done if the nearest Allied airfields were in Africa. (Neither American nor British fighters had sufficient range to support troops

in Sicily if they flew out of Tunisia.) Despite the solid reason for wanting Pantelleria's airfield, none of Ike's three British executives wanted
to take the island. It had a rocky coastline, unsuitable for amphibious
operations. It was, according to the Brits, bristling with guns. And,
for a small island, there were a substantial number of Italians there,
ready to defend the island.

Ike was undeterred and undertook a personal reconnaissance in
HMS *Aurora*. *Aurora* and her task force bombarded the island at will,
with a paltry response from the Italian shore batteries. Eisenhower was
convinced that the island could be taken at small cost to the Allies and
insisted on going ahead. Turned out that Ike was wrong. The island was
taken at a *microscopic* cost. The Italians surrendered before the Allies
stepped ashore. Only one Brit was hurt—and he was bitten by a mule.
More than eleven thousand Italians were taken out of competition
through capture, and more important, D-Day Inc. gained an airfield
for supporting its Sicilian operations.[6] All of this because the man at the
top delegated the work he needed to delegate, and at the same time,
stayed engaged with his executive team and its planning process.

WHEN DO YOU FIGHT THE GOOD FIGHT?

Back in the late 1970s, having suffered through a major oil crisis, people across
the United States suddenly became intensely energy aware. Everyone was encouraged to use less energy: turn off the lights in unused rooms, set thermostats to
use less heat in the winter and less air-conditioning in the summer. One energy-
saving measure imposed on the car companies was fleet-mileage standards,
which created a mileage average for a manufacturer's entire fleet of cars. Over
time, the standard would rise, meaning that the manufacturers would be forced
to design and build more fuel-efficient cars.

Auto manufacturers were understandably unhappy about this. Who wants
the government dictating the kinds of products and services you deliver to your
customers?

If the American car companies had followed the Eisenhower model, they would have made their case against the standards, but once the standards were in place, they would have set about to make and market the most efficient cars possible. (Foreign car companies, all of which made a more efficient mix of cars at the time, had few problems meeting the standards for the cars they sold in the United States.) Did Chrysler, GM, and Ford follow the Eisenhower model?

Nope.

Almost from the minute the standards were imposed, the car companies began lobbying to have the standards diminished and/or enacted further in the future. They rose to a design and manufacturing challenge with a political solution. And for many years, with every administration, they received extended deadlines. To be fair, Detroit's Big Three did design and build more efficient cars, but they were much less successful selling these models than their competitors from overseas were. So the American car companies spent large amounts of energy and effort on rolling back the standards whenever possible.

Then came the 1990s—and the explosion of SUV sales. SUVs are considered trucks under the fleet-mileage standards, and trucks are exempt from the standards. And because SUVs are built on truck platforms, they are much more profitable for the car companies to sell than equivalently priced cars. From the moment the Ford Explorer roared its way to bestsellerdom, the car companies' course was set. They would make SUVs and more SUVs. The profits rolled in, and the companies continued to lobby for more leniency in the fleet-mileage standards. Those profits could have been plowed back into efforts to make fuel-efficient cars that were sexy enough to compete with foreign makes. The profits could have been used to build plants in nonunion states, as the Japanese and European manufacturers did.

But that didn't happen.

Along came the gas crunch circa 2006, and then the economy tanked beginning in December 2007.

Suddenly the American car companies found themselves in a quandary—more SUVs than they could give away. Their profits disappeared, and Chrysler and

GM both went into bankruptcy in 2009, with Chrysler filing for Chapter 11 on April 30 and GM on June 1. Ford barely averted disaster by selling off many of its operations and taking on large lines of credit to secure its cash flow.

In summer of 2009, the federally sponsored "Cash for Clunkers" program allowed automakers some of their best sales months in a long time. Customers could turn in older, inefficient cars, get a cash rebate for them, and buy new, efficient cars in highly favorable deals. Only two American cars made the Top Ten list of best sellers in this program: the Ford Focus (at No. 4) and the Ford Escape (at No. 10). Vehicles from Detroit's Big Three filled the entire Top Ten list of clunkers that were traded in.[7]

If Detroit's Big Three had dealt with the fleet-mileage standards according to Ike's methodology, you have to think their chances of building *and selling* efficient cars for more than three decades would have been much better. When the economic crash hit full force in 2008, they might not have been doing the bankruptcy shuffle.

But we'll never know. Instead of accepting onerous standards and making the best of it, the car companies politicked to avoid the standards and utilized loopholes in them.

Husky was the largest operation of its type ever attempted. In terms of initial territory (one hundred miles of beachfront), it was even larger than Overlord in Normandy a year later. Husky, like England's Henry VIII trying out his multiple wives, required eight separate plans before Eisenhower decided on one. Although officially he was not supposed to participate in planning debates, Ike did more than await plan submissions. As Stephen Ambrose said, "Unofficially, . . . he was deeply involved, primarily by paying visits . . . and talking things over with the commanders."[8] The good thing about the multiple plans was that Eisenhower was absolutely confident on the eve of the operation's launch—everything that could be considered and planned for, had been. Ike felt that the more thoroughly you planned, the more easily you could improvise if you were surprised by opportunities or catastrophes.

The planning phase also realigned Eisenhower's executive team. His immediate deputies, the Brits' Alexander (overall No. 2 and land forces), Cunningham (naval forces), and Tedder (air forces) had all come to respect Ike and support him completely. Originally assigned to Ike by the senior British military chiefs as a way of having experienced British military men run things, they came to be Eisenhower men, acknowledging him as D-Day Inc.'s true leader.

PLAN FOR SUCCESS

- **Planning is the discipline that gives you flexibility**. All those endless planning sessions have a point other than producing ennui in the attendees. They allow executives to consider almost every single contingency and prepare for it. Like facing the contingency of needing to build and *market* fuel-efficient cars.

PLAN TO IMPLEMENT

- **Planning is a team-building exercise**. If working through the seemingly endless options doesn't create a sense of team, then deciding on whether to send out for pizza or Chinese food should do the trick.

Although it would be nice if every executive had the complete support of his or her superior, the reality is that superiors, even boards of directors, sometimes feel compelled to meddle in the management of a department or division or company. Instead of overseeing the manager or exec, they become involved in the functioning of the organization. Instead of making sure that the exec understands strategy, stays focused on the mission, and runs the organization accordingly, they dictate the structure of the department or decide on launch dates when the decision logically should be the exec's.

DETERMINE YOUR MISSION

- **Knock 'em out**. If your mission is to put your competition out of business, you can't afford to do it in a leisurely fashion. When opportunity knocks, go after it fast.

Eisenhower dealt with this meddling by keeping his eye on the strategy and mission, by accepting the structure imposed on him, and then working so hard and well that the men who were supposed to take over the important parts of his job became loyal to him. The military, like most corporations, is full of people who like to play games and work the politics of the organization to get ahead. Ike showed what you can accomplish by ignoring the politics and sticking to your mission.

Husky's plans continued through their eight permutations, and another executive sorting out occurred, establishing the conflict that would plague Ike through the rest of the war: Montgomery vs. Patton. Actually, the conflict was really Monty vs. Everyone Else at D-Day Inc. No one had a higher opinion of Bernard Law Montgomery than the man himself. As Michael Korda wrote, "Monty was a loner, arrogant, vain, unforgiving, professionally brilliant, and utterly convinced that he was always right."[9] Monty was fantastically cautious, putting every last detail into place before moving. Eisenhower noted that Monty waited until he had so many men and so much matériel ready before he acted, that it was almost impossible for anybody to fail in the same circumstances. There was only one problem with this style—it was slow.

Monty was the first Allied commander to defeat the Germans in battle at El Alamein, and that victory instantly made him a legend. Eric Larrabee summed up Montgomery's impact:

> El Alamein was less of a decisive battle than an icon; it was a triumphant reassertion of national valor. . . . Montgomery became a cherished symbol . . . he walked in the company of the great captains. . . . Crowds followed him, yearned to touch his sleeve. He had become a rule unto himself and could do no wrong.[10]

General "Could Do No Wrong"'s post-battle pursuit of the retreating German forces under Rommel was, to put it kindly, lacking in swiftness. Rommel's men retreated from El Alamein in good order and were able to combine with the German forces facing the Allies who had invaded in the west as part of Torch. This careful, everything-in-its place approach was a trademark of Monty's throughout D-Day Inc.'s mission, and he routinely failed to follow up swiftly enough to seize opportunities when they were there for the taking. But Montgomery was convinced that he was the most able and brilliant of all the Allied executives—he was completely dismissive of any and all Americans and, for that matter, many of his fellow Brits. Monty's arrogance led him to conclude that the executives for Operation Husky were structured in too many layers and were producing too many poor plans. He wrote in his diary, "The proper answer is to cut [Alexander, Ike's deputy and the land commander] right out of Husky. I should run Husky. With the new plan [Monty's own] it is a nice tidy command for one Army H.Q."[11]

Monty's assumption that he was now in command of Husky went over badly with the men who were actually in charge of the operation: Eisenhower, Alexander, Cunningham, and Tedder. But Ike recognized that just because Monty always thought he was right didn't mean he wasn't right occasionally. The executive structure of Husky (imposed by D-Day Inc.'s board, remember) *was* awkward and had too many layers. And Monty's major point was also on target—instead of landing forces on Sicily at the eastern and western ends of the island and then driving north to Messina, it made more sense to have the British land in the eastern "corner" of the island with the Americans landing close by in support.

Messina was the key to Sicily. If D-Day Inc. reached it quickly enough, they could trap large numbers of German and Italian forces on the island. They would control all of Sicily, and because Messina is the closest major city in Sicily to Italy, they would have an excellent jumping-off point for operations in Italy. According to Monty's plan, the British would move along Sicily's east coast to Messina, with the Americans running parallel to the Brits on their western flank, protecting them. This meant that Patton, the leader of the American ground forces, would not command his own, independent landing but instead follow the British forces into Sicily, playing a subordinate role to Monty.

Despite Monty's ego in assuming he was now in charge, and despite how he rubbed the other commanders raw, especially the erratic and brilliant Patton, Eisenhower went along with most of the major points in Monty's plan. Caving in to Monty reinforced Monty's assumption that he was the right man to be in charge and angered almost every other executive at D-Day Inc. Going with Monty's plan also set the Allies up to succeed in Sicily, but at Monty's usual slow pace, which could have meant a large number of casualties to D-Day Inc.'s forces and large numbers of the competitors' force escaping successfully to Italy, where the competition would have to resume.

Why did Ike make this decision? Two reasons: Monty's plan *was* better, and Ike was convinced that the mission could not be successful if D-Day Inc. was not a completely Allied organization. He could not play favorites to his fellow Americans. Ike wasn't about to rap Monty's knuckles when he was a hero to the British people. Dearly as Ike might have loved to put Monty in his place, Eisenhower tamped down his anger and did what he thought best to enable D-Day Inc. to succeed at its mission.

MANAGE YOUR PEOPLE

- **Be right or be in charge**. No matter how much you may dislike one of your fellow managers, if he or she is right about something, acknowledge it. Don't bother asserting your seniority or power. It rarely helps get the job done.

There may have been other complicating factors in Eisenhower's reluctance to discipline Monty. Although Ike had not been in direct command of combat units, he had allowed the Allied units, especially the Americans, to move very slowly into Tunisia. His cautious approach echoed Montgomery's. Another factor was that in D-Day Inc.'s early days, Ike was slow to fire anyone. As the Allies moved eastward into Tunisia, it became obvious that the American, Lloyd Fredendall,* needed to be replaced immediately. He was even more cautious than Montgomery and had lost to Rommel at Kasserine. And there was an aggressive, available man waiting in the wings: George Patton. Patton had led the troops ashore successfully at Casablanca and was in charge of an occupation force in Morocco, but there was no active competition in that area. Patton was doing nothing except ceremonial reviews of troops. But Eisenhower did not swap the two men, allowing the long, slow crawl into Tunisia to continue. Ike was cautious due to inexperience—Monty was cautious because it was his nature.

After the African operations completed, Eisenhower was much quicker to move his American executives to get more productive action out of those troops. But it was long after Sicily and even Normandy more than a year later that Ike finally figured out how to get Monty to move quickly: give him very specific orders and leave as little to Monty's plans and definitions of priorities as possible. But even when

---

* Fredendall was finally replaced in March 1943 and returned to the United States to assume a training command. He was never placed in charge of combat units again.

Ike reluctantly adopted this micromanaging method, Monty continued to resist, performing at a level that was mediocre, at best, due to his slow, cautious approach to every project. The ugly truth is that by most performance-assessment benchmarks, Montgomery was an underperformer. And Eisenhower failed to manage and motivate him properly. In a publicly held company, this lack of managing executives properly will cost significant losses in share value. In D-Day Inc.'s competitive environment, it cost lives.

MANAGE YOUR PEOPLE

- **Replace 'em**. It's probably the hardest thing a manager ever does—but when people don't perform, you've got to get rid of them.
- **Micromanage**. If you feel you have to keep someone (the boss's nephew, perhaps), give him very specific direction. It's a lousy way to manage, but if you're stuck, you're stuck.

Operation Husky also provided Eisenhower with a double-barreled issue from his most challenging American executive: Patton. Once D-Day Inc. moved into Sicily, Patton chafed at playing a supporting role to the slow-moving Montgomery. Patton knew he could do much better and demonstrated his brazen brilliance by breaking with the operational plan, cutting west to Palermo, and then dashing across the northern coast into Messina ahead of everyone else. Patton's success put Monty's nose out of joint. Also, Patton had only been able to go west and then swing north by leaving fellow American Omar Bradley to follow the original plan running parallel to Monty and slugging it out over brutal terrain and against topnotch German opposition.

Privately, Ike was happy with the Americans' aggressiveness, both in terms of Patton's speed and Bradley's toughness. Both had outperformed Montgomery. But Eisenhower was committed to an allied

executive structure for his Allied organization, and that meant he had
to worry about Monty's bruised ego. (Patton's leaving Bradley to continue to protect Monty's flank angered Bradley, but he was too good
a team player to make Ike's life difficult.)

Soon after thrilling most of D-Day Inc. by seizing Messina, however, Patton created a firestorm for Eisenhower. Patton slapped a
soldier in a hospital, loudly calling him a coward in front of the horri-
fied medical staff. Ike called for an investigation, hoping that a quick,
efficient inquiry would allow him to deal with the incident quietly.
His opinion of the situation: "If this ever gets out, they'll be howling
for Patton's scalp, and that will be the end of Georgie's service in this
war. I simply cannot let that happen. Patton is *indispensable* to the war
effort—one of the guarantors of our victory."[12]

Eisenhower often had to swallow hard as he put up with endless
arrogance from Monty for the sake of the alliance that was necessary
for D-Day Inc. to succeed. Now he was faced with the loss of Patton,
his indispensable man. Ike was dismayed by Patton's behavior—he
told Patton that nothing could "excuse brutality, abuse of the sick,
nor exhibition of uncontrollable temper in front of subordinates." Ike
went on, saying the incident caused "serious doubts . . . as to your
future usefulness."[13] He reprimanded Patton sharply, but unofficially,
telling him that another misstep would be the end. Ike and Patton had
been friends for a long time, and Ike was hopeful that their friendship,
as well as Patton's thirst for personal military glory, would keep the
hard-charging general in line.

The soldier-slapping incident seemed to be resolved—for all of
two days. Several reporters came to Eisenhower's office and said they
had the facts concerning Patton's abuse of the soldier. If Ike would
dismiss Patton, they would keep the story quiet.

Eisenhower responded by telling them that Patton's "emotional
tenseness and his impulsiveness are the very qualities that make him,
in open situations, such a remarkable leader of an army. The more he
drives his men the more he will save their lives."[14] Ike told them that

Patton was crucial to D-Day Inc.'s success. The reporters agreed to hold the story. Patton continued his contributions to the mission.

MANAGE YOUR PEOPLE

- **Principles before personalities**. It doesn't matter why or how big a pain in the rear someone is—if he or she contributes to the success of the mission, figure out how to work with them.

BE HONEST

- **Honesty is the best policy**. In this day and age of a ravenous news media, Ike's honesty with the press might not have worked. But you can't hide from the media. Bob Nardelli assumed he didn't have to give the press—or his shareholders—the time of day as Home Depot's CEO, and that arrogant attitude cost him his job.

Eisenhower managed to hold on to both of his prima donna executives, Monty and Patton. He was absolutely sure that both were necessary for the organization to succeed in its ultimate goals, so he made whatever adjustments were necessary. He put the mission ahead of his own emotional comfort in dealing with both men. Monty continued to do his job slowly and with an abundance of arrogance. But he played his part as the English glamour boy of the Allied team. Patton continued to cause public-relations nightmares but also thrashed his opposition at almost every turn.

Omar Bradley, the third of the three major combat commanders, followed his success in North Africa by proving in Sicily that he was quiet, tough, and exceedingly sharp. He caused none of the problems of his two better-known colleagues but was more productive than Monty and roughly as productive as Patton. He may not have been indispensable, as Ike called Patton, but Bradley was extraordinarily dependable. When Eisenhower's boss, George Marshall, asked for a recommendation for the executive in charge of the American army in England, Ike immediately and enthusiastically declared for Bradley. By the time of Operation Overlord in June 1944, Bradley, not the senior Patton, was the top executive for all American forces in France—Patton ended up working for Bradley. By the end of 1944, Bradley was in a position equal to that of Monty's within D-Day Inc.

Bradley, Montgomery, and Patton all played important roles as D-Day Inc. moved forward. Operation Husky gave Ike a very clear understanding of what each man brought to the organization and how to best use them in achieving the mission.

MANAGING YOUR EXECUTIVE TEAM

You might read the headline above and say, "Come on, how hard is it to run a team of your own guys?" ("Guys" in this usage, is not gender specific.) For one thing, you don't always get to choose the members of your own team, and sometimes, even when you do the choosing, you may make a mistake and stick yourself with a lemon. *Okay*, you're thinking, *I'm still the one giving the orders so . . . how hard can it be?* Remember, Eisenhower's actual title during much of D-Day Inc.'s life span was Supreme Commander. Talk about the ability to give orders—Ike was the supreme boss. He must have had it easy, right? Except we've already seen that wasn't true. Monty never listened to anyone but himself, and Patton promised to behave and then misbehaved time after time. Ike's supremacy didn't guarantee the kind of team he wanted. Since it's unlikely anyone reading this book has a higher title or more power than being supreme, getting your executives to be team players is a problem all managers will have to deal with at some point or another.

In the 1970s, Henry Ford II didn't like working with Lee Iacocca and ended up firing him. Iacocca took his ideas, like the minivan, to Chrysler, where he invented an entire product category within the auto market and led the company back to solvency in the 1980s. And he did it—in large part—with ideas he had tried to implement at the Ford Motor Company. Henry Ford solved his personal problems with Iacocca in the worst possible way. He dismissed Iacocca and allowed his competition to benefit from his former executive's ideas and energy. Eisenhower, by contrast, swallowed his dislike for Monty and his abhorrence of Patton's behavior and benefited from Monty's charisma with the British and Patton's brilliant aggression on the battlefield.

In another team debacle, in the mid-1990s the Walt Disney Company struggled in spectacular fashion with mismanagement of its executive team, specifically succession planning. Chairman and CEO Michael Eisner wanted to bring in a strong talent as Disney's president and heir apparent. Disney's president Frank Wells died in a helicopter crash in 1994, and Eisner had health concerns. An obvious replacement for Wells was Jeffrey Katzenberg, who was chairman of Disney's motion picture division and responsible for a string of successful movies (*The Little Mermaid*, *The Lion King*) as well as signing a deal with Pixar (*Toy Story*) and acquiring Miramax. Eisner decided to absorb Wells's duties himself and forced Katzenberg to leave in 1994. Katzenberg joined forces with Steven Spielberg and David Geffen to found Dreamworks SKG and produce the stupendous hit *Shrek* as well as Academy Award–winners such as *American Beauty*, *Gladiator*, and *A Beautiful Mind*.[15]

Eisner, meanwhile, decided that Michael Ovitz, head of the Creative Artists Agency and commonly referred to as the most powerful man in Hollywood, would make a perfect No. 2. After prolonged wooing, Eisner got his man.

Fourteen months later, Eisner fired Ovitz. Thanks to the golden parachute negotiated by Ovitz, it only cost Disney $140 million to fire Ovitz. Yup, $140 million to do his job so poorly that he was fired. All over Corporate America, a common water-cooler joke went: "Gee, I would have settled for ten or twenty million and been happy when they fired me. They could have saved more than one hundred million dollars, and I'm sure I could have screwed up as badly as Ovitz."

The firing and severance caused such an outrage that after several years two of Disney's major shareholders, including Walt Disney's nephew Roy Disney, sued the board of directors, including Eisner. Depending on who was testifying, witnesses said that Ovitz had been blocked by Eisner as he had tried to acquire a part of Yahoo!, sign new talent, and do a joint venture with Sony. Two of Disney's C-level officers had informed Ovitz they would not report to him. Others testified that Disney's senior managers had hated Ovitz and that instead of riding in a bus with his fellow executives at a corporate retreat, Ovitz chose to ride solo in a limo.

In 2005, Chancellor William B. Chandler III of Delaware Chancery Court decided in Disney's favor. But he blasted Eisner's management of his executive team, which included Disney's board: "His lapses were many. He failed to keep the board as informed as he should have. By virtue of his Machiavellian (and imperial) nature as CEO, and his control over Ovitz's hiring in particular, Eisner to a large extent is responsible for the failings in process that infected and handicapped the board's decision-making abilities."[16]

In sum: Eisner pushed away a major talent who was already in-house, hired the wrong guy, fired him at a cost of $140 million, and spent millions more of the company's money in legal fees. Although Eisner and the board of directors were vindicated, Eisner lost his position as chairman of Disney and then retired a year before his contract as CEO ran out. Jeffrey Katzenberg might not have been as successful within Disney as he was at Dreamworks, but wouldn't Disney have been better off retaining his talent than paying $140 million for a guy who didn't work out? Whatever personal issues Eisner had with Katzenberg and Ovitz, it is hard to imagine that it was more stressful or counterproductive than what Eisenhower experienced with Montgomery and Patton. But Ike retained and harnessed both men, and D-Day Inc. profited from it.

As for Disney, thank goodness that Mickey Mouse was and is more important to its future than Michael Eisner.

Patton's American forces took Messina ahead of Monty's, effectively ending Operation Husky. But even Patton's speed hadn't been enough to trap the German forces, who retreated before both Patton and Monty while inflicting significant damage as they departed. Although D-Day Inc. had been successful at gaining Sicily and now effectively controlled the Mediterranean, on a performance basis, the Germans had done much better than their competition, forcing the Allies to spend heavily in time, matériel, and men to gain their objective.

At almost the same time as Patton was taking Messina (mid-August 1943), Eisenhower was diagnosed with hypertension and ordered to spend the week resting in bed. Ike ended up taking only a day, and even that day was not completely restful. On this day off, Ike assessed his performance as D-Day Inc.'s CEO during Operations Torch and Husky. He did his self-review in front of Harry Butcher, an old friend of the Eisenhower family who served as Ike's naval aide but really filled the role of confidante.

Stephen Ambrose wrote, "It was an accurate, if painful, self-criticism, and a mark of the man that he was forthright in engaging in it." In his critique, Eisenhower said that he had made serious errors. The Torch landings shouldn't have been in Morocco and Algeria, but farther east in Tunisia. And looking back, he felt he should have launched Husky on both sides of Messina in the north of Sicily, quickly trapping the Germans on the island. But he had been too cautious, overestimating the strength of the opposition his forces would face. Instead of going straight for the heart of his competitor's operations— Tunisia in Torch, Messina in Husky—he had taken a slow-and-steady approach that took too much time and cost too many lives. Eisenhower felt he had been guilty of the same thing as Fredendall in Tunisia and Monty in North Africa and Sicily—he had been too timid. Eisenhower wrote, "Relentless and speedy pursuit is the most profitable action in war,"[17] and he had not been relentless or swift. Ambrose summed up Eisenhower's self-critique: "There were many campaigns to go, and he did not want to repeat his mistakes."[18]

BE HONEST

- **Step up**. Eisenhower was honest in his self-evaluations and always willing to take responsibility for the result of his actions. Don't waste time looking for ways to place blame. Acknowledge mistakes; learn from them; move on.

Operation Avalanche, the September 1943 invasion of the Italian mainland, proceeded almost as an afterthought. Husky had been undertaken on the premise that the next step would be decided as operations in Sicily progressed. Churchill and the British military men on D-Day Inc.'s board were all for expanding operations in the Med and taking a wait-and-see approach to launching Overlord. Their hope was that success in the Mediterranean would make operations in France unnecessary. George Marshall wanted to pull out as much of the workforce from Sicily as possible and send it to England to be reequipped and trained for Overlord, now approximately nine months away. Eisenhower usually agreed with Marshall that the entire focus of D-Day Inc. should be on France, but he also felt that Italy was too good an opportunity to batter their German competition to pass up.

Italy's head of government, Pietro Badoglio, began making noises about negotiating some kind of Italian surrender to the Allies even as Husky was still underway. (He was also negotiating with the Germans at the same time, apparently in search of the best deal he could get.) Ike didn't hesitate to see if something could be negotiated, despite his negative experience with the French admiral Darlan in North Africa. The Darlan deal had caused Eisenhower headaches with the French and with his board members in Washington and London. And it never actually had any measurable benefits for D-Day Inc. Ike was willing to try anything that might produce for his organization, however, especially anything that might save lives.

Unfortunately, the signals from Badoglio were mixed, and the negotiations weren't productive.

At the same time, the Germans were increasing their forces, especially around Rome. Eisenhower ordered Monty to move into Italy from Messina, and on September 3, 1943, the British became D-Day Inc.'s first forces on the European mainland, landing in Calabria, the southernmost part of Italy. But Montgomery was facing the same German competition that had just retreated successfully from Sicily, and he was facing them over terrain that was even worse than any of the geographical challenges in Sicily. If D-Day Inc. was going to succeed in Italy, it would need to launch another major amphibious operation much farther north on the Italian boot.

There were logistical problems with another large amphibious operation. Eisenhower's planning team wanted—and he agreed with them completely—more heavy bombers to prepare the way and more landing craft to put D-Day Inc.'s forces ashore in Italy. But the bombers were busy bombing Germany, and most of the landing craft were slated to go to England as part of the preparations for Overlord. If too many landing craft were used to go into Italy for Avalanche, it would delay operations in France for Overlord.

Another problem was that, like the landing craft, Ike did not have unlimited manpower to apply to the operation. Marshall insisted that the buildup of troops for Overlord begin in England. Many of the forces Eisenhower would send into Italy were relatively inexperienced. Finally, since the range of fighter aircraft was limited, the farthest north D-Day Inc. could go was Salerno, but it really needed to get as close as possible to Rome, approximately 150 miles to the north.

Eisenhower was as aware of the workforce limitations and of Salerno as a destination as he was the problems of insufficient aircraft and ships. He admitted in his diary that his deputies had warned him about the planes and boats and asked that he call off the invasion. But Ike decided to push ahead, even with the limited numbers of planes and boats. He wrote in his diary that the decision to go "was solely my own, and if things go wrong there is no one to blame except myself." In a note to Marshall, he said that if Avalanche failed, "I would . . . merely announce that one of our landings had been repulsed—due to my error."[19]

The landings did not fail, but it was a very close-run thing.

As usual, Eisenhower and his team had a plan for the "everything goes wrong" scenario—the invading forces at Salerno would retreat over the beach and be taken back on the landing craft that had deposited them there in the first place. Soon after the landings were made, it looked as if the worst-case scenario was about to play out. The Germans had moved into a gap between the British and American forces and looked poised to wipe out the entire force. Mark Clark, who was in charge of the action at Salerno, struggled to maintain control of his split forces. He sent a message to Ike that he was planning to evacuate his headquarters to a ship so that he could communicate more easily with his separated forces and concentrate his energies on the one that looked as if it had a chance to succeed.

Eisenhower was apoplectic. He responded to Clark that "headquarters should be moved last of all and the Commanding General should stay with his men to give them confidence. He should show the spirit of a naval captain, and, if necessary, go down with his ship."[20]

PLAN FOR SUCCESS

- **Give it your all**. Competition, as has been said before, involves risk. Sometimes "bet the farm" risk. If you make that kind of bet, stick to it. Back it up with your actions. Don't spend time looking for a way out to minimize your losses—you did bet the farm, didn't you?

Clark stayed on land, and his forces showed astounding courage in repulsing the Germans. Artillerymen refused to retreat despite being under direct attack by German tanks; U.S. and British naval vessels came in close to shore, in exceedingly shallow water, and fired their guns until they ran out of ammunition; and the men of the Eighty-second Airborne made two night parachute drops onto Clark's beachhead and went directly into action. D-Day Inc. held at Salerno.

By late September, even with Salerno secure, it was apparent that Avalanche was a strategic failure. Operations in Italy would not produce an opportunity for swift victory over the German competition. And now that D-Day Inc. was in Italy, it couldn't easily pull out. But every man and every bit of equipment that was deployed in Italy was a man or piece of matériel that could not be used in France. Within days of securing Salerno, it was obvious to almost everyone that operations in Italy would not get the job done against the Germans. Overlord was a necessity. Because Churchill was so agonized at the thought of Allied men dying on French beaches, he was the last of Ike's board members to accept this reality. But after Avalanche, despite Churchill's hesitation and continuing suggestions of alternative plans, Overlord was inevitable. D-Day Inc. focused absolutely and completely on Overlord.

Rome was not liberated from German control until June 5, 1944, and the news was all but lost in the awesome reality that was Overlord. Eisenhower and the entire D-Day Inc. organization gained valuable experience by tackling Avalanche, however, and operations in Italy did manage to tie down large German forces that D-Day Inc.'s men would have had to face in France. But there was only one way to succeed against the Germans: head-to-head competition for territory. Only one way to gain territory from the competition—take it.

That's what Overlord would do.

DEBRIEFING NOTES

STRATEGIES: DETERMINE YOUR MISSION, STAY FOCUSED

- **Focus on Your Main Purpose.** Always remember why you're in business.

STRATEGIES: PLAN FOR SUCCESS, PLAN TO IMPLEMENT

- **When the Boss Has a Good Idea—Jump on It.**
- **There Are Never Too Many Plans.** Effective advance planning for multiple scenarios is closely related to risk management, improving your chances of surviving a crisis.
- **Keep Your Options Open—Make One Decision at a Time.**
- **Planning Is the Discipline That Gives You Flexibility.** Planning allows you to consider almost every single contingency and prepare for it.
- **Planning Is a Team-Building Exercise.**

STRATEGIES: MANAGE YOUR PEOPLE (INCLUDING YOURSELF), MOTIVATE YOUR PEOPLE

- **Embrace the Madness.** If you're trapped in an illogical organization structure—embrace it and move on. It's amazing what can be accomplished if you spend your energy on doing things.
- **Replace 'Em.** If people don't perform, get rid of them.
- **Micromanage.** Okay, a few chapters ago, I said don't do this. But, if you're stuck with an incompetent (someone's relative, perhaps), give him or her very specific direction.
- **Principles Before Personalities.** If someone difficult contributes to the success of your mission, figure out how to work with that individual.

STRATEGY: BE HONEST

- **Be True to Yourself.** Believe in yourself and your vision of your organization's mission.
- **Honesty Is the Best Policy.** Yes, it is.
- **Step Up.** Acknowledge mistakes; learn from them; move on.

STRATEGY: PLAN FOR SUCCESS

- **Give It Your All**. Competition, as has been said before, involves risk. Sometimes "bet the farm" risk. If you make that kind of bet, stick to it. Back it up with your actions. Don't spend time looking for a way out to minimize your losses—you did bet the farm, didn't you?

FIVE

OVERLORD—D-DAY: SUPREME COMMANDER

Making Life-or-Death Decisions

As the Italian campaign made its grindingly slow progress through the autumn of 1943, D-Day Inc.'s board of directors turned its attention toward Overlord. Stalin and Marshall wanted to focus the organization's efforts on France. Churchill and his senior military men were still reluctant but also recognized that operations in Italy were not going to provide a quick route to success against their competition. Churchill also knew that Stalin was becoming extremely impatient and with good reason. The Soviets had been competing with the Germans for three years; the damage to their country, their industries, and their population was staggering. Stalin was convinced that only operations in France, with its close proximity to the German heartland, would relieve the relentless pressure the Soviet Union was experiencing. He wanted Overlord, and he wanted it immediately, if not sooner.

FDR, as often was the case, was taking his time deciding. D-Day Inc.'s chairman always supported Overlord as the operation that would lead to the Germans' defeat, but he realized there were logistical problems involved in pulling off the invasion. Overlord wasn't possible until the spring of 1944—there weren't enough landing craft.

Winston Churchill summed up the problem neatly when he said, "The fate of two great nations seems to be determined by some . . . things called LSTs and LCIs"[1] (LST: Landing Ship Tanks, LCI: Landing Craft Infantry). As frustrating as it was to have to wait, FDR, Churchill, Eisenhower, and all of D-Day Inc. would have to wait until more landing ships became available. At the same time, FDR didn't want the resources that were already in place to go unused until 1944, but—and it was a very large "but"—the more resources that were used for operations other than Overlord, the more losses would be incurred, and that would damage preparations for Overlord. Since Roosevelt didn't know what to do next, he delayed making decisions about D-Day Inc.

The most pressing decision FDR was dawdling over was who would be in charge of Overlord. Stalin needed the operation to relieve the pressure on his forces and believed that if the Americans and British were seriously committed to Overlord, an executive would be placed in charge. He made it very clear to both FDR and Churchill that until someone was appointed the boss, he would remain a very unhappy man. Given the gigantic effort the Soviets were making against the Germans, it was not in the best interests of the Allies to leave Stalin unhappy for a moment longer than necessary.

But Roosevelt put off making the decision. Remember, when Eisenhower first arrived in England in June 1942 as the CEO, he was considered the *acting* CEO. Ike was merely the interim executive, charged with designing and building the organization capable of pulling off Overlord. But at the time of his assignment, almost no one, including Ike himself, believed he would command Overlord. A little more than a year later, nothing had changed. Virtually every senior American and Brit believed the commander of Overlord would be George Marshall. FDR had come to trust Marshall as his go-to guy and was desperate to keep his most trusted counsel close at hand, but he also wanted Marshall to have his chance at making history in the most important command of the war. FDR said to Eisenhower, "You and I, Ike, know the name of the Chief of Staff in the Civil War, but few Americans outside the professional services do."[2]

Both FDR and Ike were aware that the field commander with the greatest success in the Civil War, Ulysses S. Grant, had gone on to the presidency. By October 1943, Eisenhower's status as acting CEO was more than sufficient to create buzz that he should be a candidate for president in the next-year's-elections. The man who was in charge of Overlord could very well make history after the war.

It speaks well of both Marshall and Eisenhower that neither man lobbied for the job. In fact, Marshall said he would gladly serve at the president's discretion. Eisenhower was perfectly willing to step down and take over as one of the American army commanders within D-Day Inc. The two American executives were not the only ones to act selflessly. British general Alan Brooke, Marshall's opposite number in England, was also considered for the top job but stepped aside due to the United States' larger contribution in men and matériel to D-Day Inc.

Stalin was not the kind of man who cared about the behind-the-scenes politics at D-Day Inc. nor the potential future consequences for the man who got to run Overlord. He just wanted the man appointed immediately. If the spot was empty, Stalin was convinced that the Americans and Brits lacked the resolve to launch the operation.

Churchill, like Alan Brooke, felt an American had to be in charge. He was far from enthusiastic about Overlord, but if it was going to happen, an American should get the top spot in the organization.

That left the decision to Roosevelt.

He was torn between his desire to name George Marshall to the job and his reliance on the man's steadiness and wisdom available to him on a daily basis as his chief of staff. FDR reviewed all the options:

- Marshall was Overlord's greatest champion on the D-Day Inc. board of directors. The British directors all respected him and listened to him.

- Even the U.S. Navy's Ernest King, a notoriously difficult personality, deferred to Marshall.
- Douglas MacArthur, who was the CEO of the U.S. military's southwestern Pacific division, was another famously difficult person who listened to Marshall.
- Eisenhower had more experience in Overlord's type of operation than any person alive, having successfully led Torch, Husky, and Avalanche.
- Eisenhower had built D-Day Inc., knew all the players, and worked well with everyone involved, especially the British.

FDR put aside his personal wishes, focused on the mission, and realized that Marshall would serve the organization better by remaining at his post. In early December 1943, Roosevelt met with Eisenhower in Tunis. FDR was returning to Washington after meeting Churchill and Stalin in Tehran. Ike met the president at the airport, and as their car drove away, FDR turned to him and said, "Well, Ike, you are going to command Overlord."[3]

MANAGE YOUR PEOPLE

- **Choose managers to fit your mission**. Sounds obvious, doesn't it? But Michael Eisner didn't do that when he pushed Jeffrey Katzenberg out and recruited Michael Ovitz to Disney. FDR, sorting through all of his personal impulses and desires, did make the right choice, based on fulfilling D-Day Inc.'s mission.

Roosevelt announced the appointment on Christmas Eve 1943. Eisenhower's title was a surprise: Supreme Commander, Allied Expeditionary Forces. Michael Korda wrote that FDR intended to reassure Stalin and to send a message to Churchill and Hitler that nothing would "interfere or delay the supreme operation of World War II: the invasion of Europe and the conquest of Germany." With the title of Supreme Commander, FDR was reaffirming the mission of D-Day Inc., and he couldn't have picked a better man. With the exception of George Marshall, no one had focused more intently on Overlord as the main operation against their German competition than Eisenhower. Korda said of FDR, "He achieved the objective that was most important to him: the concentration of the full power of the United States, the United Kingdom, and France in the hands of one man, who would use it for the sole purpose of defeating Germany."[4]

Operations in Italy were turned over to a new CEO for Mediterranean operations, General Sir Henry Maitland Wilson, with British general Alexander and American general Mark Clark in charge of the ground forces. The long, hard slog toward Rome continued even after Italy officially surrendered on September 8, 1943. The Italians would have preferred that the hostilities stop, but when two large foreign competitors have control of your entire country, your surrender doesn't do much to end the competition.

Eisenhower immediately began assembling his executive staff for Overlord. He had wanted Alexander to continue in his role of deputy commander. During both Husky and Torch, Alexander had functioned as Ike's No. 2 *and* the ground commander. But Churchill insisted that Alexander stay in Italy. Insisting again, Churchill pushed Monty as the ground commander for Overlord.

Eisenhower wanted no part of Monty as his overall deputy—instead Ike asked for and received Air Marshall Sir Arthur Tedder as his No. 2. Tedder and Ike had worked well together during the previous operations. Monty would be the ground commander *only*, and Ike even put a limitation on that. Once D-Day Inc.'s forces were past the beaches and inside French territory, Ike would come to France and take direct control of the ground forces. At that point, Monty's role in the organization would be smaller than it had been for the Sicilian operations.

Eisenhower and Churchill agreed easily on Admiral Bert Ramsay of the Royal Navy to be Ike's naval commander. (Admiral Cunningham was going back to London to become first sea lord, roughly equivalent to the U.S. Navy's chief of naval operations [CNO], then Ernest King.) Ramsay had masterminded the fleet of small ships and boats that had evacuated the British army at Dunkirk in 1940, and got along well with Americans. Air Chief Marshall Sir Trafford Leigh-Mallory would replace Tedder as the air forces executive. Leigh-Mallory's track record was solid but limited. He had been a successful fighter-pilot leader but did not understand air support of ground troops and airborne parachute operations. Both air support and airborne operations would be crucial to Overlord, and Leigh-Mallory (another Churchill assignment) was the weakest member of Ike's executive team.

MANAGE YOUR PEOPLE

- **Picking teams**. Like choosing managers (earlier in this chapter), staying focused on your mission is crucial when filling out your executive team. Ike would have preferred to not deal with Monty, but his British allies wanted Monty on the staff, so there he was. Ike structured Monty's job in a way that maximized his positive impact on the alliance while minimizing his negative impact on the operations themselves.
- Ike's new deputy for the air forces, Leigh-Mallory, was Churchill's man, not Ike's. When choosing a manager for someone else's team, you have to know what the team needs are. Churchill was more interested in a significant British presence on Ike's executive staff than on making sure that qualified men were on it.

Ike insisted that "Beetle" Smith remain his chief of staff, and Omar Bradley be the executive in charge of the American ground forces. Once Eisenhower went to France, Bradley and Monty would be equals in responsibility, if not in rank.

With Tedder, Ramsay, Smith, and Bradley on the executive team, and with Monty on it but boxed in, thanks to careful staff structuring by Ike, D-Day Inc. had a solid executive staff.

Eisenhower wanted to return to London from North Africa by early January 1944 to shift into full Overlord mode, but before he could do that, Marshall ordered him back to Washington for a brief, working vacation. The boss knew that Ike needed to be fresh in order to face what was coming at him and pushed past Eisenhower's reasons for skipping the trip. After dutifully taking his vacation, Ike arrived in London and was immediately met with problems.

The plans for Overlord, the product of eighteen months of British staff planning, were insufficient. The entry point for operations, the beachhead in Normandy, was too narrow. The initial forces were too small. American and British forces would have to land on the same beaches, which would inevitably lead to confusion due to the differences in management structure and equipment. Monty, who had reviewed the plans at Churchill's request, thought they were flawed because they had been drawn up by planners and not people with actual experience.

COMMUNICATE

- **Know your stuff**. If you don't know it, learn it. If you know what you're talking about, it generates self-confidence and gives you credibility with others. If you don't know your stuff, shut up. Faking it, even when done by the boss, does not work. A blowhard leader doesn't help his or her organization.

Typically, Monty came away from discussions with Churchill and Eisenhower believing that he was now in charge of the planning for Overlord. Given that Ike didn't even mention his initial planning discussion with Monty in *Crusade in Europe*, it is highly unlikely that any such authorization had been forthcoming.

Thanks to Ike's and Monty's reaction to the plans, however, miles of beach were added to the targeted area, widening the beachhead, and discrete zones were assigned to the Americans and British within which they could operate. Most crucially, Eisenhower added significant numbers of airborne forces to come in at the extreme western end (inland of Utah Beach near Ste. Mère Église) and the extreme eastern end (inland of Sword Beach near Caen) of the Overlord beachhead. Adding the airborne element was the result of Ike's experience in previous operations. He had the hard-won knowledge and self-confidence to overrule a group of professional planners even though they were working at the prime minister's behest. Eisenhower could agree with Montgomery without needing everyone to know that he had thought of it first or that he made the crucial changes that would increase the likelihood of success. Experience takes experience, and it's quite possible that the real payoff of Torch, Husky, and Avalanche was the experience those campaigns had allowed Eisenhower to accumulate. He had already been able to operate successfully under extreme pressure.

★ ★ ★

Although Eisenhower's staff was established, there was an organizational glitch in the Allies' structure. D-Day Inc. had its own air forces dedicated to supporting its operations, but it did not control the Strategic Air Forces. This group was responsible for long-range bombing of oil depots and refineries, factories, and military installations in Germany or German-held countries. Ike had struggled to get enough air support during Operation Avalanche when his forces were on the Salerno beachhead. He did not want to struggle again. He insisted that he have control over *all* air forces in the immediate run-up to Overlord through the invasion itself until D-Day Inc.'s forces had substantially penetrated France and Belgium. Several members of the board, especially Churchill, were not inclined to give Eisenhower this power because the board members wanted the Strategic Air Forces to continue on their own mission.

The disagreement between Ike and his board over the Strategic Air Forces centered over two things: whether Ike would have true control of these forces and the two ways he would use them—heavy-bombing attacks close to Normandy to soften the opposition, and for implementing "The Transportation Plan."

The idea of softening your opposition with artillery or bombardment now seems obvious, but almost no one not directly involved with D-Day Inc. seemed to understand how difficult getting ashore on Normandy's beaches was going to be.

Strategic bombing was a new concept in World War II. The little airplanes of World War 1 weren't capable of flying far enough or carrying heavy enough bombs to do much damage. By early 1944, long-range, heavy bombing was a given, but in a limited way. The bombing of targets to disable the competition's ability to compete was common practice. It made sense to stop the opposition from producing oil or airplanes or ships or other weapons. Many senior executives in the air forces of America and England believed that if you bombed your competition with enough thoroughness, putting forces on the ground to beat them would be unnecessary. With that kind of thinking, would you expect the air forces to want to bomb in support of advancing troops? The air force executives were thinking too small.

The other problem in deciding whether or not to utilize the Strategic Air Forces in Overlord was that except for Eisenhower and his staff, most of whom had already pulled off three extremely large-scale amphibious operations, no one knew the tremendous difficulties inherent in an operation the size and scale of Overlord. The British and U.S. air executives running the Allies' strategic bombing forces simply had no experience in amphibious projects. Through no fault of their own, they were incapable of understanding how important their support could be to Overlord.

On the other hand, Eisenhower and Tedder (his No. 2 now, his air boss for North Africa, Sicily, and Italy) did know. When D-Day Inc. began operations in North Africa and Sicily, they were not competing with a well-established foe. In both Tunisia and Sicily, the Germans had moved into the area only a little ahead of D-Day Inc. And, like Ike and company, the Germans had long supply lines to cope with. When D-Day Inc. turned its attention to Italy, specifically the Salerno operation, it found itself in a more intense competitive situation. The Germans were able to reinforce their positions in advance of the Allies' arrival. They had shorter, internal supply lines to support their forces. And they had air power—the German air force, the Luftwafte, had been built largely as a support arm for its ground forces and was well suited to the task. At Salerno, D-Day Inc. had no pre-invasion bombing and only anemic air support during operations on the beachhead. The lack of air support was one of the major factors that contributed to the almost-failure of Avalanche. Ike and Tedder did not want a repeat of that when it came time for Overlord.

Another philosophical conflict between the strategic air bosses and D-Day Inc.'s executives was how the air forces could best contribute to the success of Overlord. The executives of the strategic forces, along with Churchill and the British senior command (all of whom were on Ike's board, remember), felt they could help Overlord best by attacking oil depots and refineries in Germany, as well as munitions factories. After all, weapons that weren't made couldn't be used against you.

Eisenhower, Tedder, and Leigh-Mallory (D-Day Inc.'s air executive) were concerned with ensuring that once ashore, their forces stayed ashore. The best way to make that happen was to prevent the Germans from bringing in fresh forces. Their idea to do just that: the Transportation Plan.

The Transportation Plan was the brainchild of British professor of anatomy Solly Zuckerman, one of thousands of English scientists and technical experts who dedicated themselves to the war effort.

Zuckerman's plan called for assaults on a carefully chosen, limited number of railway centers in France. The bombing program had to be worked out in advance, extended and maintained over a period of time, but if done thoroughly would paralyze an entire region's railroads. If D-Day Inc. could chop the logistical support legs out from under their German competitors, there would be no fresh German forces. That would vastly increase the chances of the men on the beaches, which was Ike's first priority. Tedder and Leigh-Mallory both realized the potential of the Transportation Plan, persuaded Eisenhower (who took little persuading, seizing quickly on the advantages of the plan), and lobbied hard for it with Churchill and the senior British military executives.

Churchill, his war cabinet, and the senior military all hated the idea. They did not want to take the Strategic Air Forces away from their mission of damaging Germany's weapons factories and oil refineries. They did not want to give control over almost all air forces to Eisenhower—internal politics at play. Even in the wartime military, there are people who worry about allowing someone within the organization to build too large a power base. They should stay focused on what's good for the mission, instead. And Churchill and the senior British military absolutely did not want to destroy French railroads and, most likely, to kill French civilians in the process.

No one at D-Day Inc. wanted to destroy French resources and kill French men, women, and children. It was an extremely tough choice to make. But Eisenhower and his team all remembered that their ultimate goal was to stop the killing on a very large scale and to liberate people, including the French, from German control. They believed the best way to do it was the Transportation Plan. Fortunately, Charles de Gaulle, among other Frenchmen, made it known that he was in agreement with Eisenhower.

But the turf battle over control continued, and so did the reluctance of Churchill and some of the other board members to approve the Transportation Plan.

Finally, Eisenhower made it simple. Either he was given control of all the air forces and approval to implement the Transportation Plan, or he would resign from D-Day Inc.

Ike got control of the air forces and the okay for the Transportation Plan.

Despite all the conflicts Eisenhower experienced as the head of D-Day Inc., the combined issue of control of the air forces and approval of the Transportation Plan was the only time he ever threatened to quit if he didn't get his way. And he did it after multiple discussions and debates, after calmly but forcefully making his needs and plans known over and over again. The struggle over command of the air forces continued almost throughout Overlord, but Eisenhower never backed off and ended up getting what he needed.

The Transportation Plan worked. D-Day Inc. analysts set the index for railway usage in January and February of 1944 at 100. After the plan went into effect, railway usage dropped to 69 in mid-May and all the way down to 38 by D-Day. Stephen Ambrose wrote, "It [the Transportation Plan] was a resounding success. . . . It made it almost impossible for the Germans to move reinforcements to the beachhead. Eisenhower thought the Transportation Plan was the decisive factor in his victory at Overlord, and he was right."[5]

PRIORITIZE

- **If you gotta have it, get it!** If you need something from another part of your organization (even a parent company), get it. There may be some ugly political tussles, but everything will be forgiven when you succeed.
- **Remember the greater good**. No one wants to inflict widespread pain. (Okay, almost no one.) But you have to remember the greater good of your organization and your mission. In tough economic times the survival of your company, and *most* of your employees' jobs, may depend on your willingness to lay people off.

Another planning issue was the all-important "What do you do on D-Day plus one?" As almost anyone who has run anything can say, it's not enough to launch an initiative and then sit back and relax. In the early days of the "dot.com boom," more than one company put a large effort into launching its Web site and then realized it hadn't prepared itself properly for the inventory, delivery, and communications issues that success on the Internet might bring. Companies found themselves selling more product and service than they could handle. D-Day Inc.'s plans for Overlord included expanding its territorial reach beyond the beachhead, and then immediately pushing toward Germany. There would be no letup.

The directive on Overlord from the combined chiefs of staff (the senior U.S. and British military commanders, all of whom were on Eisenhower's board) was simple. As Ike described it: D-Day Inc.'s forces were "to land on the coast of France and thereafter to destroy the German ground forces."[6] Destroying the opposition was what D-Day plus one was all about. Unfortunately, there was a major conflict on the best way to do this. Stephen Ambrose wrote, "Montgomery proposed to defeat the Germans in France by outthinking and outmaneuvering them; Eisenhower wanted to outfight them."[7]

Montgomery was in charge of the eastern side of Overlord, where the British and Canadians were to move directly through northern France into Belgium and then into Germany. It was the shortest route into the heart of the competition, and Monty planned to seize ports as he moved along, securing his supply lines and making logistical support much easier. He felt that D-Day Inc.'s ground forces should attack along a narrow front—along the general route his forces were assigned—moving swiftly to cut into the competitor's territory. Monty expressed confidence that this approach would allow him to unbalance "the enemy while keeping balanced myself."[8]

There were at least two problems with this approach. Monty had demonstrated time and again during operations in Africa, Sicily, and Italy that moving swiftly was not his forte. And if D-Day Inc.

moved forward in a narrow thrust, it would make it very easy for the Germans to fall back and establish strong defensive positions. Many times in history, armies have given away territory to gain a secure defense and to survive, just as corporations have given up on markets to ensure corporate survival. In the first few years of the twenty-first century, Detroit's Big Three car companies closed down brands (Oldsmobile, Buick, Plymouth, Saturn) and sold their ownership positions in a number of foreign manufacturers (Opel, Jaguar, Volvo). Among other benefits, this allowed them to raise cash and focus more intensely on the one market absolutely necessary for their survival: the United States. For D-Day Inc. the prospect of its German competition retrenching for the long haul was too painful to contemplate. The Allies needed to finish the competition as quickly as possible.

BE HONEST

- **Know thyself**. Monty was aware of the need for movement and speed but completely ignored his own history in failing at both.

PLAN FOR SUCCESS

- **Remember what's important. Then think big**. Ike realized that he could create pressure on a massive scale by competing in a large geographic arena. He knew there were supply problems but fighting a highly mobile war would solve many of his other problems—so he made it work. Decide what you *need* to do—then figure out how to do it.

If Monty's outthink-the-Germans approach wasn't workable (not that he ever admitted it), that left D-Day Inc. with Eisenhower's

outfight-them approach. Ike wanted to engage the Germans on as broad a front as possible, fighting from Belgium down France's German border. After the slow slogs of Tunisia, Sicily, and Italy, Eisenhower was committed to mobility. "A war of movement on a vast scale was what he had in mind, one which would keep the Germans off-balance and unable to hold or form a defensive line."[9]

Ike's broad-front, highly mobile strategy required massive numbers of nonfighting vehicles, mostly trucks and jeeps. Churchill was flabbergasted at the number, approximately one vehicle for every five soldiers in France. But Eisenhower's concept included these absolute necessities:

- Basic transport for the speed of movement Eisenhower had in mind.
- Movement to engage the competition along a gigantic front.
- Engaging the Germans on a broad front would keep them out of defensive positions and would allow for the destruction of their forces.

Since Eisenhower was the boss, his view prevailed over Monty's. That turned out to be a very good thing since Monty did not push forward on his part of the front with anything resembling speed, which meant the key transportation centers, like Caen in northern France and the great port of Antwerp in Belgium, took forever to come into D-Day Inc.'s control. This lack of ports exacerbated the major drawback to Ike's mobile, broad-front strategy. Mobile operations are supply intensive, and without control of the transport centers, especially ports, it was difficult to keep the frontline forces properly supplied.

During the winter-spring of 1944, personnel problems with Ike's executive team persisted. Monty continued to believe he was in charge of planning for Overlord and was convinced that he would be

the executive in charge of all ground forces in Europe. Ike made it clear that he would take over control of the ground forces personally, but Monty ignored this. Montgomery tended to ignore anyone and anything that conflicted with his point of view.

Monty also involved himself in all kinds of activities that had nothing to do with Overlord—he suggested to the archbishop of Canterbury that a large service be held in Westminster Abbey, "in coronation regalia," to "consecrate the nation's strength." Monty laid out the details of the service to the archbishop, ensuring that he, Montgomery, would be the star. (At the instructions of the king and prime minister, the idea was disapproved.) A joke circulating at the time had Churchill meeting with the king and saying, "I'm very worried, I think Monty is after my job." The king sighs in relief and replies, "I'm very relieved to hear that; I thought he was after *mine*."[10]

After the disappointments with Montgomery's slowness in North Africa, Sicily, and Italy and months of his arrogance, even the British members of Eisenhower's team wanted Ike to fire Monty.

But the public adoration of the man was too intense to dismiss him. In modern parlance, Monty was a rock star. Ike knew there was no way to fire Monty without damaging the appearance of his Allied command—and Eisenhower wasn't going to do anything that would hurt the alliance. He continued to ignore Monty's arrogance and at the same time to use Monty's ideas. He never publicly discredited Montgomery; even in his book *Crusade in Europe*, written after the war, he treats Monty with respect. And when necessary, Ike created a structure that gave him the benefits of Monty's glamour and retained control, as he did with the decision to command the ground forces once D-Day Inc. was well established in France.

While Monty was a public-relations dream and an intra-staff nightmare, George Patton was almost the reverse. Patton was assigned to be in charge of the Third Army, which would follow Bradley's forces into France. Because the Third Army's job was a follow-up to the invasion, its timeline for assembly and equipping was further into

the future than the invasion date. In the meantime, D-Day Inc. put Patton in charge of a large phantom command, supposedly operating in eastern England—the logical place to assemble a force if the site of the invasion were to be Calais, the point in France closest to England. Its proximity to England convinced the Germans that it was the most likely place to be invaded. (Although Calais was considered as the jumping-off point for Overlord, it was quickly abandoned for a number of reasons.) D-Day Inc.'s intelligence team reinforced the German conviction that Calais was Overlord's real target by making a show of Patton playing the boss of the large shadow force that was preparing to invade Calais.

Being in charge of a fictional organization isn't much fun, however. Since there is no actual organization and no troops, there is nothing to run. Patton was restless and depressed. In the months leading up to Overlord, it seemed as if every time he spoke in public, he put his foot in his mouth. On more than one occasion, Patton misspoke, caused an uproar, and was scolded by Eisenhower: "I have warned you time and again against impulsiveness in action and speech and have flatly instructed you to say nothing that could possibly be misinterpreted." Then at the opening of a club for American servicemen approximately six weeks before D-Day in April 1944, Patton was asked to say a few impromptu words to the crowd. He spoke of the need for Anglo-American unity "since it is the evident destiny of the British and Americans to rule the world."[11]

A reporter sent out the statement on the wire services and within days the list of those offended included the Russians and the smaller nations (who were not part of the evident destiny), British editorial writers, and American congressmen of all political stripes. Patton had hit a grand slam of indignation.

The public-relations firestorm that ensued added to Eisenhower's astounding stress. He sent a message to Marshall, with whom he had discussed the Patton problem on numerous occasions, saying, "I am seriously contemplating the most drastic action."[12] Marshall told

Eisenhower that he would support any decision Ike made, to keep or to fire Patton.

Patton came to see Eisenhower within days of the incident and begged for forgiveness. At one point in the discussion, Ike thought he saw Patton's eyes getting watery. It was embarrassing, and Eisenhower ended the conversation. He considered what his next step should be. The meeting where Patton had made his "evident destiny" remark was supposed to be private, no press in attendance. Patton had spoken believing his words were off the record. Turning from the incident itself to the challenges of beating the German competition, Ike knew that Patton had competed with Rommel in Africa, and Rommel was now in command in France. Patton, unlike Monty, had a track record of being aggressive and delivering on his promises.

Eisenhower decided to keep Patton.

D-Day Inc.'s mission was to beat the Germans. No other executive on staff did a better job of that than George Patton. With the decision made, Ike told Patton, "You owe us some victories; pay off and the world will deem me a wise man."[13]

As events turned out, Ike was a very wise man on this one.

Eisenhower was also doing the intricate dance of managing up to the executive above him. Winston Churchill, in effect Ike's vice chairman, lived and worked near Eisenhower. He frequently invited Ike to lunch (an affair that invariably lasted until early evening) or to dinner (an occasion that usually didn't finish until 2:00 a.m.). Churchill was an eccentric genius, with a passion for detail, an unflinching commitment to beating Hitler no matter what, and he had more ideas than anyone knew what to do with. Some of his ideas were excellent— Churchill championed an idea to create artificial harbors by sinking old ships to form "reefs." These were code-named "Mulberries" and were in fact implemented in Overlord. (They were reasonably successful, but inadequate to cope with the ever-increasing needs of D-Day Inc.'s forces as they moved away from the shore.)

Many other ideas were, to put it tactfully, of lesser quality. But

Churchill wanted to discuss most of them with Ike, frequently in phone calls that began at midnight. Discussions with Churchill were rarely brief. All of the meetings and phone calls with Churchill were a necessary but often unproductive drain on Eisenhower's time and energy.

MANAGE YOUR PEOPLE

- **Manage up**. For a last resort, if nothing else works, you can always manage down by ordering people around. That's not an option when you manage up—in dealings with your superiors. Don't hesitate to ask for your boss's expertise if it can help. But manage the day-to-day items yourself. If you can satisfy your boss's curiosity, do it, of course. Try to anticipate his or her requests—it will create confidence in your management. If your boss is a relentless micromanager, buckle your seat belt. You're in for a rough ride, and there's nothing you can do about it.

That isn't to say that Eisenhower wanted his board to be a distant body, guiding him with a vaguely omnipotent hand. Ike was in constant touch with George Marshall.* No other member of D-Day Inc.'s board of directors had the expertise in planning that Marshall had; none of them had been committed to Overlord as *the* priority operation of the war whereas Marshall had championed it from the beginning. Marshall understood the workings of the American army and knew how its soldiers were trained. He was completely aware of the logistical challenges, especially the manufacture of the all-important landing craft. Eisenhower turned to Marshall for his experience, his expertise, and his wisdom. Because of Marshall's

---

* Ike was a direct report to Marshall in the U.S. Army, and through Marshall to President Roosevelt. But as D-Day's CEO, operating in an Allied organization, Ike really reported to the entire board. In that sense, Marshall was just one of the directors Eisenhower dealt with.

background, the majority of contact between him and Ike was productive, unlike what usually happened with Churchill.

There were two other people issues for D-Day Inc.: security and morale.

D-Day Inc. had a workforce of approximately 2.5 million troops in the months just before Overlord, all crammed together in the southern two-thirds of the United Kingdom. Ports all over England were frantic with activity. The forces continued to train, and there were large-scale operational rehearsals involving thousands of people at a time. With that many people and that much activity, the chances were high that the competition might figure out at least part of what D-Day Inc. was up to.

Eisenhower was a distant supervisor of most of the security measures employed to keep D-Day Inc. safe. Not that he wasn't concerned, but it wasn't his field of expertise, and the British had it well in hand. By the spring of 1944, British intelligence had rounded up every covert agent the Germans had managed to slip into England and were using them to feed disinformation to their German bosses.

The other major disinformation campaign, largely mounted by the British and enthusiastically supported by Ike, was the creation of the phantom force to scare the competition into defending Calais instead of Normandy. Phony harbors were built on the eastern coast of England; airfields were filled with planes made of canvas and balsa wood and painted to look real; and there were endless rows of tanks and jeeps, also cleverly painted balsa wood. Faux communications filled the radio waves. Ike's major contribution to this deception was the assignment of George Patton to be its chief executive. It never occurred to the Germans that a talent like Patton's would be used for the sole purpose of playing decoy. It worked. A month after D-Day Inc.'s forces were in France, the Germans were still holding back a large force in the Calais area. Keeping those forces out of competition for a month provided immense savings in men and matériel for D-Day Inc. and made it easier for Ike's forces to get ashore and stay ashore.

★ ★ ★

It's easy for modern executives to dismiss this gigantic disinformation campaign as romantic wartime cloak-and-dagger. But in this age of blogs, Facebook and MySpace, and Twitter, spreading disinformation isn't all that difficult. A bit of faux news written up in an anonymous blog can travel the globe almost instantly. Of course, this means corporations have to be on their guard regarding gossip and disinformation aimed at them.

Another modern tool of disinformation is *rumorware*. This is the contemporary equivalent of the phantom army that D-Day Inc. used to pin the Germans down at Calais. Rumorware is simple: Rumors—however they get started—begin circulating that a new product is coming to market soon. The new product is invariably better and sexier than anything the competition has on the market at the moment. There's only one thing wrong with these rumors—they're not true. Either the product is not quite as wonderful as the rumors make it out to be, or it's not coming to market quite as soon as was represented in the rumor.

What's the point of rumorware? If it works, it keeps consumers from buying the competition's product as they wait on the glorious new bit of rumorware—your new product or service—to come true.

★ ★ ★

While Eisenhower was not the controlling hand behind the counter-espionage and disinformation campaigns such as Patton's phantom army, he was very active in dealing with leaks from within D-Day Inc. itself. The organization's headquarters had more than sixteen thousand people reporting for work. The possibilities for breaches in security were stupefying. In March 1944, less than three months before the launch of Overlord, documents including data on the strength of the forces, targeted territories, equipment, and the tentative date of the operation were found in the Chicago post office.

A dozen postmen in the office saw some or all of the documents. It turned out that this was not espionage but homesickness: a sergeant daydreaming of home accidentally addressed the package to his sister instead of the War Department in Washington DC.

In April 1944, a U.S. Army Air Force general went to a cocktail party. *In vino veritas*, because after a few drinks, the general began talking about D-Day, which he announced would begin before June 15. He even offered to take bets on the date. When Ike found out, he acted forcefully, "busting" the general to the rank of colonel and sending him back to the States. The now colonel pleaded for mercy. He was a West Point classmate of Eisenhower's and an old friend, but Ike sent him packing in his reduced rank.

A month later, a U.S. Navy officer got drunk and supposedly revealed a large number of details similar to what the Air Force officer had. Eisenhower had no power over naval officers,* so he asked the man's superiors to handle the situation as they thought best. The good news was that the officer, while drunk, did not reveal anything that was not common knowledge in the newspapers. The bad news for the officer was that his superiors were as angry about his loose lips as Eisenhower was—he was sent back to the States as well.

Ike said of these kinds of security breaches: "I get so angry at the occurrence of such needless and additional hazards that I could cheerfully shoot the offender myself."[14] Like any CEO, Eisenhower was not able to stop all leaks of confidential information. What he could and did do, was model the keeping of confidences himself and harshly discipline anyone who broke security on confidential information. Ike was constantly frustrated by the lack of perfect security; he could only hope that the organization had *enough* security. Fortunately for D-Day Inc., it did.

---

* The U.S. Navy was a separate service, and its officers reported to Eisenhower on D-Day operations but not on matters of discipline. The U.S. Air Force was still part of the U.S. Army during World War II, so Ike had direct control over its officers who worked for D-Day Inc.

Another people issue that Eisenhower and his executives dealt with was the morale of D-Day Inc.'s workforce. There were approximately 2.5 million people in the organization, many of them, such as the Americans and Canadians, a long way from home; others, such as the Brits, French, Poles, Czechs, and Dutch, were weary from years of struggling against the Germans. Ike and his team were asking these men to go in harm's way. As the countdown to D-Day proceeded, the training and the operational rehearsals finished, leaving these millions of men with nothing to do but anxiously wait, wondering if they would ever see home again. Eisenhower also worried that they would never go home. Stephen Ambrose wrote: "It made him heartsick to think about 'how many youngsters are gone forever,' . . . he could 'never escape a recognition of fact that back home the news brings anguish and suffering to families all over the country.'"[15]

MANAGE AND MOTIVATE YOUR PEOPLE

- **Care for your people**. If you're not capable of feeling concern because it's the right thing to do, *act* concerned for pragmatic reasons. It's a timeworn cliché but nonetheless important for being clichéd: *People are your most important resource*. Without them, your company is going nowhere.

Ike's concern for the troops led him, in the months before Overlord's launching, to visit twenty-six divisions, twenty-four airfields, five ships of war, and depots, shops, hospitals, and other installations, according to Ambrose. "He made certain that every soldier who was to go ashore on D-Day had the opportunity to at least look at the man who was sending him into battle; he managed to talk to hundreds personally."[16] At every visit, he asked the men their names and where they were from. He looked them in the eye, and shook as many hands as he could. Bradley, Montgomery, Patton, Tedder, and other D-Day Inc.

executives made as many visits as they could. For all of his other flaws, Monty was terrific at these visits—he stood on the hood of his jeep and asked the men to gather around, then said, "Take off your helmets so I can get a look at you."[17] He pointed at one of the men and asked, "What's your most valuable possession?" The soldier gave the semi-official reply, "My rifle, sir." Monty responded, "No it isn't, it's your life, and I'm going to save it for you."[18] The troops—and who could blame them?—loved this.

"All the visits paid off. On the eve of D-Day, [Ike's chief of staff, Beetle] Smith reported that the confidence of the troops in the high command was without parallel."[19]

PEOPLE FIRST—YOUR PEOPLE

If this idea of visiting your frontline workforce sounds familiar, it should. It used to go by the term "management by walking around." Actually, visiting with employees isn't the only way to connect to them; enlightened company policies can pay dividends with employees, customers, and shareholders. Herb Kelleher, the cofounder and former CEO of Southwest Airlines, is renowned for caring for employees. In 2001 the *New York Times* quoted Kelleher:

> You have to treat your employees like customers. . . . When you treat them right, then they will treat your outside customers right. That has been a powerful competitive weapon for us. . . . We've never had layoffs. We could have made more money if we furloughed people. But we don't do that. And we honor them constantly. Our people know that if they are sick, we will take care of them. If there are occasions of grief or joy, we will be there with them. They know that we value them as people, not just cogs in a machine.[20]

According to the *New York Times*, Southwest has been the great success story of the airline business—the only company that has been consistently profitable through these tumultuous times, even as many competitors have filed for bankruptcy or gone out of business. Although it is unionized, Kelleher managed to handle negotiations without anger. He didn't see the pilots as enemies because they were in the union. To Kelleher, they were employees first, union members second. In fact, when he retired as Southwest's chairman in 2008—he gave up the CEO position in 2004—the pilots ran a full-page ad in *USA Today* that said, "The pilots of Southwest Airlines want to express our sentiment to Herb that it has been an honor and a privilege to be a part of his aviation legacy."

Prior to the economic meltdown in September 2008, Southwest had been profitable for seventeen straight years. As of April 2009, the company was suffering through its third red-ink quarter in a row and was making cuts in spending. Those cuts did not include layoffs—employees were offered a buyout program.[21] Despite the poor economy, a year after the meltdown began, Southwest's stock was up approximately 12 percent versus an industry average of -0.23 percent year-to-date. Its market capitalization was $7.2 billion versus an industry average of $5 billion. Looks as if there's something to the "treat your employees like customers" theory of Kelleher's.[22]

For the men of Overlord, the hard part of the operation would begin as their planes and ships departed for France. For Eisenhower, the hard part would come before those departures. Ike had to make some tough decisions. *Tough* might be too gentle a word. *Brutal* or *agonizing* would probably be more appropriate. The one thing that distinguishes the CEO from all other executives is that he or she is the person in the organization with the final say, the person empowered to decide on the fate of employees by choosing to lay off a large portion of the workforce, for instance. When the pressure is cranked up to the maximum—whether due to a bad economy, a regulatory setback, a staggering loss in court, or a disaster like a factory explosion—the CEO still has to make the decisions necessary not only to the survival of the company but to its future success. On a smaller scale, this is true of the executives who manage any business unit.

Eisenhower was the chief executive of the biggest, most daring business unit of the war. Other executives, such as FDR and Churchill, had even greater responsibilities, but none with the immediacy of Ike's responsibility to D-Day Inc. He wasn't dealing with the normal pressures and risks of business, wasn't deciding on launching a new product or service into a new part of the globe nor on whether or not to issue a dividend for the quarter nor on closing a plant and making layoffs. Ike's decisions concerned where and when to send thousands of young men—to be hurt and, in too many instances, to be killed. But he was the CEO of D-Day Inc., and those decisions went with the job. Eisenhower thought of himself as a corporate head. He frequently referred to the price or the cost of operations and believed it was necessary to justify the expenditure of human life to his stockholders, who happened to be the American and British peoples. Whatever he decided about those young men had to be justified to all of his countrymen and his allies.

Eisenhower faced two gut-wrenching decisions in particular:

- whether or not to send the U.S. Army's 82nd and 101st Airborne Divisions into action on the western extreme of Overlord, in support of Bradley's forces on Utah Beach
- the specific date to launch the entire invasion

Using the two Airborne divisions in support of operations on Utah Beach had been one of Eisenhower's major contributions to the plan for Overlord, and the question of whether or not to cancel their deployment came up at almost the last minute. On May 29, 1944, a week before Overlord was supposed to start on June 5, intelligence came in that the Germans were reinforcing the area inland of Utah Beach. Eisenhower's air exec, Leigh-Mallory, begged Ike to call off the Airborne units—he estimated that losses for the two divisions might be as high as 70 percent, a staggering rate that meant more than ten thousand men hurt or killed. If the losses were even close to that high, the Airborne couldn't possibly succeed in supporting Bradley's forces on Utah, and the losses on the beach would also be horrific. If the Airborne operations were canceled, it made sense to cancel the landings at Utah. Canceling Utah would create a domino effect of last-minute adjustments on a massive scale moving east along Overlord's fifty miles of beach.

Operational plans for D-Day were detailed down to the minute, and had taken eighteen months to construct. The idea of rearranging them all with only seven days to accomplish the new plan for launching was beyond comprehension. But if the Airborne and Utah Beach operations weren't canceled, the possible losses would be unbearable. Eisenhower would find himself trying to justify wasting tens of thousands of young lives after he had been forewarned of the impending disaster. Ike said, "It would be difficult to conceive of a more soul-racking problem."[23]

Eisenhower went to his tent to make the decision on his own. He already knew that Bradley wanted the Airborne support and that Leigh-Mallory wanted to cancel the operations. War, like major business initiatives, is about risk. Ike assessed the risks:

- Without the Airborne, Utah could fail.
- Without Utah, Overlord could fail.

The possibility of failure was so devastating that nowhere in D-Day Inc.'s plans was there an evacuation plan in case Overlord failed. Not having a fallback plan is not a best practice for any business, but if failure is not an option under any circumstances, why bother with fallback plans? Also, the unspoken but understood fallback plan for Overlord was to retreat over the beaches as the English had at Dunkirk. The unspoken but understood fallback plan for many businesses is closure of the plant or the division or the company and layoffs of all employees. When the stakes are that high, no wonder the fallback plans go unspoken. Eisenhower concluded that as bad as the risks for the Airborne divisions were, the risk to Overlord was much greater. The Airborne would go in as planned; Bradley's men would operate on Utah Beach as planned. The risk would have to be taken.

The second decision—when, specifically, to launch Overlord—at first glance seemed easier. After all, the United States, the United Kingdom, and Canada were all committed to go. The only decision was "when"—not "if." But the risk factors involved in "when" were so complex that if the decision was incorrect, it would lead to failure. In addition to the complications of getting the forces onto the airplanes and the ships at exactly the right moment—men rode the railroads all over the United Kingdom for days to make the journey from their bases to the correct airfields and ports—there were a number of weather and tide factors that had to be weighed:

- The Airborne forces needed darkness until they arrived over their zones and parachuted in—afterward they wanted moonlight.
- The tides had to be low at approximately dawn so that defensive obstacles placed in the water would be visible and could be dealt with.
- D-Day Inc. needed a "long" day—lots of daylight in which to operate.
- The tides had to be low again near the end of the day for follow-up forces to land before dark—this tide factor reduced the number of suitable days in any month to six.
- Warships and bombers needed good visibility to identify their targets.
- Low winds had to be blowing from the English Channel into France, to clear the beaches from smoke and maintain visibility.
- Three quiet-weather days had to follow D-Day to facilitate a quick buildup in follow-up forces.

- Calm seas. The last thing Ike or his executives wanted was for the men aboard the landing ships arriving too seasick to fight.

Eisenhower was an optimist, but he wasn't crazy—he and his executive team were well aware that there was no way all of the factors would line up perfectly. Cornelius Ryan said that Ike "schooled himself, in countless dry runs with his meteorological staff, to recognize and weigh all the factors which would give him the bare minimum conditions for the attack."[24]

Eisenhower said, "The desirability for getting started on the next favorable tide is so great and the uncertainty of the weather is such that we could never anticipate really perfect weather coincident with proper tidal conditions, that we must go unless there is a real and very serious deterioration in the weather."[25]

The tides would be suitable on June 5, 6, and 7, 1944, and then again beginning on June 19. On the nineteenth, however, the moonlight conditions would not be good for the Airborne. And if the weather shut down the nineteenth completely, Overlord would have to wait until July. Since the two hundred thousand men arrived at their ships and airfields on June 3 and 4, if Overlord was postponed until either June 19 or July, Ike would have to order the holding of all the men in isolation in the cramped spaces on their ships and at their airfields in an attempt to keep the secret of D-Day intact. It also meant that thousands more assigned to arrive in France in the days immediately after D-Day—men already headed to the ports and airfields—had to turn around and go back to their bases, to be held in isolation there.

The possibility of delay had all of D-Day Inc.'s executive team on edge. "So terrifying was the thought of postponement that many of Eisenhower's most cautious commanders were even prepared to risk attack instead on the eighth or ninth [of June]."[26] Eisenhower was worried about the men. He said, "Those people in the ships and ready to go were in cages, you might say. . . . They were crowded up, and everybody was unhappy."[27] If the weather was bad enough, however, D-Day Inc. couldn't use the advantage of air superiority—and that was crucial. D-Day Inc. was sending gigantic forces into France, but the German forces waiting to receive them were much larger. Overlord was dependent upon air support for success. Without it, D-Day Inc. would likely be overwhelmed.

Talking of the decision on when to send his men into France, Eisenhower said, "Those fellows meant a lot to me. But these are the decisions that have to be made when you're in a war. You say to yourself, I'm going to do something that will be to my country's advantage for the least cost. You can't say without any cost. You know you're going to lose some of them, and it's very, very difficult."[28]

But Ike, like all corporate leaders, was paid to make the tough decisions. He knew that the success of his organization was going to require sacrifice. He was painfully aware that the level of his personal sacrifice—the constant, agonizing, never-ending stress—was nowhere near what he asked of his people. But . . . being able to make the final decision is what separates the manager of a business unit from the people who work for him or her. Eisenhower never backed away from that responsibility. He just hoped—and prayed—that when he made the decision, it would be the correct one.

★ ★ ★

D-Day itself was originally scheduled for June 5, the first of the three days that had the proper tides and had a chance of moonlight after the Airborne had arrived. The final weather conference was held at 4:00 a.m. local time on June 4. On the assumption that Overlord would begin on June 5, many ships were already under way. It was raining steadily, and the water was choppy. Most landing craft were relatively small, flat-bottomed boats with very little stability and no overhead covering to keep the crowded men and equipment dry.

The men aboard were soaked through, and many were seasick. As Ambrose described it: "To the men . . . whose transports and landing craft had left harbor, the smell in the air was vomit."[29]

At the weather conference, Ike and his senior staff assembled at Southwick House, the naval headquarters in Portsmouth, to listen to their meteorological committee's report. Group Captain J. M. Stagg made his report as he had been doing for Ike on a daily basis for a month. The report for June 5 was terrible: a low-pressure front was moving in, and there would be stormy conditions with a very low cloud base and substantial winds.

Eisenhower asked his executives, his team of experts, for their opinions. Admiral Ramsay thought that the landings would be difficult but could be managed. The heavy seas would make naval gunfire supporting the forces going ashore highly inaccurate. Tedder and Leigh-Mallory, the two airmen, wanted to postpone. The low cloud cover ruled out air support. Montgomery believed delay was worse than any weather conditions and wanted to launch Overlord. Ike mulled over Stagg's report and the opinions of his team. He stated that without air support Overlord was too risky and asked if anyone disagreed with that. There was no disagreement.

Ike postponed for twenty-four hours, hoping the weather would improve.

After the decision to postpone was made, Eisenhower spent a great deal of time in his trailer, what he called his "circus wagon"[30] near Southwick House. Most of the other generals and admirals had much nicer accommodations, several of them staying in large manor houses. But Ike wanted to be close to the ports and his men, so he had ordered the establishment of a small headquarters made up of tents and trailers. Ike's personal conference room was a large tent outside his trailer. The trailer itself, like Eisenhower's uniform, was not ostentatious. The trailer had no frills and no touches of ego—no framed pictures with famous men, no special orders, and no citations on the walls.

Ike's uniform was a standard uniform, with his insignia of rank (four stars), his unit patch on the shoulder, and a single line of ribbons over one breast pocket. Compare this with Patton's silver helmet; Monty's beret; MacArthur's slouch cap, oversized pipe, and sunglasses; or the row after row of ribbons many other officers wore. With Ike there was a simple, personal feel to the man and to his quarters—the only homey touches to the trailer were pictures of his wife and son and a collection of well-worn Western novels that he liked to read for relaxation. It was his retreat between moments of decision.

On June 4 at 9:30 p.m., Eisenhower and his executives reassembled to hear the latest on the weather from Stagg. The news was very good. The storm would break and D-Day Inc. would have a thirty-six-hour window for operations. The air forces would be able to operate during the late-night hours of June 5 and the early morning of June 6 despite scattered clouds.

Leigh-Mallory, the air executive, didn't like the sound of that. If the clouds hampered the air ops, the ground forces could be left exposed. He wanted to postpone until June 19. Ike polled his team. His chief of staff, Beetle Smith, said, "It's a helluva gamble, but it's the best possible gamble."[31] Tedder, Eisenhower's No. 2 and an airman like Leigh-Mallory, wanted to postpone. Monty wanted to go.

The decision was back in Ike's hands, where it had always been.

Watching Eisenhower, Smith was aware of the "loneliness and isolation of a commander at a time when such a momentous decision was to be taken by him, with full knowledge that failure or success rests on his individual decision."[32] Ike began pacing—he often paced as he came to decisions. No one said anything; the French doors of the room were rattling loudly, thanks to the wind, and the rain continued to pour down. The weather at that exact moment argued that Overlord needed to be postponed.

Eisenhower said, "I am quite positive that the order must be given."[33]

Ramsay, D-Day Inc.'s naval executive, rushed to send the necessary orders to the massive fleet. Ike went back to his trailer to sleep, woke up about five hours later at 3:30 a.m., and went back to Southwick House for one final weather conference with his executive team.

The storm had continued; if it went on much longer there would be no choice for Eisenhower. He would have to recall the ships and postpone D-Day. At the conference, Stagg confirmed the storm would break soon and that Overlord could launch. The bad news was that the good weather window he had predicted for operations had shrunk—it was possible the initial forces would get ashore and then be stranded without the follow-up forces able to land later in the day. Or even the day after.

Ike paced and polled his executives. Smith and Monty wanted to go. Ramsay thought naval gunfire would be difficult but that they should launch Overlord. The two airmen, Tedder and Leigh-Mallory, were very reluctant—and since air support was crucial to the success of Overlord, their opinions weighed heavily on Eisenhower. And there was also the possibility that Stagg and his committee were wrong. The storm might not break. D-Day Inc. could leave weak, seasick men on the beaches with no air cover and no naval-gunfire support. If the storm didn't break, Ike would be sending his forces to slaughter. He had made the gut-wrenching decision the night before; now he had to make it again.

He paced and did not speak. To the men in the room, it seemed as if the silence went on for a long time. Finally, Ike stopped pacing, turned to his executives, and said quietly, "Okay, let's go."[34]

The conference room emptied as Eisenhower's team left to launch Operation Overlord. Within seconds Ike was alone. His job had been to make the decision, and once the decision was made, his executives' jobs were to execute that decision. There was no way for one man to run all the different components of an organization as massive as D-Day Inc. Having given the order to proceed with Overlord, Eisenhower found himself alone and virtually powerless. Ike said,

"That's the most terrible time for a senior commander. He has done all that he can do, all the planning and so on. There's nothing more he can do."[35] But Ike had built a strong, capable executive staff—it was time to delegate, to let his executives do their jobs.

PLAN TO IMPLEMENT

- **Decide**. Nothing is more important for a manager than making decisions. Remember your mission, consider your options, balance the possibilities, and decide. Then don't waste time second-guessing yourself.

MANAGE YOUR PEOPLE

- **Delegate**. If you've made the correct choices in building your executive team—or the correct management moves with the team members foisted upon you—go ahead and delegate. Your people can handle it.

WAR OF THE WEB—USING YOUR ADVANTAGES

When Microsoft decided to battle Netscape for Internet supremacy, Microsoft was in a position analogous to D-Day Inc.'s going up against the Germans. (This is said without in any way equating Netscape with the Nazis.) Netscape was hugely successful and utterly dominant. The Associated Press described Netscape's Internet browser, Navigator, as "the world's first commercial Web browser and the starting point of the Internet boom."[36] As of August 1996, Netscape had complete control of its territory—"at least an 80 percent share of the Internet browser market."[37]

Microsoft felt it absolutely had to get into the browser arena. Netscape's threat went beyond the operating system, where Microsoft was dominant. Whichever company controlled the browser would set the tone for, and likely control, the world of networked computing. In the mid-'90s Microsoft already dominated the personal computer market—its real growth potential lay in networked computing. If Netscape became dominant in networked computing first, well . . .

Eisenhower also faced a competitor with complete control of its territory. He had two major advantages over that competitor: air superiority and the mass-produced mobility of jeeps and tanks. Air superiority would allow D-Day Inc.'s forces to gain a toehold in Europe even though they were confronted by a much larger force, already entrenched in defensive positions. And America's astounding industrial muscle would produce enough noncombat vehicles, like trucks and jeeps, that Eisenhower would be able to move too quickly for the Germans to counter properly.

Microsoft had two similar advantages in competing with Netscape. Microsoft's operating system, Windows, was every bit as popular as Navigator—"used by more than 80 percent of all personal computers"[38] in 1996. Microsoft's version of air superiority was Windows—the company included its browser, called Internet Explorer, with Windows. Every new personal computer came with Internet Explorer already installed on it, and people with older computers could download Microsoft's browser for free.

The second advantage that Microsoft had was almost the same as D-Day Inc.'s: sheer muscle. D-Day Inc. relied on the manufacturing base of the United States; Microsoft assigned more than five hundred programmers to work on its Internet projects, allowing it to move much more quickly than the smaller Netscape.

Approximately a year after Microsoft had launched Internet Explorer, it had only 10 percent of the browser market[39] but was gaining share. Sticking to its plan to give the software away and integrate it into Windows (despite significant legal challenges), two years later Forbes was declaring: "By the autumn of 1998 Microsoft had won the war."[40] About five years after debuting Internet Explorer, in November 2000, Microsoft had 86 percent of all browser use[41] and Netscape had become a dwindling part of America Online (AOL). Microsoft deployed its versions of air superiority and manufacturing muscle extremely effectively, virtually wiping out its competitor.

PLAN FOR SUCCESS

- **Take advantage**. If you have something your competition doesn't—take advantage of it. Microsoft saw its future growth threatened by Netscape and beat its opponent by doing things Netscape couldn't: integrating the browser into Windows, offering it for free to existing Windows customers, and devoting more manpower to produce and refine the browser than Netscape could.

BE HONEST

- **Own up**. You made the decision; now accept responsibility. There's an old saying on the streets: "Don't do the crime if you can't do the time." Being in charge is, ironically, the same. Don't take your paycheck if you can't make decisions and then accept the responsibility.

On June 5, after the 3:30 a.m. weather conference and final decision to launch, Eisenhower had breakfast and then went to Portsmouth harbor to watch the ships depart and the loading of the follow-up forces into more ships. Early in the morning, the rain stopped and the wind died down—it looked like Stagg's report of the weather improving was correct. Ike returned to his trailer, played checkers with his naval aide, had lunch, and then sat down to write one of the

most stunning documents of the entire war—a press release to be
used in the event that Overlord was a failure:

> Our landings . . . have failed . . . and I have withdrawn the troops.
> My decision to attack at this time and place was based upon the
> best information available. The troops, the air, and the Navy did
> all that bravery and devotion to duty could do. If any blame or fault
> attaches to the attempt it is mine alone.[42]

Given the horrible magnitude of what the press release contained,
it is astonishingly concise and complete. (The entire release is about
double the quotation above.) Eisenhower cut to the chase, stating that
Overlord had failed and ended with the withdrawal of the men. He
explained the basis for his decision in one sentence. He acknowledged
and praised the immense sacrifice made by the men of D-Day.

And then Ike accepted the entire responsibility for the catastrophe.

No alibis, no excuses.

He could have been forgiven for mentioning the factors of
weather, tides, and moonlight, for noting Overlord's complex shipping and air schedules, for rationalizing the decision by explaining
that it had been made in consultation with the absolute best minds
in this business. Eisenhower would have been within his rights to
point out that war is risky, but that the stakes—freedom from Nazi
tyranny—required risk.

If Overlord failed, and this release were sent out, it would mean
many more months, possibly years, before the Allies could rebuild
D-Day Inc. and remake the attempt. Hundreds of thousands of
people would die in the interim. If Overlord failed, it would be the
great disaster of the war, probably of the entire twentieth century.

Eisenhower was keenly aware of all that—he called Overlord "the
great crusade." And yet, he wrote the press release accepting all the
blame, knowing that if it had to be released, he would be known as
the man who had wasted thousands of lives in Overlord and failed to

save thousands of lives under the Nazi hand. People around the world would never forgive him.

In less than one day, Eisenhower had demonstrated what makes for truly great leadership: making the tough decision and accepting responsibility for the decision.

★ ★ ★

Typical of Ike, one of the last things he did on June 5 was visit the soon-to-be-departing troops at an airfield. He went to Greenham Common, where the Screaming Eagles of the 101st Airborne were about to board their planes in the evening. The 101st was one of the divisions that would parachute in to support Bradley's forces at Utah Beach—the operation that D-Day Inc.'s air boss, Leigh-Mallory, begged to have canceled. It's hard to imagine Eisenhower's frame of mind as he spoke to these young men who had a projected 70 percent casualty rate hanging over their heads—a death sentence. Whatever he was thinking, Ike asked the men where they were from and what their names were. He told a group of enlisted men not to worry, and the response from a Texan was, "Hell, we ain't worried, General. It's the Krauts that ought to be worrying now." With another group an enlisted man shouted, "Now quit worrying, General, we'll take care of this thing for you."[43]

Eisenhower stayed to watch the 101st board their planes, then waited to see every one of the planes take to the sky. He turned to his driver, Kay Summersby, who saw tears in his eyes. He spoke softly, "Well, it's on."[44]

★ ★ ★

Late on the night of June 5, Admiral Ramsay, D-Day Inc.'s British naval executive, wrote a final entry in his diary for that day: "I am not under [any] delusions as to the risks involved in this most difficult of all operations. . . . We shall require all the help that God can give us & I cannot believe that this will not be forthcoming."[45]

DEBRIEFING NOTES

STRATEGY: COMMUNICATE

- **Know Your Stuff**: If you don't know it, learn it. If you don't know your stuff, shut up. Faking it does not work.

STRATEGIES: DETERMINE YOUR MISSION, PRIORITIZE

- **If You Gotta Have It, Get It!**: If you need something from another part of your organization, get it.
- **Remember the Greater Good**: You have to remember the greater good of your organization and your mission.

STRATEGIES: BE HONEST, DETERMINE YOUR MISSION, AND PLAN FOR SUCCESS

- **Know Thyself**: Admit what you can and cannot do. You'll save yourself a lot of pain in the long run.
- **Remember What's Important**: Decide what you *need* to do— then figure out how to do it.
- **Own Up**: You made the decision; now accept responsibility.

STRATEGY: PLAN TO IMPLEMENT, MANAGE, AND MOTIVATE YOUR PEOPLE

- **Choose Managers to Fit Your Mission**.
- **Picking Teams**: Stay focused on your mission when filling out your managerial team.
- **Manage Up**: Try to anticipate your boss's requests—it'll create confidence in your management. If your boss is a relentless micromanager, hang on. There's nothing you can do about it.

- **Care for Your People**: *People are your most important resource.* Without them, your company is going nowhere.

STRATEGIES: DETERMINE YOUR MISSION, PLAN TO IMPLEMENT, MANAGE YOUR PEOPLE

- **Decide**: Nothing is more important for a manager than making decisions. Remember your mission, consider your options, balance the possibilities, and decide.
- **Delegate**: If you've made the correct choices in building your team—go ahead and delegate. Your people can handle it.

STRATEGIES: PLAN FOR SUCCESS, PLAN TO IMPLEMENT

- **Take Advantage**: If you have something your competition doesn't—take advantage of it.

★ SIX ★

OVERLORD:
ACTIONS AND RESULTS

Moving Decisively Toward the Endgame

Looking at a map of Normandy, the designated beaches of Operation Overlord stretched from the westernmost beach, Utah (American), and then eastward to Omaha (American), and on to Gold, Juno, and Sword (all three being assigned to the British and Canadian forces) at the easternmost tip. The 82nd and 101st Airborne Divisions had arrived overnight via parachute and huge gliders inland of Utah Beach, right around the town of Ste. Mère Église and north of the town of Carentan. Their drops were scattered and mostly off target. In the morning "many of them would be found dead, drowned by the weight of their equipment in rivers and ponds, or hanging lifeless from the limbs of trees."[1]

Many men landed and were immediately engaged in fierce fire-fights with competition they couldn't see. But the casualties were not even close to British air marshal Leigh-Mallory's 70 percent prediction. It was a member of the 101st who had told Eisenhower to not worry, they were going to take care of things. And they did, making adjustments to the situational realities, gaining one objective after another.

When Ike woke up early on June 6, first reports from the Airborne

were good. The risk he had taken with their lives had paid off. Thanks
in large part to the Airborne's performance inland of Utah,* Bradley's
forces were able to secure their objectives on the beach. Later in the day,
Leigh-Mallory apologized to Eisenhower for his grim projections—he
was sorry that he had added to the burdens Ike already carried.

The British and Canadians made solid progress inland from Gold,
Juno, and Sword; and the British Sixth Airborne Division had seized
two urgently needed bridges. Although the British and Canadians
didn't quite achieve Monty's overly aggressive goals (not a surprise to
students of Montgomery), they were doing very well.

The major D-Day concern for Eisenhower was Omaha Beach.
Difficult currents and smoke from the naval bombardment caused
confusion, with many of the Americans landing in the wrong place.
Even worse, the oldest division in the U.S. Army, the First Infantry
Division, known as the "Big Red One" for their unit shoulder patches,
had slammed directly into the extremely well-established German
352nd Infantry Division. The 352nd's presence was a complete surprise, but shouldn't have been. If D-Day Inc.'s intelligence operation
had done its job better, the Big Red One would have been prepared
for its opposition instead of surprised by it. The Big Red One found
itself pinned down on the beach with no place to go but back into
the water. The Germans, however, never moved to shove them back.
The Big Red One established the thinnest of holds on Omaha Beach,
but it was enough.

By the evening of June 6, the men who had landed ashore numbered 156,000, and more were on the way—the number doubled in
less than a week. Casualties for the entire day were 2,500, a ghastly
price for each family who paid it, but colossally less than what anyone
at D-Day Inc. had expected.

---

* On Utah Beach a bit of history was made when the only general to arrive with the first
wave was also the son of President Teddy Roosevelt, Brigadier General Theodore
Roosevelt. At almost the same time, Teddy's grandson and General Roosevelt's son,
Captain Quentin Roosevelt, landed in the first wave at Omaha Beach.

PLAN FOR SUCCESS

- **Know your competition**. Understanding where and how your competition operates can save you precious resources when you go head-to-head with them. If you don't understand your opposition, you'll be forced to slug it out—on prices, length of contract, scope of service agreements, etc. Understanding the competition is often the easier and softer way to success.

Ike's announcement to the press, issued by an aide at about 9:30 a.m. on June 6, was typically simple and brief: "Under the command of General Eisenhower, Allied naval forces, supported by strong air forces, began landing Allied armies this morning on the northern coast of France."[2]

BE HONEST (NOT SELF-AGGRANDIZING)

- **Don't waste time tooting your own horn**. Your success will speak much louder and more compellingly than anything you can possibly say.

Once again he gave credit to the people of D-Day Inc. by singling out the navies, air forces, and armies. Once again he emphasized the allied nature of his organization. Simple as this announcement was, the impact was astounding. In Britain, people stopped what they were doing and began singing "God Save the King!" In Philadelphia, they rang the Liberty Bell. Joining it were church bells all across America and Canada. All over Europe, people heard the news on either Radio Berlin (which didn't have the same kind of positive spin as Allied media did) or the BBC. Even the people in POW and concentration camps heard the news. (If "the grapevine" worked in concentration camps, and it did, no wonder it is so effective in the modern office.)

In West Point, New York, Ike's wife, Mamie, was watching their son, John, graduate with the rest of his class at the United States Military Academy. When "John finally went up to the podium to accept his diploma, the name Eisenhower elicited a rapturous ovation."[3]

On June 7, as the follow-up forces were already coming ashore, Eisenhower sailed from England aboard HMS *Apollo* to Omaha Beach. Bradley came to the ship to update his boss. Although the news was generally good, there was an overall lack of transport vehicles, tanks, artillery, and general supplies like food and ammunition. For many complex reasons, the lack was especially acute on Omaha Beach. The Germans continued to fire on both Utah and Omaha, and there was a serious danger that the gap between the two beaches (about twelve miles) could be exploited by the enemy, cutting Utah off from all the other D-Day Inc. forces.

PLAN TO IMPLEMENT

- **Follow-up**. Ike and company were all about following up—their initial forces were insufficient to succeed at their mission. The Germans were incapable of follow-up, in large part due to D-Day Inc.'s plans and also due to Germany's messy management.

Thanks to decisions Eisenhower had already made, however, D-Day Inc. had time on its side. Because Ike had insisted on and gotten the Transportation Plan (the bombing of the French railroad system), the Germans were almost completely incapable of deploying their reserves. And, unlike D-Day Inc., which had a clear executive structure with one man in charge, the German executive in charge, Erwin Rommel, was handcuffed by Adolf Hitler, who micromanaged

German operations from a distance without all the necessary facts at hand. Hitler didn't allow Rommel to deploy the few reserves he did have, giving the Allies more time to build their beachhead.

In sharp contrast to Hitler's methods, Ike, after assessing the situation with Bradley, decided that instead of pushing straight inland from Utah and Omaha, the American forces should move into the gap between their beaches and link up, forming a larger and more stable unit. This was the one major change to the plan Eisenhower made, and it was completely in keeping with the way he operated. Ike came to the area of operations, gathered facts, and decided.

D-Day Inc. continued to bring its forces into France at a mind-boggling rate. By July 23, less than seven weeks since the first day of Overlord, there were more than 1.3 million men and 170,000 vehicles in France. The lack of support vehicles, food, and ammunition had largely been resolved thanks to the Herculean efforts of the American and British navies, which were supporting the operation by moving supplies over the beaches and through the artificial harbors (the "mulberries," created by filling the hulls of old ships with cement and then sinking them). A storm in late June had damaged the mulberries, however, and left almost 300 boats and small ships wrecked on Normandy's beaches.

D-Day Inc. badly needed a major port to ease its supply crisis but didn't have one. The original plans called for the Americans to swing west from the beaches to seize the port of Cherbourg, while Monty (the executive in overall charge of ground forces, and the direct boss of the British and Canadians) was supposed to seize the town of Caen with its vital crossroads throughout the region and then continue east, pushing toward the deep-water port of Antwerp.

The Americans were stalled in the hedgerow country of northern France. The hedgerows were as old as the Roman Empire, originally used to mark boundaries. They were mounds of earth, topped by densely grown hedges, often with sunken roads running alongside them. Between the height of the hedgerows and the hedges' overgrowth above the roads, visibility was limited at best. Stephen Ambrose described the hedgerows this way: "There were, on average, 14 hedgerows to the kilometer in Normandy. . . . All through the Cotentin Peninsula, from June 7 on, the GIs labored at the task. They heaved and pushed and punched and died doing it, for two hedgerows a day. No terrain in the world was better suited for defensive action."[4] Tanks could, in some instances, climb them and crash through the hedge, but doing so exposed the tanks' soft underbelly to waiting Germans, who fired antitank weapons at close range into the tanks, usually killing all aboard.

PLAN TO IMPLEMENT

- **Know the market**. Every market has barriers to entry, such as cultural, linguistic, geographical, and political realities. Find them in advance and prepare for them. It is impossible to gauge how badly D-Day Inc. was hurt by its lack of preparation for the hedgerows.

Despite all the massively detailed plans for Overlord, the hedgerows had not been understood or properly anticipated. It took weeks of painful fighting to adjust to the realities and begin cutting through this terrain. By the time the Americans finally took the port of Cherbourg on June 27, the Germans had damaged the port facilities badly enough that it would take some time for D-Day Inc. to begin using it as a supply port.

As slow and painful as the American performance was in the hedgerows, it was still better than Monty's performance at Caen. Montgomery had declared he would take Caen by the end of D-Day. Most of the executives thought this was overly optimistic, but Monty insisted it was possible, so other plans were tied to the early acquisition of Caen. As the weeks passed without success there, Monty explained the situation by claiming that his plan had *always* been to pin

the Germans at Caen, grinding them down, which allowed Bradley's forces to flank them and take Cherbourg. Monty's critics (both then and now) said that he changed plans to deflect charges of failure at Caen. Given his history of overpromising at the beginning of operations and then redefining his plans afterward to custom-fit the new realities, it's easy to believe Monty was covering his derriere, behavior that is familiar to most people in Corporate America.

PRIORITIZE

- **Get what you need from your people**. Ike didn't need Monty to pin down the Germans at Caen. He needed Monty to seize the town and then exploit its crossroads to pressure the competition more broadly. But Eisenhower failed to give Monty a direct order. Bad move. If you need your managers to produce, assign them benchmarks: dates, quantities, revenues, whatever makes sense for your company. But be specific.

Fed up with Monty's delaying and Bradley's crawl through the hedgerows, Eisenhower returned to Normandy to put a charge into his executives in the field. He spent five days visiting the troops, looking over the battlefield, and meeting with Omar Bradley's team of commanders. Eager to see as much as he could himself, Ike grabbed a jeep, climbed behind the wheel, and drove off with only one aide and an orderly. His inspection of the American frontline (inland of Utah Beach, west and south of Ste. Mère Église) was so in-depth that he actually crossed over the line into German territory. (Nothing happened, although it's hard to imagine modern CEOs sneaking into their competitors' plants or territory, especially if the competition has a standing "shoot on sight" order.) As important as anything else about Ike's five-day visit was the effect on morale. "The GIs were delighted to see Eisenhower driving the jeep and shouted and whistled as he drove past."[5]

Ike was not happy about what he had seen. He worried that an American breakout from the hedgerow country in the northwest of Normandy was not possible—and if there was no breakout, he could not fight the highly mobile, high-speed war he had planned. Eisenhower was convinced that mobility and speed would defeat the Germans more quickly. "A breakthrough at this juncture will minimize the total cost," he told Bradley.[6]

Tedder and Smith, Ike's No. 2 and his chief of staff respectively, both blamed Monty for the sorry state of D-Day Inc. His stalemate at Caen was bogging down all of D-Day Inc.'s efforts. The two men pleaded with Eisenhower to force Monty into action. Ike wrote a letter to Monty that was more of a reminder of the objectives of D-Day Inc. and less of a direct order. If the letter had an effect, it was a negligible one. Monty continued to move slowly and cautiously, leaving D-Day Inc. stalemated.

MANAGE AND MOTIVATE YOUR PEOPLE

- **Support your people**. Ike recommended Bradley for command even when he was junior to other men. Bradley justified the recommendation in spades, delivering the breakout from Normandy. Patton caused nothing but trouble until Ike was able to utilize his special gifts. After that, Patton racked up one success after another.

Finally on July 18, Monty went after Caen with everything he could muster. A gigantic air bombardment helped, and within two days Monty finally took Caen. But the cost was high: 401 tanks and 2,600 casualties. Monty called a halt to the initiative and declared positive results. But there had been no breakout. Neither the British and Canadians under Monty nor the Americans under Bradley had moved out of the Normandy beachhead. Ike was livid and "thundered that

it had taken more than seven thousand tons of bombs to gain seven miles and that the Allies could hardly hope to go through France paying a price of a thousand tons of bombs per mile."[7]

When the breakout came, it was thanks to Omar Bradley, who always delivered the goods for Eisenhower. Bradley planned to take St. Lô, a crossroads town for northwest Normandy that sat at the center of a network of good roads—roads that allowed tanks and trucks to travel at relatively high speeds. St. Lô was D-Day Inc.'s exit from the hedgerow country. Eisenhower was so pleased that he wrote to Monty, "Now we are pinning our hopes on Bradley."[8]

Determined that Montgomery would launch an attack near Caen, in the eastern part of D-Day Inc.'s operational area, at the same time Bradley did, Ike flew to Monty's headquarters. Beetle Smith was impressed with his boss's presentation, writing that Eisenhower wanted "an all-out coordinated attack by the entire Allied line, which would at last put our forces in decisive motion."[9] Monty was not impressed. But he did as he was told and launched an attack in support of Bradley, who after a short, vicious fight, took St. Lô.

Eisenhower finally had the chance to fight a broad, mobile war. And he had the right man to do it: George Patton. In short order, the Third Army was activated with Patton taking over. Courtney Hodges took charge of the First Army as Bradley was promoted to become the executive in charge of the Twelfth Army Group—Patton's and Hodges's immediate boss. Ike had spent a lot of energy and emotion protecting George Patton from the consequences of his own bad behavior and words, convinced that when the opportunity came, Patton would prove to be the best field executive at D-Day Inc. Ike's efforts paid off—Patton's Third Army slashed through the Germans at astonishing speed, cutting south from Normandy, then east, then north. Hodges' First Army was also moving quickly on Patton's left.

On August 7, Eisenhower established a tented headquarters in the town of Mortain in Normandy, where he and Bradley expected the Germans to counterattack. The two men decided to hold Mortain with relatively few forces so that Patton's rush to the south could continue. If the Germans succeeded in pushing through at Mortain and cut the Third Army off, Eisenhower planned to keep Patton supplied via airlift.

The Germans did counterattack at Mortain, but the Americans' defensive positions held there, and the Germans were forced to retreat from their operation due to the pressure from Patton in the south. The Canadians were also moving down from the north (near Caen), and the two Allied armies were creating a pincer, trapping the German forces. Hodges's First Army also gave chase, coming from the southwest (Mortain), tightening the space in which the Germans had to operate. With the Germans scrambling to escape the pincers, Monty had a chance to break out to the east toward the Seine, but he failed to take advantage of the opportunity, angering both Eisenhower and Patton. On August 19, however, the pincers closed at the town of Falaise, almost thirty miles southeast of the Normandy beaches, trapping fifty thousand Germans and leaving ten thousand dead.*

PLAN TO IMPLEMENT

- **Speed kills**. Ike knew he could beat the Germans by pressuring them with as many forces as he could bring to bear—which required a broad front and swift movement—and that meant refusing to be stalemated. At Falaise, quick action by Hodges and Patton won a large victory for D-Day Inc. Monty's slow, carefully planned movement lost the even bigger victory that was there for the taking. Perfecting your plans can take time and dissolve your opportunities. Don't wait too long to act. Remember: speed kills.

---

* Ike's forces were international: the forces that actually closed the pincers were the First Polish Armored Division, operating with the First Canadian Army, and the Second French Armored Division, serving in Patton's Third Army. It was appropriate that the Poles and the French sealed the first major victory in France.

It was a smashing victory and a vindication of Ike's strategy of attacking in strength all along the front with mobile forces.

D-Day Inc.'s success at Falaise was pretty much the end of German operations in France. Over the next three weeks, Montgomery finally began moving with a swiftness to match the Americans—covering two hundred miles in the last week of August alone. The Americans' First and Third Armies swept through France almost to the German border, and the First Army scored a huge symbolic victory by liberating Paris.

At almost the same time, Romania surrendered to the Soviets and joined the Allied effort by declaring war on Germany. The Germans pulled out of Greece. The Red Army drove to Yugoslavia, inflicting seven hundred thousand German casualties. In Italy, after the Allies had liberated Rome on June 5, they had continued to drive north, driving the Germans back.

The Allies also landed in southern France west of Cannes and began driving rapidly north. Additional follow-up troops continued to come into Normandy, adding the Ninth Army to Bradley's group. In England, the American 82nd and 101st Airborne Divisions, who had supported Bradley at Utah Beach, and the British Sixth Airborne, who had supported Monty near Caen, were formed into the First Allied Airborne Army, creating an experienced, successful, mobile reserve force that could be deployed almost anywhere Eisenhower wanted to use them.

All of this success in Europe, however, raised expectations of quick and easy success. Many members of D-Day Inc.'s board, the press, and the American and British peoples all thought final victory over the Germans would be achieved in no time.

Even D-Day Inc.'s staff fell prey to this kind of thinking. The intelligence department of the executive staff (G-2) issued a summary on August 23 stating: "Two-and-a-half months of bitter fighting have brought the end of the war in Europe within sight, almost within reach." Patton said he would cross the German border in ten days.

Monty added, "One really full-blooded thrust toward Berlin is likely to get there and thus end the German war."[10]

Eisenhower didn't share in the optimism. He knew that it would take a lot of effort to break the Germans' control of Europe. Ike wrote in *Crusade in Europe*: "Our own populations and their governments might underrate the task still to be accomplished, and so might slacken the home-front effort . . . I not only brought this to the attention of my superiors, but . . . held a press conference, predicting that there was one more critical task remaining . . . the destruction of the German armies." Unfortunately, Ike went on, his words were "swept away in the general rejoicing . . . and even among the professional leaders . . . there grew an optimism, almost a lightheartedness." that ignored the very ugly realities still facing D-Day Inc.[11]

This is akin to a CEO worrying over quarterly financial reports coming out that will fail to meet the expectations of the Wall Street analysts. Many companies have reported solid profits only to see a drop in stock value when earnings, although good, weren't quite as good as the analysts had predicted. Ike was practicing spin control in an effort to keep everyone's morale up—he knew that defeatism could pop up the minute D-Day Inc. ran into any obstacles to victory. And there were millions of obstacles in the gray uniforms of the Wehrmacht still out there.

There was another obstacle to success facing D-Day Inc., and it was a two-headed hydra inside the organization: issues concerning who was in charge of the ground forces and what strategy the company would follow.

In late August, Eisenhower announced that as of September 1, he was becoming the Allied ground commander in addition to his role as CEO of D-Day Inc. Omar Bradley remained in charge of the American Twelfth Army Group, while Bernard Law Montgomery continued as the executive of the British and Canadian Twenty-first Army Group. This made Bradley and Monty equals—both men would report directly to Ike. It was, effectively, a demotion for Monty—one that had been preset when Eisenhower acquiesced to Churchill's demand that Montgomery be the overall ground commander.

Monty was outraged—he had been the ground commander for Overlord and the Normandy breakout. He was responsible for a huge Allied victory, never mind that others, including Eisenhower, had contributed heavily to the planning and that Bradley, with Ike's urging and support, was the man who achieved the breakout. Churchill and Alan Brooke, Britain's senior army man and Monty's version of George Marshall, were outraged—as was the British public. Eisenhower was well aware of Monty's popularity from the top of the British government to the public at large—it was the reason he never seriously contemplated firing the man, even when the British generals at D-Day Inc. pleaded with him to do so. Brooke wrote in his diary, "This plan [of Ike's] is likely to add another 3 to 6 months to the war."[12]

Outrage or no, Ike was determined to take control of the ground campaign. He'd told Churchill that he would months earlier, and now that D-Day Inc.'s forces had broken out of the beachhead, it was time. And while most of Britain was angry at the decision, Ike's staff was solidly behind him: The Brits, Tedder and Leigh-Mallory, along with American Beetle Smith, had thought that Eisenhower's assuming direct control of the ground campaign was the most effective way to push Monty into action. Bradley and Patton both encouraged Ike to take command of the ground campaign.

Why was the issue of command of the ground campaign of such importance, aside from ego and reputation? Was Ike trying to prove to the world that he had what it took as a commanding combat general? Was he finally getting even with Montgomery by demoting him? Did it make a major difference if Ike controlled the ground campaign directly?

Michael Korda wrote, "Ike simply sensed the need for one person to control the battle, and believed that it was his responsibility." Monty assumed that ego was at least part of the equation for Eisenhower, but that assumption went against Ike's career to that point. He had always been willing to step aside if he believed it was the best course. And the best course was the exact reason Eisenhower felt he must be in direct control. His vision of how to beat Germany was very different from Monty's, and Ike couldn't implement his vision by remote control.

It was the old broad-front-versus-the-narrow-front debate all over again.

Monty, Brooke, and Churchill all wanted a narrow front, a concentration of forces, slicing through Europe in a northeasterly direction, through Belgium into the Ruhr area of Germany, its industrial heartland. They believed that if D-Day Inc. could control the Ruhr, Germany would collapse. Remember, the British leaders' very different mind-set was caused by one reality: they had been competing with Germany for five years, two years longer than the Americans. They were operating from a smaller industrial base and with a smaller population from which to draw their forces. Their resources were dwindling as the competition continued. Monty, Brooke, and Churchill wanted to husband their people and resources as much as possible—and a concentrated, narrow-front approach did that.

Eisenhower didn't think it was that simple. A single, concentrated force was vulnerable on its flanks because the Germans could counterattack so effectively that they would sever supply lines and destroy the leading D-Day Inc. forces. And even if the concentrated attack worked as planned and penetrated to the Ruhr, D-Day Inc. didn't have the port facilities to supply its forces beyond the Rhine.

The supply problem acted as a huge brake to operations—the farther from Normandy the forces went, the harder it was to supply them. The supply system was stretched to the maximum due to other problems. Because of the limited port facilities, if D-Day Inc. wanted to build advance air fields to continue their air support as its forces moved closer to Germany, those building supplies and engineers would displace supplies needed by the frontline forces. When D-Day Inc. did reach the Rhine, they would need bridging equipment. But if the bridging equipment came forward, supplies for the frontline would have to wait.

Pipelines were built from Cherbourg to Paris and from Marseilles to Lyon (a fantastic achievement by the U.S. Army Corps of Engineers) to deliver oil closer to the frontline forces, but every bit of matériel and every engineer who traveled to make the pipelines a reality meant that supplies or troops intended for the frontline did not. There wasn't enough capacity to advance without a major port like Antwerp, which just happened to be on the list of Monty's objectives—an objective he had failed to achieve.

DETERMINE YOUR MISSION

- **Delegate when possible. Otherwise do it yourself.** In a perfect world, your managers are committed to your vision for achieving your mission. But if they aren't, you have to lead the way.

With the problems of a single force's vulnerability and the supply challenges in his mind, Eisenhower remained convinced that the broad-front approach was best. Supply was a problem with this approach too, but the German competition couldn't exploit multiple forces on a broad front the way they could a single force. Ike's strategic thinking on the type of front differed from the Brits largely because he was an American. America was already providing the majority of forces for D-Day Inc., and the balance would continue to weigh more heavily on the American side as operations continued. The U.S. industrial base was producing at previously unimaginable rates, supplying the U.S. military with everything it needed, and supplying many of the Europeans, including the British and French, with huge quantities of matériel.

No one had ever seen industrial production on this scale before; the British couldn't comprehend that they were now in a resource-rich position and couldn't apply that to their strategic thinking. But

Eisenhower understood that the ever-increasing American forces and the never-ending supplies provided him with enough muscle to tackle the Germans everywhere he could confront them. It was a huge strategic advantage, and Ike had no intention of squandering it in the narrow-front approach.

Given Monty's convictions about the narrow front, it only made sense that Eisenhower would assume control of the ground campaign to ensure that his vision was carried out. Monty argued the point energetically. He was convinced that he was the better man for the job, that Ike wasn't much of a soldier, and that being CEO of the entire organization was more than enough job for any one man to handle—the ground boss should be an individual committed solely to the ground campaign. Monty's conviction that he was the best man for the job wasn't completely delusional. He had a long track record of success that stretched back to the previous world war. And until Ike took charge of D-Day Inc., Ike had no experience running a large operation actively engaged in combat. But his final point was the most telling. Eisenhower planned to be the CEO of D-Day Inc. and president of its largest, most active operating division. If you were constructing a business organization, you probably wouldn't structure it that way. But there are cases where the right individual can handle both jobs—even do both jobs well. Ike was the right individual, but that wouldn't be proved until months had passed. (And Montgomery never admitted that it was proved.)

Typical of Monty, he made his point about the executive structure of the organization in a condescending lecture, face-to-face with Eisenhower. Monty also told Ike that his broad-front strategy would be a failure. (Note to executives: Rudely telling your boss how his job should be defined and that his strategic plan for the entire organization will fail is not recommended practice for enhancing your career.) To give Montgomery his due, he also offered to step aside and serve under an American (other than Eisenhower) if the core of the problem was that Ike felt he needed an American commanding all ground forces—Monty just felt Eisenhower shouldn't hold two jobs at once. Like Marshall and Ike, Monty was completely committed to the success of D-Day Inc.'s mission, and like those Americans, he was willing to step down if it would help the cause, probably the only high point in his lecture.

Eisenhower had experienced enough of Monty's diatribes that he managed to not explode. He informed Monty that his mind was made up and he would assume control of the ground campaign, but then spent an hour engaged in a debate with Monty about how Monty and Bradley's Army Groups should operate relative to each other.

MANAGE YOUR PEOPLE

- **Be unselfish**. If you're the right person for the job, go for it. If you're not, please get out of the way. Voluntarily.

Monty, still trying to get his narrow-front strategy in place, wanted absolute priority over Patton in supplies, which would require Patton's Third Army to stop its forward movement. Monty also wanted the First Allied Airborne Army assigned to him, and Bradley's First Army assigned to him as well. Finally, Monty wanted a directive that would send him to Antwerp, Brussels, and into the Ruhr area. If Monty could get these items, he would be in *de facto* control of a narrow-front campaign.

Eisenhower wasn't going to go that far but felt some concessions were warranted. Monty's Twenty-first Army Group would have priority in supplies, although supplies would continue to go to Patton to allow limited operations. The Airborne Army was assigned to Monty's control, and Hodges' First Army (part of Bradley's Army Group) would be under Montgomery's authority in terms of coordinating its operations with the British and Canadians—a lot of verbiage that, in effect, gave control of First Army to Monty.

This was not one of Eisenhower's shining moments as a manager. He and Monty were in complete disagreement as to strategy, and yet he granted Monty several priorities that left D-Day Inc. semi-following Monty's single-thrust strategy. Ike allowed his acerbic subordinate to wear him down. Despite Eisenhower's insistence that he would be the ground commander and that D-Day Inc. would follow his broad-front strategy, he had ceded too much control to Monty for the organization to follow his vision.

COMMUNICATE

- **Be clear**. It's great to find agreement. But not at the cost of fuzziness regarding your organization's goals. Without clear communication, you will fail to meet your goals.

Additionally, Ike failed to communicate clearly with Monty and the rest of his executive team at D-Day Inc. about Monty's receiving a supply priority, controlling the Allied Airborne Army, and having powers of coordination regarding the U.S. First Army. The news of these decisions led to more problems of understanding, more arguments, and weakened morale among his executives. Arthur Tedder, Ike's No. 2 and a Brit, disagreed with the concessions to Monty, as did Generals Bull and Strong, Ike's staff officers in charge of operations (G-3) and intelligence (G-2). Bradley and Patton were so angry that Patton, ever the intemperate man, urged Bradley to join him in issuing Eisenhower an ultimatum: give us back our supplies and the First Army or we resign.

Bradley was deeply disappointed with Ike but had no intention of dispensing ultimatums. Instead he met with Eisenhower for two days during which he argued that First Army should remain within his Army Group. When Ike finally issued the directive concerning the new arrangements, Bradley had won. The directive authorized Monty to coordinate with Bradley regarding the British and Canadian Army Group and the American First Army—exactly what they would have done without the directive. The entire back-and-forth left Monty, Brooke, Bradley, and Patton convinced that Eisenhower had a bad habit of agreeing with whomever he last spoke to.

While Ike did try to find agreement with everyone, he was fully capable of holding to a decision. He was adamantine about taking control of the ground campaign and about the broad-front strategy. But Eisenhower also wanted to reduce conflict among the Allies, and he too often ended up appeasing the people he spoke with and failing to communicate his decisions properly. Alan Brooke, not an Eisenhower admirer, said Ike was "an arbiter balancing the requirements of competing allies and subordinates, rather than a master of the field making a decisive choice."[13] This led to the executives of D-Day Inc. leaving meetings feeling that Eisenhower agreed with them, regardless of how he actually felt. The sense of agreement was a great way to keep a bunch of strong-willed men working in alliance. It was a poor way to run strategic operations.

Ike took over the ground campaign on September 1. Also on that day, Churchill promoted Montgomery to field marshal. This was done at least in part to salve the wound of Monty's demotion, and it left Ike in the position of bossing a man who outranked him, five stars to Ike's four. The promotion led Monty to increase his efforts to get his narrow-front plan implemented. Even though Eisenhower had granted him priority in supplies, Monty felt he wasn't getting his required share. Even as he gave Monty the priority, Ike encouraged Bradley to continue operations, and Bradley immediately let Patton loose.

By the time Eisenhower had taken charge of ground operations and Monty had been promoted, Patton was already one hundred miles east of Paris. But his allotment of gas had been seriously cut back, and there was a serious danger of running out of fuel. Patton insisted

that the Third Army continue its advance "until the tanks stop and
then get out and walk."[14] He assumed, probably correctly, that Ike
wouldn't leave him high and, literally, dry—Eisenhower would give
him more fuel, even if it came out of Monty's allotment. Ike did, in
fact, give Patton more fuel at a September 2 meeting of Eisenhower,
Bradley, Hodges, and Patton at headquarters. Eisenhower also okayed
Third Army operations toward Mannheim and Frankfurt and decided
to detach Hodges's First Army from Monty's flank and assign it to
Patton's left.

Montgomery was livid. He argued that Eisenhower was mis-
allocating supplies and that the misallocation would prolong the
war, a pretty serious charge to throw at your superior. There was
a back-and-forth of communications, with Monty sputtering that it
was difficult to resolve this kind of thing without talking face-to-face.
Would Ike mind coming to see Monty to discuss it? It was tactless
and rude of Monty—he was the subordinate looking for a handout;
he should have gone to Eisenhower.

Monty's request was even worse on second glance. On a routine
trip between the headquarters of different units, Ike had been injured
when the small plane he had been flying in made an emergency landing on a French beach. Eisenhower got out of the plane to help the
pilot push it above the tideline and wrenched his knee in the wet sand.
He was ordered to a week of bed rest, and the knee was put in a cast.
The pain persisted throughout the war, and was occasionally so bad
that Ike had to rest in bed for a day or use crutches or a cane. Monty
knew of the injury, but rebuffed Eisenhower's counter-invitation for
Monty to come see him. Ever accommodating, Ike flew to Monty.

In *Crusade in Europe*, Eisenhower described the meeting in even,
businesslike terms, talking about his certainty that a single-thrust
initiative could never work, and the supply problems confronting all
of D-Day Inc., not just Monty's Twenty-first Army Group. Ike said
the need for the port of Antwerp was utmost—it would do more to
solve their supply problems, and therefore beat the Germans—than

anything else. Stephen Ambrose, while not contradicting anything that Eisenhower said, had a very different picture of the meeting. Ike never mentioned that his leg was so painful he could not get out of the airplane, so the meeting with Monty took place in Eisenhower's B-25. Ambrose wrote, "Pulling Eisenhower's latest directive from his pocket, waving his arms, Montgomery damned the plan in extreme language, accused the Supreme Commander of double-crossing him."[15]

"As the tirade gathered in fury Eisenhower sat silent. At the first pause for breath, however, he leaned forward, put his hand on Montgomery's knee, and said, 'Steady, Monty! You can't speak to me like that. I'm your boss.' Montgomery mumbled that he was sorry."[16]

The moment of apology derailed Monty's tirade but was immediately followed by an outlandish proposal. Monty brazenly insisted that if he got all the supplies he was asking for, he could make a single thrust through the Dutch city of Arnhem to Berlin itself. Eisenhower, according to Tedder, who was at the meeting, thought "it was fantastic to talk of marching to Berlin with an army which was still drawing the great bulk of its supplies over beaches." Ike refused to consider the proposal, later writing in his diary, "Monty's suggestion is simple, give him everything, which is crazy."[17] The two men sat in the B-25 for another hour, arguing as to what to do next. During that discussion, Monty proposed a two-pronged operation that was only slightly less daring than his Arnhem-to-Berlin extravaganza. It would be called Market-Garden.

In the first prong, Market, Monty wanted to drop the First Allied Airborne Army into Holland to seize key bridges from the Germans. The second prong, Garden, would see his Second Army smash its way up sixty-four miles of highway that connected the bridges. The final bridge crossed the Lower Rhine at Arnhem and would allow D-Day Inc. to spring into Germany. Market-Garden would have the advantage of surprise—the Germans most likely were prepared to counterattack along the shortest route into Germany, well north of this operation's key bridges and highway. And it would employ the

Airborne Army in a mass attack from the air, something Eisenhower, along with D-Day Inc. board members George Marshall and Hap Arnold (boss of the U.S. Army Air Force), wanted very badly.

The idea of the major attack from the air also added to the surprise; it would be a first for the Allies. Torch, Husky, and Overlord had all been amphibious operations with some airborne elements—Market-Garden was predominantly an airborne attack with an armored element. But D-Day Inc. had a long string of firsts: Torch, Husky, and Overlord had all presented unprecedented challenges that had been met successfully.

Another factor in Ike's consideration of Market-Garden was the personal war of wills going on between him and Monty over the lack of speed and daring in all of Monty's operations. Eisenhower had chafed at Monty's slow, cautious approach to everything since North Africa, then in Sicily and Italy, and most recently at Caen and the struggle to break out from the Normandy beachhead. Ike had spent enormous amounts of time and energy pushing Monty to be more aggressive. But Montgomery had rebuffed his boss almost every single time. Now the British field marshal was proposing Market-Garden, a plan Bradley categorized as "one of the most imaginative of the war." Bradley also said of the plan, "Had the pious, teetotaling Montgomery wobbled into [headquarters] with a hangover, I could not have been more astonished than I was by the daring adventure he proposed."[18]

Market-Garden had a number of significant problems. Eisenhower had observed that the narrow-front strategy was easily stopped with effective counterattacks and could result in the loss of the lead forces. This operation was a narrow, single-thrust movement, requiring an armored column to travel sixty-four miles along a single roadway in German-held territory—making it very easy to attack the column. Another weakness in the plan was that for it to succeed, all the bridges had to be taken from the Germans and held long enough for the armored column to arrive at each bridge. Since all of the bridges needed to be available for the column to move swiftly, there would be separate parachute drops in the vicinity of each river crossing. Every drop increased the probability of some forces landing off target or losing necessary equipment during the course of the drop. The Market-Garden plan also required that the lightly equipped Airborne forces hold off the heavily equipped Germans already in the area. If the armored column was delayed in its progress along its single, exposed roadway, the Airborne could be left in a very ugly position.

The difficulties with the highway, bridges, and multiple drops were the tactical threats to Market-Garden's success. The biggest problems with the operation were strategic. If Market-Garden went ahead, Monty needed the absolute priority in supplies he had wanted earlier. Bradley's Twelfth Army Group would all but stop in place while it waited for Monty to finish. The broad-front strategy had to be put on hold, at least for a short period. Because of the direction Market-Garden took, a gap was created in the Allies' line, and Hodges's First Army needed to move north, away from its supporting position to Patton, stretching D-Day Inc.'s defensive positions very thinly. Finally and most important, Market-Garden would in no way help the critical supply situation.

What Eisenhower really needed Monty to do was capture Antwerp immediately, if not sooner. He had to have a deepwater port with the facilities to supply his ever-growing, ever-moving armies. Without Antwerp, it wasn't possible to drive deep into Germany. Without increasing its supply capability, D-Day Inc. was looking at a stalemate that extended the war by months. Market-Garden intensified the supply problem without alleviating it, even if the operation was a complete success. Antwerp's port facilities should have been Monty's one and only priority.

Ike, fully aware of the operational issues of Market-Garden, as well as the strategic issue of Antwerp, approved the operation. In return, Monty agreed that Antwerp was at the very top of his to-do list. In less than two weeks, Market-Garden produced a disaster. Stephen

Ambrose described Ike's decision: "The result was one of the great mistakes of the war . . . The man both immediately and ultimately responsible for that failure was Eisenhower."[19]

PRIORITIZE

- **Do what you need to. Ignore the rest**. Eisenhower's approval of Market-Garden is like a manager approving a shiny new Web site when most of his business is via an 800-number call center—and the call center is in desperate need of a technology upgrade and training for its workers. Or like buying a new fleet of cars for a delivery service when you need trucks to handle the heavy loads you often deliver. Don't waste your time on shiny and new until you've met your core needs.

DEBRIEFING NOTES

STRATEGIES: DETERMINE YOUR MISSION, PLAN FOR SUCCESS, AND PLAN TO IMPLEMENT

- **Know Your Competition**. Understanding the competition is often the easier and softer way to success.

STRATEGY: BE HONEST (NOT SELF-AGGRANDIZING)

- **Don't Waste Time Tooting Your Own Horn**. Your success will speak much louder and more compellingly than anything you can possibly say.

STRATEGIES: PLAN FOR SUCCESS, STAY FOCUSED, AND PLAN TO IMPLEMENT

- **Know the Market**. Every market has barriers to entry. Find them in advance and prepare for them.

- **Follow Up**. After all the planning, and the launching of the plans, you have to continue in your efforts. (And yes, follow-up should be part of your plans.)
- **Speed Kills**. Perfecting plans takes time and dissolves opportunities. Don't wait too long to act.

STRATEGIES: PRIORITIZE, COMMUNICATE

- **Get What You Need from Your People**: Assign benchmarks to your managers: dates, quantities, revenues, whatever makes sense for your company. Be specific.

STRATEGIES: DETERMINE YOUR MISSION; MANAGE AND MOTIVATE YOUR PEOPLE

- **Delegate When Possible. Otherwise Do It Yourself.**
- **Be Unselfish**: If you're the right person for the job, go for it. If you're not, get out of the way.
- **Support Your People**. As has been said before, people are your most important resource—why wouldn't you support them?

STRATEGY: COMMUNICATE

- **Be Clear**. Without clear communication, you will fail to meet your goals. Clear enough?

STRATEGIES: DETERMINE YOUR MISSION, STAY FOCUSED, AND PRIORITIZE

- **Do What You Need To. Ignore the Rest**: Don't waste your time on shiny and new until you've met your core needs.

SEVEN

LOSING FOCUS

Keeping Clear Regarding Risk vs. Reward

The Market-Garden concept was brilliant and daring almost beyond belief. But, as is true with so many plans, the devil was in the details. Eisenhower's impatience after more than a year of Monty's go-slow, be-careful methods was understandable. Dazzled by the brilliance of the plan and the possibility that D-Day Inc. could be operating across the Rhine by the end of September, less than three months after stepping onto the French beaches, Ike approved the operation.

To ensure that Monty didn't revert to his tortoiselike habits, Eisenhower approved the plan on the condition that it go as soon as was possible. Ike committed all the supplies Monty needed, as long as Market-Garden happened quickly.

With Eisenhower's approval in his pocket, Monty outlined the concept to Lt. General Frederick Browning, one of Britain's Airborne masters. Like all military men, Browning could read a map—the equivalent of the modern business executive being able to read a spreadsheet—and see the crucial facts of the situation. The plan called for the Airborne Army to seize "a series of crossings—five of them major bridges including the wide rivers of the Maas, the Waal, and the Lower Rhine—over a stretch approximately sixty-four miles long . . . they were charged with holding open the corridor—in most places a single highway . . . over which British armor would drive. All of the bridges had to be seized intact if the armored dash was to succeed." Browning asked Monty how long it would take the armored forces to reach the farthest bridge at Arnhem over the Lower Rhine. Monty told him two days, and Browning said the airborne forces could hold for four days. Even with that two-day safety margin, Browning felt compelled to add, "But, Sir, I think we might be going a bridge too far."[1]

Browning and the executive in charge of the First Allied Airborne Army, Lewis Brereton, gathered to begin the detailed planning. Aside from the overarching concept, Monty had given them only one condition: the operation had to happen ASAP, if not sooner. As Brereton and Browning began to plan, the devilish details began making themselves apparent:

- *Lack of enough planes for the drop.* The air forces didn't have enough planes to drop the entire First Allied Airborne Army simultaneously, which meant multiple trips to make multiple drops—further complicating an already complicated situation. Brereton needed three days to transport the entire force to its assigned areas.

- *Lack of surprise.* After the first day, the Germans would be fully aware of what D-Day Inc. was attempting. The drops on the second and third days would be made against a competitor who was ready and waiting.

- *Different mix of forces and supplies for each.* Maxwell Taylor's 101st Airborne Division (American) was dropping nearest the oncoming armored thrust. They would be relieved first, which meant they needed to seize their objectives the quickest. Their drop requirements called for a lot more men than equipment to facilitate that.

    Gavin's Eighty-second Airborne (American) would have to wait longer and was assigned two of the wide-river bridges, the Maas and the Waal, which required specialized equipment. Their drop requirements had a much heavier mix of equipment.

Finally, the British First Airborne was to hold the bridge at Arnhem over the Lower Rhine. They were at the far end of the route for the armored thrust; they would be relieved last and needed to hold the longest. The First had the largest force, being joined by the Polish First Parachute Brigade, and the Fifty-second Lowland Division, which would be flown in to reinforce the operation as soon as local airfields had been secured.

★ ★ ★

Planning a major operation of any sort presents an opportunity to manage risk—executives have a chance to play the "What if . . . ?" game and assess the risk/reward balance. If the risk is too high and the reward too small, canceling an operation beforehand—painful and expensive as it may be—frequently results in less harm to an organization than going ahead with the plan. Admittedly it's a balancing act. Sometimes the only way to succeed is to put a stake in the ground in the form of a decision to act, and then refusing to pull the stake out until the operation is over. But risk assessment needs to be an ongoing process, moving along hand in glove with planning. No matter how firmly the stake has been driven into the ground, if the risk/reward formula is out of whack, the stake has to be pulled out—the decision needs to be rescinded.

The U.S. financial markets gave dramatic proof of the need to manage risk and take corrective steps in September 2008. The markets came tumbling down in large part due to many organizations—such as AIG, Citigroup, Fannie Mae, and Freddie Mac—failing to account for the extreme risk involved in the many credit instruments they were holding in their portfolios. A stream of financial industry CEOs made the trek to Washington, where they were forced to admit in front of Congress and the media that some of the instruments were so complicated, they didn't fully understand how the instruments worked. It's very hard to manage the risk inherent in a product or service when you don't know how it works. These companies had embraced the rewards of their investments without properly assessing the risk attached, and the companies and the entire American economy suffered for the lack of comprehensive risk management.

As the plans for Market-Garden went forward and the challenging details piled up, it should have been clear that the risks were too high for the reward. Remember: the operation was never designed for the one objective D-Day Inc. absolutely needed—Antwerp and its port facilities. Eisenhower applied a risk/reward formula to the operation, but applied it incorrectly. He felt that being able to cross the Rhine was an opportunity he couldn't let the organization pass on. Operating past the Rhine intensified the supply problem, however, and made the need for Antwerp more urgent.

PLAN FOR SUCCESS

- **Don't use a hammer for everything**. Use your strategic tools. With Market-Garden, D-Day Inc. fell into a rut of using one, and only one, strategic tool. Almost everyone was so involved in making the plan happen that every warning sign was ignored.

STAY FOCUSED

- **Lose focus and fail**. Ike forgot the mission. D-Day Inc.'s job was to beat Germany—and it had to have Antwerp to do that. Anytime you forget your mission is a time you are going to fail to advance your mission.

PLAN TO IMPLEMENT

- **Manage risk or fail**. Operation Market-Garden, AIG, Citigroup, the junk bond traders of the '80s . . . if you don't understand the risks you're running, get someone who does. And listen to them.

COMMUNICATE

- **Lose communication and fail**. If communication doesn't work up and down the management chain, very little else will work too.

The people doing the planning were following orders to figure out a way to make the operation happen. No one questioned the operation's failure to support the mission (beat the Germans) or mentioned that this was not a plan to succeed (they had to take Antwerp to do that). The failure here was the complete lack of communication regarding risk. While Brereton and Browning were painfully aware of how difficult the operation was becoming, the risks they perceived were not presented to Eisenhower in any form of risk matrix. D-Day Inc. did not have a formal process to assess and manage risk.

The Airborne Army executives weren't the only ones who saw the risks piling high. Miles Dempsey—in charge of the British Second Army, which supplied the armored forces to make the sixty-four-mile dash—was very worried. Dempsey's intelligence staff used reports from the Dutch resistance to create a very worrisome estimate of the situation. German forces were increasing in size in the drop area near Arnhem, and some Panzer units were refitting in Holland. As armored forces, Panzers were much more heavily equipped than the

D-Day Inc.'s Airborne forces, which meant that holding the bridges would be much tougher. Montgomery believed that once Second Army smashed through the hard outer crust of German defenses, it would be met with little resistance from weak forces. D-Day Inc.'s intelligence confirmed his view. When Dempsey made his intelligence estimate known, he was ignored—another example of risk improperly assessed at the top and a failure of communication.

Instead of worrying about whether Market-Garden helped the mission of D-Day Inc. or assessing the risk, Eisenhower seemed exclusively focused on making sure that Monty kept moving at a quick pace. Within days of Ike's approving the operation, Monty complained (again) that he was not receiving enough supplies and that the operation could not possibly be launched until at least September 23, 1944. Eisenhower dispatched Beetle Smith to see Monty, who then promised Monty that he would receive one thousand tons of supplies a day plus transport. Assured of having the matériel he needed, and believing that the opposition in Holland would be light, Monty set a launch date of September 17—only a week after Ike had approved the plan. Eisenhower may have believed he was getting what he wanted: quick action. There's an old saying: Be careful what you want—you may get it. Ike was about to get it.

The operation started perfectly. The weather was exactly what was needed, the first-day drops were on-target, the 101st seized its objectives, and the Second Army moved out along the highway. Within days, everything was wrong. The weather over England grounded the air forces—no reinforcements and no air support for the forces in Holland. The weather over Holland, however, was fine, so for a rare few days, the Germans enjoyed uncontested superiority in the air and wreaked havoc with D-Day Inc.'s forces.

The Panzer forces that Dempsey had tried to warn his fellow managers about turned out to be exactly where he thought they were. Resistance to the armored dash was heavy and incredibly effective. Most of the highway the British Second Army was using was elevated—and the Second Army's vehicle silhouettes made fantastic targets. And as the Germans knocked out more and more tanks, the roadway was blocked. The single, elevated highway became a gigantic death trap with no cover.

The Eighty-second Airborne took its assigned bridges but at great cost—boats needed for a river crossing couldn't be trucked up the highway due to the hammering the poor Second Army was taking. When the boats finally arrived, the Eighty-second's Third Battalion, under Major Julian Cook, was forced to make the river crossing in broad daylight. The casualties were enormous; boats were blown out of the water, and some sank from overloading. When the men reached the far side of the river, there was no cover for them on the beach. The situation quickly progressed from bad to worse: There weren't enough boats for the entire unit to go in one crossing, so the engineers driving the boats had to turn around under heavy fire, pick up the rest of the battalion, and go back. The additional crossing under fire was astoundingly heroic and horrifically costly in human life. But Cook's men took the bridge and moved on to their next objective.

As the Second Army struggled to make its "dash" up the highway, the Germans counterattacked both the 101st and 82nd Airborne Divisions. The Germans were much stronger than Monty or most of the execs at D-Day Inc. had thought, and without feeling any pressure from the stalled Second Army, they went after the Americans.

As ugly as the situation was for the American Airborne Division, it was downright terrible for the British First Airborne. The German resistance in Arnhem, where the last bridge of Market-Garden stretched over the Lower Rhine, was fierce. The Brits and the Polish First Airborne Brigade were caught in a days-long firefight with Panzer units who were much more heavily armed than they were. They were only able to secure one end of the bridge. But they could not be reinforced since they were unable to capture local airfields. Without the airfields, the Fifty-second Lowland Division couldn't reach them, and the Second Army's armored column was bogged down miles away on the highway. Monty had promised relief for the First Airborne in two days. Browning had thought they could hold out for four. They held out even longer, but it didn't matter. The Second Army never reached them.

The First Airborne and Polish First Airborne Brigade were evacuated via the river in a mini-Dunkirk—shattered units. Casualties for the Brits and Poles at Arnhem totaled 7,578. Casualties for Market-Garden totaled more than 17,000, according to Cornelius Ryan. That 17,000 figure is almost double what D-Day Inc., with a much larger overall force engaged, suffered on D-Day, June 6.[2]

PLAN FOR SUCCESS

- **Don't be seduced**. Daring is for bullfighting. It can be handy in business projects too, but it can be a little too exciting for your own good. Don't go for the overly aggressive plan just because it's a way to get things moving.

STAY FOCUSED

- **One step at a time**. Eisenhower should have pushed Monty for necessary objectives like Antwerp instead of approving a wild scheme with promises of quick success.

Ryan summed up Market-Garden by quoting Montgomery's memoirs: "In my—prejudiced—view, if the operation had been properly backed from its inception, and given the aircraft, ground forces, and administrative resources necessary for the job—it would have succeeded in spite of my mistakes, or the adverse weather, or the presence of the 2nd SS Panzer Corps in the Arnhem area. I remain Market-Garden's unrepentant advocate."[3] In other words, everyone else was to blame.

It is understandable that in a man's memoirs he might be a little hesitant to take responsibility for squandering thousands of lives on a project that could never have advanced the mission of the organization. But Monty never showed that he could learn from his mistakes—it is highly unlikely that he showed a more enlightened side in private. Eisenhower, you may remember, engaged in heavy self-analysis at the end of the North African campaign and did adjust his thinking and behavior as a result.

Bernhard, the prince of the Netherlands, was interviewed by Ryan and had this reaction to Market-Garden: "My country can never again afford the luxury of another Montgomery success."[4]

Eisenhower doesn't seem to have done the kind of soul-searching post–Market-Garden that he did as the North Africa campaign finished. He was at a different point in his learning curve by late September 1944—he'd been in command of gigantic combat forces for approximately a year and a half; he could learn the lessons he needed to know quickly. His comments about Market-Garden were limited to a brief description of the action and comments such as "We were inordinately proud of our airborne units. . . . When, in spite of heroic effort, the airborne forces . . . were stopped in their tracks, we had ample evidence that much bitter campaigning was still to come. . . . It was now vital to avoid any further delay in the capture of Antwerp's approaches."[5]

Ike acknowledged the operation was a failure and accepted the blame for it. As Alan Brooke—D-Day Inc. board member, chief of the Royal Army, and not one of Eisenhower's admirers—said, "I feel that Monty's strategy for once is at fault. . . . [He] ought to have made certain of Antwerp in the first place. . . . Ike nobly took all the blame on himself as he had approved Monty's suggestion to operate on Arnhem."[6]

Winston Churchill blamed the weather—both Monty and Ike

felt it was a crucial factor as well—and wrote, "Heavy risks were taken in the Battle of Arnhem, but they were justified by the great prize so nearly in our grasp."[7] What Churchill ignored, writing many years later in the rosy glow of victory, was that even victory at Arnhem did not solve D-Day Inc.'s supply problem. The organization simply did not have the resources to continue operating the way it needed to. There was only solution to the problem: Antwerp.

DON'T BE SEDUCED

While it's hard to imagine any serious, successful American businessperson getting seduced by a wondrous new idea, it does actually happen once in a while. You may remember a little thing called the dot-com boom in the late 1990s—it seemed as if every corporation was rushing to create a Web site and that any new product or service with ".com" at the end of its new name was guaranteed success. In the early days of this boom, Amazon's stock value kept increasing even as the company reported one red-ink quarter after another. Why? The promise of the dot-com future was too bright to ignore. (To be fair, Amazon has had profitable quarters since then.)

The shiny luster of the Internet is the only way to explain how Gerald Levin, Time Warner's chairman and CEO, agreed to join his company with Steve Case's AOL in January 2000 in "the largest merger in corporate history."[8] The combined unit was 55 percent owned by AOL, 45 percent Time Warner, even though AOL's value at the time was $108 billion, $3 billion less than Time Warner's. Dab an old-style media company with a bit of Internet pixie dust, and poof! The wonderful synergy of content (Time Warner) with Internet (AOL) was magical indeed.

"This is a fabulous deal," Arthur Hogan, chief market strategist of Jefferies & Co. in Boston, told *Forbes*. "It lends credibility to the entire Internet sector. It gives the merged company the best of both worlds: AOL's growth and Time-Warner's revenues."[9]

Ed Clissold, assistant market strategist at J. C. Bradford in Nashville, also speaking to *Forbes*, said, "AOL is the Internet company that's the farthest along on the road to profitability. This deal will set a standard that other companies will have to follow."[10]

"Everybody wanted to do this deal, but only Levin had the guts to do it," said Barry Hyman, senior market analyst with Ehrenkrantz King Nussbaum in New York, to *Forbes*. "This year, we'll see Internet companies form the alliances and ownership patterns that will determine the future of the entire industry."[11]

Not so fast . . . like Operation Market-Garden, there were flaws to this thinking. Not all Internet companies were created equal. Despite AOL's amazing success to that point, there were flaws in its business model. AOL began life as an Internet-service provider (the company that actually allows people to "get on" the Internet) as well as an online community. AOL had a browser built into its software and had a preset community of services and products available to its users, or "members," as AOL called them.

The problem with this model was simple: In the early days of Web sites, many people needed a service that took them by the hand and led them through the bewildering online universe. In addition to AOL, Prodigy and CompuServe also provided Internet access and pre-built communities. By 2000, millions of people had become experienced enough that they were more than willing to tackle the Internet on their own—they could get a free browser from Microsoft and buy their Internet access more cheaply from broadband providers like Earthlink or their phone company or their cable TV company. Web sites like Google and Yahoo! allowed regular visitors to customize their experience and use those sites if they still needed handholding. Prodigy and CompuServe were, to all intents and purposes, gone. AOL—despite terrific numbers in its filings and stock value—was already in decline. The company was going to need to redefine itself, and soon.

Well, hey! Merging with an old-line media company will cause you to redefine yourself, right?

Maybe, except that in the case of Time Warner and AOL, the dot-com bust started in 2001, Google and Yahoo! were booming as Web presences, and there was an ongoing culture clash between the merging entities. In December 2001, Levin announced that he was leaving AOL Time Warner. In 2002, the company "reported a one-time write-off of $99 billion—at the time the largest corporate loss ever reported. At its nadir, the firm boasted a meager market cap of $48 billion—$171 billion less than at the time of the merger."[12]

In May 2003, barely two years after the merger, Steve Case departed as chairman of AOL Time Warner. A few months later the corporation's name was changed back to Time Warner. Talk about trying to hide your shame . . .

In July 2009, *Forbes* reported that "Time Warner boss Jeffrey Bewkes seems to be making a savvy move by unloading digital media subsidiary AOL in a public offering. Time Warner reported this morning that AOL is bleeding subscribers—revenues for its paid Internet access service have fallen 70% since 2006—as well as digital ad revenue, which fell 24% in the three months ended June 30, compared to last year."[13]

Levin and Case were dazzled by the possibilities of the "new" and didn't look at the basics. A realistic appraisal of the large numbers of dot-com companies with high stock values and no profits should have made anyone realize that the odds were high against a merger of online and old-line working out. A cold-eyed look at AOL's fading business model should have made Levin and the Time Warner board hesitant about the merger.

But, as with Eisenhower and the executives at D-Day Inc., there was no assessment of the downside risks involved, no balancing of the risk/reward equation.

Now that everyone at D-Day Inc. had finally realized there was no success without Antwerp and the supplies that could come through that port, all efforts turned to seizing and opening the port. The lack of supplies made it very difficult for the Americans in the south to move forward, and the British and Canadians were going to need everything they could get their hands on to take Antwerp.

Monty's forces had taken the city in early September 1944, before Market-Garden launched. Unfortunately, that was not enough. Antwerp sits on the Scheldt River, at the southern end of a very long estuary, approximately fifty miles from the open sea. It was possible to control the city of Antwerp but not be able to use the port because the competition had assumed defensive positions in the estuary, exercising control over the waterway. In September the Germans were not well positioned in the estuary to seal off the port, but Monty didn't act to secure it. Instead he ignored Antwerp's estuary to go after Arnhem with Operation Market-Garden. It was early October 1944 by the time D-Day Inc. was firmly on the Antwerp track. The Germans had not been idle in the preceeding month; they now completely controlled the estuary. The port was sealed and useless—it took weeks of brutal fighting, mostly by Monty's Canadians, to push the competition out of the estuary.

Antwerp's port finally opened to service on November 28, 1944, almost ten weeks after Eisenhower had approved Market-Garden and allowed Monty to ignore D-Day Inc.'s priorities. In those ten weeks, there was very little forward progress made by any of D-Day Inc.'s forces. Bradley's Army Group was more or less stuck in place without enough supplies to push deeper toward Germany. Monty's force had enough supplies to operate, but virtually all of them were going into the effort at Antwerp. After carving its way through France at mind-boggling speed, D-Day Inc. found itself in a momentary stalemate.

Montgomery's bravura regarding Market-Garden wasn't just for the public and for postwar audiences. What had happened in no way humbled him, despite the fact that for the second time in three months most of the executives at D-Day Inc. were calling for his head. (The first time was during the prolonged effort to take Caen.)

On October 9, Eisenhower sent a cable to Monty that "of all our operations on our entire front from Switzerland to the Channel, I consider Antwerp of first importance, and I believe operations designed to clear up the entrance require your personal attention." Monty replied that "operations [in Antwerp] are receiving my personal attention." Ike responded, "Let me reassure you that nothing I may ever say or write with respect to future plans . . . is meant to indicate any lessening of the need for Antwerp."

Later in the day, Beetle Smith, a man renowned for his forcefulness, telephoned Monty to follow up, asking when Ike and his C-level officers could expect action around Antwerp. Stephen Ambrose described the call: "Heated words followed. Finally Smith, 'purple with rage,' turned to his deputy General Morgan, and thrust the telephone into his hand. 'Here,' Smith said, 'you tell your countryman what to do.' Morgan . . . told Montgomery that unless Antwerp was opened soon, his supplies would be cut off."[14]

Given the failure of the previous month, and the clarity of the communications of October 9, most executives in Monty's position would be extraordinarily eager to assure their bosses that they understood what was required of them and would make it happen. Not Monty. He lashed out by writing to Beetle Smith, saying that the problem with Market-Garden was a lack of coordination between his force and Bradley's. The solution, according to Montgomery, was simple—give the American Twelfth Army Group to him. Playing office politics and making a blatant power grab isn't usually a good career strategy— doing it when your boss has expressed his displeasure with you and issued a clear set of priorities for you is almost beyond belief.

Monty was asking for control of the ground campaign, in effect asking Eisenhower to give up a significant part of his job, and was still trying to maneuver all of D-Day Inc. to support his narrow-front strategy. (If Ike had handed the U.S. Twelfth Army Group to him, it would have constituted a de facto switch to Monty's strategy as opposed to Eisenhower's.) "It was obvious that a crisis had been reached and the time had come to have it out with Montgomery."[15] Ike asked British brigadier general John Whiteley, who knew Monty well, to write a letter in response to the latest outrage. Beetle Smith, Whiteley's immediate boss, reviewed the letter, and Eisenhower sent it out to Monty over his signature.

The priority, Ike said in the letter, was Antwerp. It needed to be opened as a port immediately. According to Eisenhower, D-Day Inc.'s crucial board members, Alan Brooke (Monty's boss in the Royal

Army) and George Marshall (Ike's boss in the U.S. Army), both agreed that Antwerp was the sole priority. "The Antwerp operation does not involve the question of command in any slightest degree"[16]—meaning Bradley kept the Twelfth Army Group, and Monty stayed where he was. Eisenhower elaborated on his vision for the executive structure of the ground campaign and the strategy D-Day Inc. continued to follow (Ike's broad-front approach). Eisenhower also discussed the Allied nature of the organization they worked for and laid out a simple and effective methodology for corporate managers everywhere:

> It is the job of soldiers, as I see it, to meet their military problems sanely, sensibly, and logically, and while not shutting our eyes to the fact that we are two different nations, produce solutions that permit effective cooperation, mutual support, and effective results. Good will and mutual confidence are, of course, mandatory.[17]

Typical Eisenhower, acknowledging the difficulties of working within an Allied framework and proposing exactly how to manage the challenges of doing so.

The crucial words, however, came earlier in Ike's letter: "If you . . . feel that my conceptions and directives are such as to endanger the success of operations, it is our duty to refer the matter to higher authority for any action they may choose to take, however drastic."

There it was. Do what I tell you to do, or we'll let our board decide who stays or goes. Arrogant as Monty was, he knew that even Churchill and Brooke would support Eisenhower if they were presented with a "him or me" choice. The United States was supplying the majority of the manpower and the vast majority of the resources for D-Day Inc. The CEO had to be an American, and there was no way the board could allow a British executive to emasculate the CEO.

Montgomery, for all of his faults, was no fool. He also had come to the conclusion that he would not be able to reach the Rhine anytime soon and had already shifted his forces to concentrate more completely on Antwerp. He replied to Eisenhower, "I and all of us will weigh in 100 percent to do what you want. . . . You will hear no more on the subject of command from me." Monty signed off, "Your very devoted and loyal subordinate."[18]

Finally, all quiet on the western front, to borrow a phrase.

PRIORITIZE

- **Playing politics is stupid**. There's no way you are working in the best interests of your organization when you play office politics. The very nature of office politics means you are advancing your agenda over the needs of the company. D-Day Inc. had to have an American CEO—so every minute Monty spent fighting Ike was wasted time and effort.
- Likewise, D-Day Inc. board members like Churchill and Brooke made things worse by listening to Monty through back-channel communications and by their continued argument against the American-endorsed broad-front strategy. They should have taken a note from Ike's career: he had not wanted D-Day Inc. to launch Torch (North Africa), but once his board decided on it, he wasted no time and dedicated himself to the project.

Monty's devotion and loyalty were of short-term duration. Within two months, Eisenhower needed to resettle the intertwined issues of strategy and command. The important point for executives to glean from this is not that Ike failed to resolve the issue once and for all. All organizations and their CEOs face ongoing challenges that, by their very nature, cannot be resolved. Ongoing challenges are like chronic illnesses that can't be cured, only dealt with on a day-by-day basis. Regarding the early October management crisis at D-Day Inc., Stephen Ambrose wrote: "Eisenhower continued to make the decisions and enforce his will. . . . He was sure he took everything into account, gathered all relevant information, and had considered all possible consequences. Then he acted. This is the essence of command."[19]

Why didn't Eisenhower just fire Montgomery? His C-level officers, including the Brits, wanted him to. His top field executives, Bradley and Patton, would have rejoiced. Monty was uncooperative, arrogant, and unpleasant in the extreme. And, most important, he consistently over-promised and under-delivered. Patton was the most challenging of all Ike's American executives, but Patton delivered. It makes sense to put up with an executive as frustrating as George Patton when the executive produces the kind of results that Patton consistently produced. But Monty? Based on results, it was impossible to justify keeping him on. So . . . why keep him?

It was simple. Eisenhower didn't measure Monty's contributions to D-Day Inc. against the usual benchmarks of territory gained or competition put out of action. Ike never lost sight of the fact that D-Day Inc. was an alliance. The organization had to succeed as an alliance. Montgomery was the visible face of the alliance. Crucial British board members, Churchill and Brooke, were fans of Monty. The shareholders (the British public) loved him. The British press loved him—and since D-Day Inc.'s "home office" was in England, the British press was more important to the organization than the American media.

There were other English generals who were more competent than Monty—Harold Alexander, who had been Eisenhower's deputy and ground commander in Torch and Husky, for instance. But no one had the public impact that Monty had—no one else even came close. Firing Monty would be akin to a golf club manufacturer dumping Arnold Palmer as its spokesman because he was no longer a competitive golfer. Monty, like Palmer, was a legend. It's very difficult to assess the value of a legend, but almost everyone can see that legendary status is extremely valuable. Monty was a competitive asset, not necessarily on the battlefield, but in the boardroom and with shareholders.

No one comprehended this better than Eisenhower. If the short form of D-Day Inc.'s mission statement was "Beat the Germans," the slightly longer form was "Beat the Germans as Allies." Monty's ultimate value to the organization was that he was the active, in-combat face of the British part of the alliance. Strategies No. 3 and 4 are: "Stay Focused"—know and get what you need to succeed; and "Prioritize"—do what you need to do for success; nothing else matters. Keeping Monty on the D-Day Inc. executive team fulfilled both of those strategies, and keep him Ike did.

Most executives would do well to remember to stay focused and prioritize. Almost all of us find ourselves working with people we could strangle with glee. (If you feel you have *never* had this feeling toward another manager or key employee, you need to look long and hard at Strategy No. 10: "Be Honest.") But, before you wrap your fingers around the offending person's throat and begin to squeeze, ask yourself if your company receives any value from him or her. Remember—be honest. If there's value there, please reconsider your strangulation strategy and spend some time thinking of ways to maximize that value. If there's no value, let me suggest firing instead of strangling. (Unless your career goals include sampling the social life in prison, in which case, strangle away.)

In addition to the ongoing management struggles with Monty, Eisenhower spent a great deal of time in the autumn of 1944 taking care of other personnel issues. During October and November, Ike tried to visit every division in D-Day Inc., visiting with as many men as possible, as well as the officers, who were D-Day Inc.'s frontline managers. This wasn't just a case of showing his face to the troops and bolstering their morale with a quick handshake and a smile—Eisenhower was gleaning information that he put to use as a matter of policy; Ike wanted "equality of treatment as between officers and enlisted men."[20] This equality meant five things:

- Officers weren't entitled to more leave than enlisted men.
- Officers couldn't use jeeps for recreational purposes unless something similar was provided for the men.

- Captured wine should be distributed exactly the same to officers and enlisted.
- Generals should travel aboard the ship with their men instead of flying on ahead.
- Generals should travel frequently by road, with the stars on their vehicles hidden so there was no preferential treatment, and discover what conditions truly were, and make efforts to correct problems.

Eisenhower summed up his policy: "Officers must invariably place the care and welfare of their men above their own comfort and convenience."[21]

MANAGE AND MOTIVATE YOUR PEOPLE

- **Your people are your company**. Take care of them like the precious resource they truly are. Herb Kelleher of Southwest argued that employees come before customers and shareholders. Eisenhower went a bit further—they are more important than executives too.

Ike's visits to the front had paid dividends in the past, for instance, when he ordered the halftracks forward in Tunisia, and they continued to do so in France. Conditions for the enlisted men did improve, and in early December, Eisenhower was able to say, "The morale and condition of our troops stay remarkably high."[22]

The enlisted men weren't the only beneficiaries of Ike's close concern. Eisenhower made a point of meeting the senior managers of his divisions and corps (one-, two-, and three-star generals). "In certain instances these officers themselves do not realize that they are momentarily exhausted."[23] Ike had these men take long leaves to ensure they could rest and be productive on their return to duty. Just as George

Marshall had ordered Eisenhower to take a vacation before beginning Overlord, Ike now did the same for the executives making the urgent decisions for the men of D-Day Inc. Burnout is a serious problem for managers operating under intense stress; a little personal scrutiny by the chief executive and a resulting vacation can often save a productive career.

There was also a compassionate motive for some of these executive moves. Eisenhower relieved two generals and sent them back to the United States because each man had lost his only son in the war. "This shock and distress, coupled with the abnormal strains always borne by an active Division Commander, are really more than any one man should be called upon to bear."[24] Sending the generals home was the right thing to do for the two grieving fathers and sent a message to the rest of the organization: you are not just a body in a uniform—we care about you. That message was one of the major differentiators between D-Day Inc. and its German competition.

In addition to personnel issues, the other ongoing problem Eisenhower faced in the autumn of 1944 was expectations. Prior to June 6, Churchill had told Ike "Liberate Paris by Christmas and none of us can ask for more."[25] Fortunately for the Parisians, D-Day Inc. beat that deadline by four months—Charles de Gaulle walked down the Champs-Elysées on August 25. Even with the failure of Operation Market-Garden and the ongoing supply problems, the Germans had been pushed back almost to their borders by late September—much earlier than anyone had expected. And until approximately the middle of October, Churchill, Brooke, Monty, Patton, and others believed that a push across the Rhine deep into Germany was possible. The across-the-Rhine faction all were convinced, supplies be damned, that if you pushed deep enough and hard enough into German territory, the Germans would collapse.

The conviction that the Germans were on the verge of collapse ignored certain realities. Operation Market-Garden demonstrated that the Germans still had plenty of fight left in them. Their resistance to the First Allied Airborne Army had been withering. Also, D-Day Inc. had done the competition a huge favor by driving it back to its own borders—German supply lines were much shorter than they had been previously, their lines of communication were internal to their own territory, and they could take advantage of defensive positions built earlier, most notably the Siegfried Line.

Yes, the Germans had absorbed staggering losses in France and Belgium—"losses that would have certainly broken the resistance of any nation, army, or leader not sustained by sheer fanaticism."[26] But the Germans *were* sustained and driven by sheer fanaticism at the top. And the CEO of the German forces facing D-Day Inc. was Karl Gerd von Rundstedt, the same man who had knocked France out of the war entirely and sent the British scrambling over the beaches at Dunkirk in 1940. Unlike Hitler, who seemed to vacillate between mad genius and insanity, Rundstedt was the consummate, professional military man. In autumn 1944, "Rundstedt's stern, old-fashioned professionalism took hold from top to bottom of the German armies in the west."[27]

Rundstedt's competence, a still-robust German industrial base, shorter supply lines, and internal communications combined to create a simpler, improved operational situation for the Germans. Germany's situation resembled a modern conglomerate that sells off some of its operating divisions and subsidiaries to focus on one or two core competencies. Assuming the conglomerate is still competitive in its remaining competencies, it has a good chance of competing success-fully. Germany was an extremely able competitor within its new, limited focus of operations.

D-Day Inc., on the other hand, was still bogged down with long supply lines, unable to use Antwerp, arguing about strategy at its top levels, and making incremental progress toward its final goal. Monty's forces were able to open the estuary north of Antwerp, and the port was finally in use in very late November. Bradley's Army Group had moved a little closer to Germany, despite the shortage of oil. Patton's Third Army had captured more than twenty-five thousand Germans in November, and Hodges's First Army and William Simpson's Ninth Army had each captured more than fifteen thousand in the same month. But D-Day Inc. had lost the initiative, something no military or corporate organization ever wants. In *The Supreme Commander*, Ambrose called his chapter on these months, "A Dreary Autumn." Korda titled his chapter on the same time frame, "Stalemate."

Eisenhower wanted to break the stalemate, just as he had wanted to achieve a breakout from the Normandy beachhead in June. The board of D-Day Inc. and its C-level officers desperately wanted to break the stalemate as well, and the old debate about strategy and command started again. Beginning in late November, there was a flurry of letters back and forth between Monty and Ike, culminating in a meeting on November 28, 1944. "Montgomery reported to Brooke that Eisenhower had agreed that his [Ike's] plan had failed and 'we had suffered a strategic reverse,' and had further agreed to abandon 'the doctrine of attack all along the front and concentrate our resources on selected vital thrust.'"[28] Monty seems to have been convinced that Eisenhower's patiently hearing him out meant that Ike agreed with him. It did not.

Monty followed up the meeting with a memo to confirm what had been decided on in the meeting. He began the memo with a slap in the face: "We have . . . failed; and we have suffered a strategic reverse. We require a new plan. And this time *we must not fail*."[29] He went on to describe the need for a single thrust, although his new single thrust had two parts, one going north of the Ardennes and the other going south of it. The Ardennes is a densely forested, mountainous area covering large parts of Belgium and Luxembourg and a small part of France. The woods and mountains made it, in theory, unsuitable to modern combat operations.

In 1940, the Germans had assumed the French did not defend their side of the Ardennes and swept through the area into France as part of their successful blitzkrieg. Now Monty was assuming it was a logical dividing point for D-Day Inc.'s operations because of the topography—as if what the Germans had done in 1940 was a fluke not to be repeated. "Perhaps Monty was so anxious to get his own way over the 'single thrust' that he simply failed to consider the possibility of Rundstedt's attacking first."[30]

Eisenhower fired back with his angriest letter to date to Monty. He made it clear that he didn't agree with virtually a single point made by Monty at either the meeting or in the follow-up memo. He refuted Monty's claim that D-Day Inc. had failed to-date, pointed out that Normandy had been a great success, implied that Monty's performance at Caen had been disappointing while explicitly praising Bradley as the man responsible for the breakout. Montgomery replied with a letter that, while not a full apology, indicated a bit of repentance. He had not meant to indicate that the past was nothing but failure. Ike, as usual, was generous in his response. "You have my prompt and abject apologies for misreading your letter."[31]

Less than a week later, the debate erupted again. On December 7, 1944, the third anniversary of the attack on Pearl Harbor, Eisenhower met with Bradley, Tedder, Smith, and Montgomery. "Monty was at his worst, haughty, pedantic, and still harping on his idée fixe—being returned to the position of Ike's commander of ground forces, with Bradley (and the American forces) serving under him."[32] Monty wanted there to be a large, single thrust aimed at the Ruhr. He was clear in his presentation that Ike's strategy of simultaneously moving north and south of the Ruhr toward Frankfurt had no chance of succeeding. Eisenhower allowed Monty to interrupt him and contradict him at several points in the meeting, but insisted that he, Eisenhower, remained the ground commander and that the Americans under Bradley moved in the direction of Frankfurt. The drive toward the Ruhr was the primary drive, but Bradley's southern thrust was also large in size. Ike remained convinced that mobility was a tremendous asset for D-Day Inc., and he intended to exploit it.

The other major continuing difference between Eisenhower and Montgomery was their conflicting assessments of their competition.

Ike was convinced that the Germans were capable of stiff resistance, possibly even mounting a substantial counterattack. Monty dismissed the Germans' ability to remain competitive and ignored the evidence of Operation Market-Garden, where the Germans had thwarted a major D-Day Inc. initiative.

Monty wrote angry, disappointed (and disloyal) letters to Brooke and British secretary of war Sir James Grigg. He said, "I personally regard the whole thing as dreadful. . . . In my opinion he [Eisenhower] just doesn't know what he is doing."[33] The letters triggered another meeting a few days later, this time with Eisenhower, Tedder, Churchill, Brooke, and the British heads of the military services—with the exception of Tedder, all on Ike's board of directors. Brooke asked Eisenhower to present his plan for operations aimed at getting over the Rhine and then penetrating Germany. Brooke said later, "I disagreed flatly with it, accused Ike of violating principles of concentration of force, which had resulted in his present failures." Brooke continued in the same vein to Eisenhower's face, "highly critical, and extremely loud."[34]

To Brooke's dismay, it was Churchill who ended the argument by saying he agreed with Ike. Churchill was probably bowing to reality. There was no way that Eisenhower would be presenting this plan if it didn't have the backing of FDR and George Marshall. Since the Americans were the majority of D-Day Inc.'s workforce and becoming a larger majority almost by the minute, and the Americans were producing and distributing the vast majority of supplies, the views of FDR and Marshall had more weight than any others on D-Day Inc.'s board. Arguing with Eisenhower, when he had their backing, was a waste of time, and Churchill was way too cunning a politician to waste time on fruitless debate. Brooke was so upset he "seriously thought of resigning" since Churchill seemed dismissive of his viewpoint. Montgomery pouted at his headquarters in Holland and refused to send any of his staff to participate in planning at D-Day Inc. because he refused "to be involved in an unsound procedure."[35]

Given the American preponderance in men and matériel; the

crucial support on the board of FDR, Marshall, and even Churchill; and most important, Eisenhower's persistence in keeping to his strategy, you could easily think that the meeting with Churchill and Brooke finally ended the debate. You would be mistaken. It's astounding but true—the strategy debate continued almost to the end of the war, which was still six months away. Which begs the question: Why did Ike allow it to continue? After all, he was the boss, and he had the support of the two most important members of his board.

Ike worked in a military organization where the giving and taking of orders was routine. He had already proved his decisiveness by ordering the launching of Torch, Husky, Avalanche, and especially Overlord. When British air marshal Leigh-Mallory pleaded with Eisenhower to cancel the Airborne operations within Overlord, he listened and then reaffirmed his earlier decision that the Airborne must go—end of discussion. He demonstrated his backbone by promoting Omar Bradley over his senior, George Patton, and making him equal to another senior man, Bernard Montgomery. When necessary, Ike successfully rapped Patton's knuckles on many occasions. Sooner or later, he had to discipline Patton again, but the intervals between outrageous outbursts was usually measured in months, highly productive months. With Monty, the intervals tended to last days, sometimes hours. So, why did Ike, who was extraordinarily capable of being firm, put up with the constant questioning of his strategy? Questioning that went to the heart of whether or not D-Day Inc. would succeed at its mission.

The answer is to be found in Eisenhower's convictions and personality. As mentioned before, Ike was convinced that victory was only attainable for an Allied organization. Being allies, functioning as a team was all-important to him and came naturally to the man. Ike was friendly; he wanted to get along with people and usually did. He enjoyed working with people and believed they would be more effective if they could work well with each other. His leadership style as an executive was to gather as many facts as possible, listen fully to the informed opinions of others, and decide. Eisenhower was self-confident enough that he could listen to criticism, open-minded enough that he could change his mind when he heard a good idea, and sympathetic enough that he always wanted to let everyone have his or her say. And that is exactly where he went wrong.

Let's digress to contemporary Corporate America for a moment. In one of my past jobs, I worked at a company that had recently installed customer relationship management (CRM) software. Our company could track all of the interactions a customer had had with us, a complete customer history. But there was more. The software could handle billing, shipping (electronically through our Web site or physically by generating pick lists and labels for shipping), and inventory. Customer phone calls could be logged in the system; letters to and from customers could be stored in it. The new software, in my opinion, was a pretty cool piece.

During the implementation of the software, several e-mail alerts were sent out to the staff—the future users—explaining what was going on as the software was being installed. Staff members were asked what kind of features they needed, and when a beta version of the software was ready, the staff was asked to test the software and report any issues they had. To sum up, the staff was kept informed at every stage of the way and had input into the CRM software's implementation.

Even with all of this preparation and communication, when the CRM software went live, the first couple of months of using the new system were bumpy. All kinds of little problems popped up. We quickly discovered the truth of what Ike had said: "Plans are worthless, but planning is everything."[36] No matter how much you plan, reality will always throw you a curve. Fortunately, we were ready for the curve balls because we'd planned for them. A system was in place to log all the problems, fix them, and inform our company's staff that the problems had been fixed. After the CRM software was live for about sixty days, the frequency of complaints was way down; all the major problems had been solved, and most of the minor ones too.

What was frustrating about the CRM implementation was even

after months of preparation and planning, months of informing the staff of what was coming, months of collecting their input on what they wanted in the new system, months of testing by the staff, and then more months of fixing the live system, we still had people complaining about problems that had been fixed and making claims about the system that were factually untrue. CRM meetings were held once every week or so, and staffers arrived with a laundry list of problems they had previously complained about—in some cases complained about six or seven times. Problems were being fixed expeditiously, which meant the complainer had already been informed—at least four or five times— that the complaint had been fixed. But the complainers continued to complain, and the company continued to hold CRM meetings to allow for these seemingly endless and incorrect moanings and groanings.

After a while, the guy running the CRM project stopped holding the meetings. They were pointless—nothing new ever came up. The staff, feeling they were not being listened to, complained to the CEO, who in turn made the CRM guy resume the meetings. The CEO acknowledged that most of what was said in the meetings was pointless, and repetitiously pointless at that, but at least staffers felt they were listened to.

What's the moral of this little story? No matter how hard you try to communicate or engage your people in the process, no matter how much you listen to your people, no matter what changes you make as a result of what you heard, there will always be people in your organization you cannot make happy. That includes the people on your management team. It's just my opinion, but if 80–85 percent of your people are happy, you're doing great. That last 15–20 percent of unhappy folks . . . you have to accept there is virtually no power on earth that could make them happy, and you should manage them in whatever way is least damaging to the rest of the organization.

In the story above, the CEO felt that staffers should have a venue to complain endlessly so they felt listened to. But if they felt they had been heard, why didn't they stop complaining? Why did they still have the need to be listened to? It was a vicious cycle, and the only way the CRM guy could escape it was to move off the CRM function at the company. The new CRM guy became the designated complainee.

MANAGE YOUR PEOPLE

- **It ain't a debate club**. Listen to your people. Gather facts and ideas from them. Then decide. Unless some major new fact or facts come into play, stick to your original decision.

Eisenhower seemed unable to accept the idea that Monty, and by extension Brooke, couldn't be satisfied. Ike felt that if he listened to them just one more time, if he gave them another opportunity to vent rudely and loudly, if he calmly explained again what he wanted and his reasons for wanting it, they would eventually accept his ideas and follow his lead. But that never happened. Eisenhower allowed the debate to continue and accomplished nothing but wasting time and bruising egos. Monty and Brooke never came to agree with Ike—even after the war, their memoirs amply demonstrated their anger toward and disrespect for Eisenhower. After the first two or three instances of this discussion, Ike should have said something like, "I hear you, I appreciate your thoughts, but I don't agree with you. Since I'm the one who is paid to make the decisions, we're going to do it my way. Discussion closed."

Sometimes, enough is enough.

The debate in December 1944 did not close with any sense of resolution. It merely adjourned momentarily due to Churchill's support of Eisenhower's position. Before the arguments could resume, 250,000 Germans intervened by surging through the Ardennes. The Battle of the Bulge, the deadliest fight for the Americans in the entire war, had begun.

DEBRIEFING NOTES

STRATEGIES: DETERMINE YOUR MISSION, PLAN FOR SUCCESS, STAY FOCUSED, PLAN TO IMPLEMENT, AND COMMUNICATE

- **Stay Focused**: Anytime you forget your mission, you're going to fail in your mission.
- **Fail to Communicate and Fail**: If communication doesn't work, very little else will work too.
- **Manage Risk or Fail**: If you don't understand the risks you're running, get someone who does. And listen to them.
- **Don't Be Seduced**: Don't go for the overly aggressive plan just because it's a way to get things moving.
- **One Step at a Time**: Push for necessary objectives instead of approving daring schemes with promises of quick success.

STRATEGIES: DETERMINE YOUR MISSION, STAY FOCUSED, AND PRIORITIZE

- **Playing Politics Is Stupid.** You're not working in the best interests of your organization when you play office politics.

STRATEGIES: MOTIVATE AND MANAGE YOUR PEOPLE

- **Your People Are Your Company**: Here we go again—take care of your employees like the precious resource they truly are.
- **It Ain't a Debate Club**: Listen to your people. Gather facts and ideas from them. Then decide. End of discussion.

EIGHT

"NUTS"

Never Giving Up—*Ever*

When Eisenhower had traveled to the December 7 meeting with Tedder, Smith, Bradley, and Montgomery, he noticed how thin the defensive lines in the Ardennes were and asked Bradley whether or not the defensive positions should be reinforced. Bradley did not want to reinforce the Ardennes because he would have to weaken Patton's Third Army and Hodges's First Army to do so. Bradley also felt that if the Germans attacked in the Ardennes, the Americans could counter effectively along the German flanks and stop any forward progress. As an added precaution, Bradley had not allowed any major supply installations to be placed in the Ardennes, so the enemy couldn't overrun anything valuable.

Patton was about to attack along the Saar River, near the French border with Luxembourg. Hodges was already engaged in operations against the Roer River dams east of Aachen, Belgium. Eisenhower said, "Both Bradley and I believed that nothing could be so expensive to us as to allow the front to stagnate. . . . My basic decision was to continue the offensive to the extreme limit of our ability." Ike approved Bradley's defensive arrangements and unflinchingly accepted the blame for what happened: "The responsibility for maintaining only four divisions on the Ardennes front and for running the risk of a large German penetration in that area was mine."[1]

The German penetration wasn't large—it was gigantic. A quarter million men, almost fifteen hundred tanks, and more than two thousand artillery pieces were unleashed on the Ardennes and those thinly held American lines on December 16. Ironically for Eisenhower, he had been informed the day before that he was being promoted to General of the Army, a newly created five-star rank equal to the highest rank in the British, French, Soviet, or German armies. A little more than three years earlier, Ike had been an anonymous staff officer, a mere lieutenant colonel, six rungs below the pinnacle he occupied as General of the Army. Now, as the Germans burst upon his forces in one last, desperate attack, there was no military man anywhere in the world who outranked him. He quickly demonstrated how well deserved the promotion was.

The first days of the battle were immensely successful for the Germans. Although Eisenhower and Bradley had thought the Germans might launch a significant operation, they had no idea just how capable the Germans still were. Because Hodges's and Patton's forces were aligned to operations of their own, there were no reserves for Eisenhower to deploy. On top of the poor tactical situation on the ground, the weather was terrible and D-Day Inc. had no air support. The one factor, air superiority, that could have been the great equalizer had been eliminated, and for the first time since June 6, the Americans were facing a foe that was more numerous, more mobile, and better equipped than they were. If the Germans could push through the Ardennes to the river Meuse, they could seize the bridges and D-Day Inc.'s massive supply dumps and shift the competition entirely in their favor. A successful German push would be a disaster, and in the first few days of battle, it looked like a real possibility.

Despite all the bad news, the poor weather, the lack of air cover, and the poor positioning of his forces, Eisenhower felt he had been handed a terrific opportunity. "If things go well we should not only stop the thrust but should be able to profit from it."[2] Ike made a series of calm, calculated decisions to capture that profit:

- The commanding general of the Services of Supply and all his quartermasters and engineers would move forward to the river Meuse to establish defensive positions and prepare the demolition of all bridges if a worst-case scenario unfolded, increasing the available troops for Eisenhower and improving defensive options.
- D-Day Inc. would not retreat beyond the Meuse no matter what.
- Reserve forces would not be used on a piecemeal basis as reinforcements for battered units but would be held to be deployed in a focused, powerful counterattack.
- The Eighty-second and 101st Airborne Divisions would be deployed to hold two key towns in the Ardennes. The Eighty-second would protect the small town of Stavelot, which provided access to a large number of fuel and supply dumps, something the Germans had to have if they were going to continue operations in this battle. The 101st would protect Bastogne, an unremarkable little town that happened to be a key crossroads to most of the area. Bastogne was an absolute necessity for victory for either side.
- Monty would break off operations and begin squeezing the northern flank of the German operation. Patton would also break off and squeeze from the south, enabling D-Day Inc. to pinch the Bulge in their lines and turn it into a giant trap.

On December 19, 1944, Eisenhower, Tedder, and other D-Day Inc. executives met with Bradley and Patton. Ike began the conference by saying: "The present situation is to be regarded as one of opportunity for us and not of disaster. There will be only cheerful faces at this conference table."³

Korda wrote: "Patton, who grasped Ike's strategy intuitively, smiled broadly and said, '[L]et's have the guts to let [them] go all the way to Paris, then we'll really cut 'em off and chew 'em up.'"⁴

That was a bit more opportunity than Eisenhower wanted, but all the generals smiled, recognizing the possibilities. As the Germans extended operations deeper into the Ardennes, it was like a boy crawling out on a tree branch to grab an apple at the end of the limb. The farther out the boy climbs, the more the limb bends under his weight. As Rundstedt's forces advanced deeper into the Ardennes, the long, fragile limb of his supply lines became more and more compromised. And as long as the Americans refused to yield Bastogne, the Germans' operational abilities were dangerously limited.

STAY FOCUSED

- **Setbacks are opportunities**. This sounds like the kind of thing Grandma needlepointed on a pillow, but it's true. A setback gives you a chance to look hard and honestly at yourself and to move in ways you might not have been willing to before the setback.

MANAGE YOUR PEOPLE

- **Stay calm**. It allows you to think.
- **Stay optimistic**. It is contagious.

Eisenhower made another key decision at this meeting: he wanted the U.S. First and Ninth Armies to hold in the north, assuming a defensive position and giving up some ground if necessary to shorten their lines. At the same time, Patton's Third Army smashed north at high speed toward the 101st Airborne at Bastogne. Both Patton's drive and the 101st's fight to hold Bastogne became the stuff of legend. Neither would have happened without Ike's calm yet quick decision making.

The Third Army was already attacking eastward when Eisenhower reassigned them to a northern path directly into the heart of the Ardennes. It's very difficult to break off an attack and not be sliced to pieces by your opposition; it's almost impossible to wheel away from your competition and without breaking stride head in another direction completely. Given the bitter winter conditions and the complete absence of air support, the potential for disaster was high.

STAY FOCUSED

- **Know what you need to succeed.** It only took a quick look at the map for both the Americans and the Germans to realize that Bastogne was a must. Most corporate challenges don't "map out" so obviously. But it is crucial to separate what you need from what you want.
- **Get what you need to succeed.** Eisenhower and Bradley committed the necessary resources to maintain their grip on Bastogne. Make sure you have whatever you *must* have to attain your company's goals.

"Patton performed exactly the kind of miracle that Ike knew he was capable of at his best, and switched his troops from their eastward attack to move north in miserable weather over frozen, rutted, backwoods roads that wound through hilly, heavily wooded country to attack the southern flank of the German salient and punch open a corridor to Bastogne."[5] It was the greatest moment of Patton's career, a fitting payback to Eisenhower for retaining

Patton as a D-Day Inc. executive. Ike had suspected that a day would come when he would need a "miracle" and that only Patton could deliver it.

In the long history of the American military, there have been few more heroic moments than the monthlong siege of Bastogne. Because of its crossroads, the town was the key to the Battle of the Bulge. The Americans held Bastogne; the Germans had to have the town. Eisenhower released the 101st Airborne Division from its reserve status, and Bradley immediately sent it to Bastogne to join with elements of the Tenth Armored Division. The Americans arrived in Bastogne before the Germans did and were promptly surrounded. (Traveling around Bastogne instead of through it was difficult and time-consuming—even though by surrounding the town, the Germans now controlled the roads, they absolutely had to control the town too.) The weather prevented almost all supply drops from the air, the temperature hovered around zero, and the ground was blanketed with snow at least ankle-deep. The conditions gave the phrase "a cold day in hell" an entirely new and real meaning.

The Americans were badly outnumbered and heavily under-armored compared to their competition. The one-plus division of Americans faced fifteen German divisions, four of them armored, and heavy artillery. German bombardment was frequent and devastating. Casualties mounted quickly, and the majority had to go untreated because the Germans had captured the medical supplies and doctors. The situation couldn't get any worse.

But the Americans refused to give in.

The difference in urgency between battle and business competition is huge. Fortunately, no one in Corporate America deals with anything so desperately important as the life-and-death struggle of combat. And it's almost impossible to imagine any business operating under conditions as extreme as those faced by the U.S. Army at

Bastogne. But I'm not suggesting that leaders look to this astounding American victory for operational tips or a guide to success. The lesson to be learned from Bastogne is simple: commitment.

Sometimes the only thing that keeps an organization from failing is its people's refusal to fail—their commitment to their mission. If the Americans at Bastogne had been committed to their survival and not the mission, they would have surrendered and marched off to German prisoner-of-war camps. But their commitment was so deep that they refused to fail—to surrender. How do you foster the kind of commitment that refuses to fail? Do what Herb Kelleher did at Southwest or what Eisenhower did at D-Day Inc.—treat your employees as if they are truly the most important part of your business. The day may come when you need your employees to accept a reduction in salary or work uncompensated overtime or tackle a project outside their comfort zones.

Fred Smith didn't create FedEx because he needed the money (he came from a well-to-do family)—he just couldn't let go of an idea he had first written about in a college paper at Yale. He couldn't let go even after he'd lost almost all of his initial investors' money. His commitment to the idea was rock solid and led to the company's guarantee: "If we don't get it there, we don't get paid."

That kind of commitment, whether it's at Bastogne or FedEx, is developed only by treating your employees extremely well. Smith said,

> If you're going to run a high service organization, you have to get the commitment of the people working for that organization right at the start. If you don't, you'll never be able to deliver at the levels of expectations of the customer. You can't make people do what's right. You can lead them, and you can empower them to make the right decision, but if you don't produce a culture that allows them to do that, then all the rest is just bumping your gums as one of my old business partners used to say.[6]

STAY FOCUSED

- **Use what you have**. Ike and the executive team at D-Day Inc. knew what their force was capable of, and they utilized it. Either build the workforce you need or adapt your strategies to fit the force you have.

MANAGE AND MOTIVATE YOUR PEOPLE

- **Empower your people**. This is especially important with your frontline managers and workers. They'll become aware of opportunities you'll never see. This means you have to give them the room to fail and encourage them to keep improvising.

Eisenhower and many of the executives at D-Day Inc. talked the talk and walked the walk on this issue, and while there's no measurable benchmark of morale success equivalent to dollars of profit earned, it's hard to argue with an absolute refusal to surrender in the face of overwhelming odds.

The U.S. Army, not just D-Day Inc., believed in empowering absolutely. Army leaders all understood that their forces needed to be thoroughly trained and grounded in military doctrine. But there was also a consistent emphasis on empowering the frontline forces to exploit opportunities that presented themselves, even if exploiting them meant ignoring doctrine.

The men of the 101st Airborne had no training on working with tanks. But the combat team from the Tenth Armored Division had tanks. If the two couldn't work together effectively, it would exacerbate the Americans' already wretched situation. Colonel William Roberts, the executive in charge of the 10th's combat team, moved among the

Airborne troops, giving them a crash course on the capabilities and limits of tanks and how best to use them. The 101st's officers thought the tanks should be used as static mini-fortresses; Roberts explained that mobility was the key to successful deployment of tanks. Despite no training or experience with this kind of operation, a squad from the 101st worked in tandem with a single tank to take out a German roadblock that threatened to separate the 101st from Bastogne.

Part of this improvisational spirit was an inherently American trait. Way back in August 1776 at the Battle of Brooklyn, George Washington discovered that his American troops could retreat faster than his British adversaries could chase them. The Americans were loosely organized, mostly without formal training or military indoctrination—and that made them flexible and fast, unlike their more restricted competition. Washington recognized what a valuable asset this flexibility was and adapted his strategy to take advantage of it throughout the rest of the Revolutionary War. Any organization reflects the traits of the population(s) it draws its workforce from. As a result, the Americans had the knack for this kind of on-the-fly adjustment, and their German competitors did not. Patton demonstrated the knack on a macro scale by shifting the Third Army from an attack toward the east to the north; on a smaller scale, the men of the 101st and Tenth showed they could work together without any previous training or experience.

The Americans demonstrated a can-do attitude that was reflected in such seemingly minor operations as vehicle repairs. German engineering, even in the 1940s, was a thing of beauty. German combat vehicles, such as tanks, outshone their British and American counterparts in the weight of their armor, speed, and heavier cannons. Their noncombat vehicles were equally sublime by comparison. There was only one little problem with all of them: uptime. The simpler, lighter, longer-ranged American vehicles spent a lot more time in action. And, when the vehicles broke down, many American GIs, with years of experience on family cars, farm tractors, trucks, or hot rods, could pop the hood and fix the vehicles without resorting to trained mechanics at the motor pool. The complexly engineered German vehicles defied the repair talents of the average German soldier.

The Americans were improvisational, flexible, and mobile—and Eisenhower counted on that. The Germans were rigid and hierarchical, a top-down structure of command and control. When Ike needed an entire army disengaged from one battle and sent charging off in a new direction, all he needed to do was tell George Patton, "Go get 'em." Patton had organized and trained his troops to handle something that according to military doctrine was so difficult as to be impossible. Unconstrained by doctrine and enthusiastically supported by the boss, Patton's Third Army succeeded. By contrast, when Erwin Rommel needed the Panzer reserves to stop Overlord, he had to ask for Hitler's permission to use them—and he never received it.

Eisenhower didn't create the American spirit, but he knew it existed and, like most of the American executives at D-Day Inc., he fostered it whenever possible. As mentioned earlier, during the hedgerow fighting in June 1944, tanks couldn't climb the hedgerows for fear of being destroyed with an antitank shell fired directly into their lightly armored bellies. Frontline troops came up with a number of innovations:

- They utilized explosives to blow a hole wide enough to allow a U.S. Sherman tank to go through the hedgerow, using phosphorus shells to burn out enemy machine-gun nests and saturating the hedgerows with .50-caliber shells. The infantry then followed the tank through the hedgerow and secured the area.
- They drilled holes into the hedgerow. It took too much explosive to blow a hole wide enough for a tank if the explosive was laid on the outside bank of the hedgerow. A tanker suggested mounting pipes on the front of tanks and using them to drill holes and plant the explosive in the holes.

- They prepacked explosives into used 105mm shell casings, making it easier to insert the charges into the holes in the hedgerows.
- They welded large pipes and leftover steel from the Germans' beach obstacles to the front of tanks, allowing tanks to plow directly through the hedgerow without wasting time on explosives.[7]

All of these ideas worked, and all were figured out and then implemented by the junior managers and frontline forces. Corporations want to make sure that ideas and information flow up as well as down, and that frontline workforces are empowered to make changes (and sometimes mistakes). Look at how many innovations in hardware and software came from computer companies' front lines.

On December 22, 1944, after the Germans had bombarded and attacked Bastogne for several days, General Fritz Bayerlein, the boss of the Panzer Lehr Division, sent his attaché, Lieutenant Helmuth Henke, with a note to the American in charge, Brigadier General Anthony McAuliffe. Bayerlein's note demanded an "honorable surrender to save the encircled U.S.A. troops from total annihilation."[8] Henke spoke good English and was ordered to go with three other men to the American lines under flags of truce and deliver the surrender ultimatum to the American boss.

The Germans waved white flags and were allowed to approach the American lines, where Henke explained his mission. He was blindfolded and taken to McAuliffe, to whom he handed the note. He waited for McAuliffe to read and reply to the note and then was taken back to the American lines. When the blindfold was finally removed, Henke read McAuliffe's official response.

It said, "Nuts."

Henke understood. Has the idea that "failure is not an option" ever been expressed more eloquently?

"Nuts" has become emblematic of everything the Americans did at

Bastogne. In January 1945, McAuliffe was awarded the Distinguished Service Cross, and the citation highlighted not only his successful leadership but also his men's heroic action:

> The President of the United States takes pleasure in presenting the Distinguished Service Cross to Anthony Clement McAuliffe (0-12263), Brigadier General, U.S. Army, for extraordinary heroism in connection with military operations against an armed enemy while serving as Acting Commander, 101st Airborne Division, in action against enemy forces from 17 to 26 December 1944, at Bastogne, Belgium.
>
> During this period General McAuliffe was in command of the 101st Airborne Division during the siege of Bastogne, Belgium, by overwhelming enemy forces. Though the city was completely surrounded by the enemy, the spirit of the defending troops under this officer's inspiring, gallant leadership never wavered. Their courageous stand is epic.
>
> General McAuliffe continuously exposed himself to enemy bombing, strafing, and armored and infantry attacks to personally direct his troops, utterly disregarding his own safety.
>
> Brigadier General McAuliffe's courage, fearless determination and inspiring, heroic leadership exemplify the highest traditions of the military forces of the United States and reflect great credit upon himself, the 101st Airborne Division, and the United States Army.[9]

Two items jump out from the citation—a leader is only as good as the people who work for him or her, and leaders need to model the kind of behavior they expect. The citation singles out McAuliffe's personal direction of his troops, "utterly disregarding his own safety." If you want your people to demonstrate commitment, you have to model it yourself.

Two days after McAuliffe's "Nuts" reply to the Germans, he received a much more welcome communication. On Christmas Eve at about 10:00 p.m., George Patton sent a message: "Christmas present is on its way. Hold out!"[10] Patton was a day late, but on December 26, the Third Army broke through to Bastogne, a huge relief for the 101st and the Tenth's combat team. But Bastogne continued to be a focus of German energy. Within days, Hitler said, "Bastogne must be taken at all costs." If by some chance the Germans captured it, they could possibly change the course of the battle, and if the battle went their way, it was possible the Germans could continue their push through the Ardennes, across the Meuse River, and into France itself. The war itself would be reshaped. The Germans continued to attack and shell the town, but once the Third Army arrived, any realistic chance for the Germans at Bastogne had vanished.

MANAGE AND MOTIVATE YOUR PEOPLE

- **You commit first**. If you need commitment from your people—especially the extreme commitment of salary cutbacks, furloughs, and benefit cutbacks— you should go first. Take a severe cut in your own salary. Don't give yourself any bonuses until you've already given them to your people.

Very shortly after Hitler's "at all costs" comment, the entire Battle of the Bulge began to shift in favor of the Americans. The fighting remained fierce, but Eisenhower refused to panic. On a personal level, his refusal was demonstrated by the way he dealt with rumors of the assassination plot against him. The Germans had organized groups of English-speaking German soldiers, dressed them in American uniforms, given them captured American jeeps to drive, and sent them out into the American lines. Their mission was to cause confusion by issuing false orders and to capture key bridges and crossroads. They were quite successful.

As D-Day Inc. became aware of this program of sabotage, the

rumor developed that a group of these agents had been ordered to kill Eisenhower. Immediately, armed guards were placed around Ike. He couldn't leave headquarters, virtually a prisoner in his own office. After two days of captivity, Ike emerged from his office and declared, "I'm going out for a walk. If anyone wants to shoot me, he can go right ahead. I've got to get out!"[11] With that, Ike left via the back door and walked around in the deep snow.

Eisenhower's refusal to panic had manifested itself strategically as well. He insisted that the Bulge represented an opportunity for D-Day Inc. and made a large number of moves to take advantage of that opportunity by placing the Eighty-second and 101st Airborne Divisions in key towns, reassigning the U.S. First and Ninth Armies to Monty (he was north of the Bulge in D-Day Inc.'s line and was better positioned to take charge), and sending in reinforcements to key locations throughout the Ardennes. Ike and his air commanders knew that eventually the weather would cooperate, and it had cleared just before Christmas, restoring D-Day Inc.'s control of the skies and making life very difficult for the Germans on the ground. All of these efforts began to produce positive results. The Germans failed to capture any major supply or oil depots, and the long extension of their supply lines over the Ardennes' inadequate roads began to hamper their operations.

As the German push began to slow, Eisenhower set up his counter move. He instructed both Monty (north of the Bulge) and Bradley (south of the Bulge) to hold with minimum forces and gather their reserves to push against the German flanks—in other words, to pinch off the Bulge and trap the German forces inside it.

Unfortunately, as usual with any situation involving Montgomery, there were bruised egos to deal with. Because the German push had all but cut off Hodges's First Army and Simpson's Ninth Army from Bradley's forces south of the Bulge, it made complete sense for Ike to reassign Hodges and Simpson to Monty for the duration of this battle. Neither Hodges nor Simpson liked Monty—why should they be different from everyone else?—but they now had to take orders from him. Bradley resented having two armies taken from his command and assigned to Monty, whom he disliked so intensely he barely spoke to the British officer.

Ike sent a cable to both Hodges and Simpson, "congratulating them for what they had done so far and pointing out that 'your good work is helping create a situation from which we may profit materially.'" He asked them to remain calm, determined, and optimistic. Getting to the point, he added, "'Now that you have been placed under the field marshal's operational command I know that you will respond cheerfully and efficiently to every instruction he gives.'" Ike went much further to assure Bradley that the reassignment of the two armies was not a veiled criticism. Eisenhower cabled George Marshall and requested that Bradley be promoted to general, a four-star rank. In explanation of the request, Ike said that Bradley had "kept his head magnificently" and acted "methodically and energetically."[12]

Eisenhower was realistic enough to know he couldn't keep his entire management team happy all the time, and he wasn't trying to accomplish that. He just wanted his executives to put aside their differences long enough to carry out his directives. For the most part, he was successful in this. The one exception, as always, was Montgomery.

Within days of giving Monty the American First and Ninth Armies, Eisenhower received word from the British officer that he had a new plan for attack, utilizing a very large portion of his forces. Ike's reaction: "Praise God from whom all blessings flow."[13]

Eisenhower was correct about the source of all blessings; he was badly mistaken that Monty's new plan was one of them. Montgomery, in his usual fashion of over-promising and under-delivering, almost immediately began modifying his statement and his assessment of the situation, looking for wiggle room. A day after informing Ike that a new plan was coming, Monty said that he was sure the Germans would make one more major attack. Monty wanted to stop the initiative and then counterattack. But he wanted to go after the tip of the Bulge, pushing the Germans back instead of trapping them by going after their flank as Ike had directed.

COMMUNICATE

- **Learn from your mistakes**. If you try to reason with one of your managers time and time again and it never works, isn't it time to realize you're making a mistake by doing so? Maybe it's time to try something else.
- **You are the boss**. Don't forget that you are the boss, and your employees are not. If requests and suggestions aren't proving to be effective communications with your people, issue orders. If things go badly, and they sometimes do, do you want to be responsible for results produced by someone who didn't follow your strategy?

Eisenhower told Monty that Rundstedt would either begin pulling all of his forces out of the Bulge or use his infantry to hold the line while he withdrew the more powerful and valuable armor, which he could then deploy as reserves. Ike urged Monty to attack quickly and attack at the flank—the opportunity of capturing immense resources and crippling the competition wouldn't last forever. Monty repeated that he needed to deal with the German attack first and then—and only then—launch his own. "Eisenhower grumbled that there would be no attack."[14] The discussion continued and finally ended when Monty agreed that if there was no German initiative in the next two days, he would launch his own against the flank on January 1, 1945.

On the second day of the promised two-day waiting period, Monty sent his chief of staff, Francis "Freddie" de Guingand, to inform the D-Day Inc. executives that Montgomery would not be moving until at least January 3, 1945. De Guingand, representing Monty's views, said that Eisenhower had misunderstood; there had been no agreement on a January 1 attack. Ike snapped back, "There was!"[15] Eisenhower was frustrated and believed Monty had lied to him. Worse, he worried that a terrific opportunity was about to be squandered, that Monty would move too slowly to pinch the Bulge and trap the retreating Germans. Ike finally wrote the kind of blistering letter he should have sent to Monty months earlier, demanding that Monty live up to his promises for action against the Germans or be fired. Incredibly, de Guingand talked him out of sending the note. Everyone at D-Day Inc. liked de Guingand—unlike his boss, he was affable and reasonable. But after the many misrepresentations and arguments by Monty, the behind-the-back politicking, the slow progress in battle time, and again, for Ike to pocket the letter to Montgomery when D-Day Inc. was at the brink of a fantastic success or gigantic failure was staggering. Enough should have been enough.

But it wasn't. Eisenhower allowed de Guingand to confer with Monty and explain how urgently Ike wanted immediate action against the German flank. On New Year's Eve, de Guingand met with Monty and then returned to D Day Inc. headquarters to confer again with Ike. De Guingand informed Eisenhower that Monty was holding to his belief that the Germans were about to move, and he planned to let them come and then counterattack. De Guingand repeated that Ike had misunderstood about the launching of an initiative against the German flank on January 1.

Omar Bradley, in the mistaken belief that Monty would launch operations on January 1, was already attacking in the south, moving to pinch off his side of the Bulge. But without any pressure from Monty, the Germans could move their armor to the south to hold off Bradley while they began retreating from the Bulge. The fantastic opportunity to finish off the competition was about to slip away.

As bad as Monty's handling of his part of the battle was, he did something worse. In the middle of this debate about what he was going to do and when, Monty sent a letter to Eisenhower "damning the Supreme Commander's policies and demanding that he,

Montgomery, be given full control of the land battle. And, of course, there must be a single thrust, in the north, with Patton held where he was."[16] Not even a month had passed since the showdown where Ike had threatened to take their disputes to the board of directors and Monty had apologized. And here was Monty, not only refusing to do what his boss wanted, but saying once again that he, Monty, should be the boss of the land campaign. To top off this astounding display of arrogance, Monty had the temerity to write out a directive for Ike's signature, making all of Monty's ideas come to pass.

Eisenhower was not amused. He issued his own directive that negated every single point of Monty's, restoring control of the U.S. First Army to Bradley and insisting on the broad, double thrust into Germany. "The one thing that must now be prevented is the stabilization of the enemy salient. . . . We must regain the initiative, and speed and energy are essential."[17] In a cover note with the directive, Ike wrote to Monty that he did not agree with Monty regarding Monty's running the land campaign with Bradley reporting to him. He informed his British subordinate that he had planned an advance on a broad front and ordered Monty to read the directive carefully.

Eisenhower went on to say that if they continued to disagree so strongly, he would feel compelled to bring the matter to the board, leaving Monty to conclude what would happen to him should the board be forced to choose between the Brit and the American. Ike wrote, "The confusion and debate that would follow would certainly damage the good will and devotion to a common cause that have made this Allied Force unique in history."

In effect, Eisenhower was saying, "I can play along for the sake of the alliance. Can you?"

At the same time, de Guingand worked on Monty, trying to help his boss by getting Monty to cooperate with *his* boss. De Guingand was blunt, telling Montgomery that the general feeling at D-Day Inc. was bitter—that Monty should be fired. Monty wasn't buying that; he was sure that he was irreplaceable, even asking who could take his spot. De Guingand said that a replacement was already in mind: Harold Alexander, who'd been Eisenhower's deputy for Torch and Husky, and had proven to be an aggressive leader in the Italian campaign. "The notion of replacing Monty with Field Marshal Alexander seems to have occurred to Ike—an astute one, since however big a hero was to the British public, nobody, including the prime minister, could complain about replacing him with a figure so universally admired as Alexander."[18]

"Montgomery paled. . . . He began pacing his trailer, finally turning to de Guingand to ask, 'What shall I do, Freddie? What shall I do?'"[19] De Guingand, like an executive assistant magically pulling a contract out of thin air for the boss to sign, handed Monty a message to Eisenhower. He told Montgomery to sign the message, and for once Monty did exactly as he had been told. The message acknowledged that Ike had to balance many factors that were unknown to Monty and asked Ike to tear up the letter that had demanded control of the ground campaign.

On January 3, Monty finally went into action. His attack was not all Eisenhower had wanted, but it was much better than what Monty had initially proposed. The Bulge would not be completely eliminated for almost a month, but when the battle was over, the Germans had lost almost half of the men, tanks, and artillery that had begun the attack. The losses were devastating, especially the tanks, since now the Germans had no armored mobility to counter D-Day Inc.'s tank forces and Ike's highly mobile, fluid strategy. The losses at the Bulge hurt on another front—those forces were no longer available to stop the Soviet forces in the east. The Red Army was closer to Berlin than D-Day Inc., and now the Germans had very little in the way of reserve to deal with that approaching calamity.

As great as the success was, Eisenhower's fears of squandering a great opportunity were partially realized. Bradley's forces had performed very well, but Monty's slow start allowed many Germans to escape the Bulge. As large as the final tally was—about 120,000

German casualties—it could have been larger, meaning fewer competitive forces to deal with later.

While the Battle of the Bulge was finally over, the recriminations were only beginning. Montgomery got the post-battle bitterness off to a resounding start with a press conference. Churchill had approved the idea of a press conference, and the prime minister reviewed and approved Monty's speech. But Churchill "could hardly control Monty's delivery, which Monty's own intelligence chief described as 'disastrous.' 'Oh God, why didn't you stop him?' asked one distinguished British war correspondent who was an appalled witness to the press conference."[20]

Monty seems to have pushed every possible button. He wore a red Airborne beret, which was, to say the least, insensitive—the Airborne loathed him after what had happened at Market-Garden. His tone toward Eisenhower and the Americans was patronizing, and he falsely described British forces as "fighting on both sides of American forces who have suffered a hard blow." The British did not fight on both sides of the Americans, and the implication that they had saved the day was especially painful to the American leaders and their men. Almost no British soldiers had been involved in the Bulge; British casualties for the entire battle were fewer than fifteen hundred—American casualties were greater than seventy-five thousand, more than fifty times as many casualties as the British. To top off his performance, Monty said it was an interesting battle and compared it to his legendary success at El Alamein. He said of the Bulge: "I think possibly one of the most interesting and tricky battles I have ever handled." And then the ultimate comment—Monty said the "GIs made great fighting men, when given proper leadership."[21]

Stephen Ambrose wrote that nearly every American officer in Europe was furious: "As they saw the battle, they had stopped the Germans before Montgomery came onto the scene. . . . Far from directing victory, Montgomery had gotten in everyone's way and botched the counterattack."[22]

Almost twenty years later, Eisenhower, who tended to be an ally and a gentleman even in his memoirs and postwar interviews, said, "This incident caused me more distress and worry than did any similar one of the war."[23]

The Battle of the Bulge was a huge success for D-Day Inc., but success with a very bitter aftertaste. Both the success and bitter aftertaste were due to Eisenhower. First, the negatives: He allowed Monty to argue, debate, and stall in following his strategy. Monty is certainly to blame for his pathetic performance, but Eisenhower has to take the blame for letting Montgomery get away with it.

But the drama of the Ike vs. Monty conflict shouldn't overshadow the astounding success of the Battle of the Bulge.

Eisenhower stayed calm in the middle of a turbulent competitive situation and exploited his opponent's weaknesses. He was so effective at this exploitation that the only drawbacks were the ones inherent in his own management team. The moral of the Ike vs. Monty story: get your managers to do what you want, or get rid of them.

In late January 1945, the Battle of the Bulge had turned decidedly Eisenhower's way, and he had been promoted to five-star rank* and was now entitled to an extra $255 a month—adjusted for inflation, worth a bit more than $3,000 in 2009. Only three other soldiers had been named to this high rank, newly created at the time to honor the senior military commanders of World War II:

- General of the Army George C. Marshall, CEO of the U.S. Army, member of the D-Day Inc. board of directors
- General of the Army Henry H. "Hap" Arnold, CEO of the U.S. Army Air Force, member of the D-Day Inc. board of directors

---

* Omar Bradley would be named General of the Army in 1950. The other non-Army five-star officers from the war were: William Daniel Leahy, chief of staff to the commander in chief, U.S. Army and Navy, the President of the United States during WWII; Ernest Joseph King, CEO of the U.S. Navy and a member of D-Day Inc.'s board of directors; Chester William Nimitz, CEO of the U.S. Navy's Pacific Fleet; and William Frederick "Bull" Halsey Jr., CEO of the South Pacific area.

- General of the Army Douglas MacArthur, CEO of the
  Southwest Pacific Theater, former CEO of the U.S. Army

The promotion could have led Ike to indulge in a bit of satisfaction on a personal level. His career in the army had begun more than thirty years previously at West Point, and now he was one of the four highest-ranking officers in the entire outfit, with the greatest assignment of any of them. But when Ike mentioned the promotion to his wife, Mamie, in a letter, he thought it was amusing that, while he had the new rank and pay, there was no finalized design for the insignia yet. (Five stars in a circle became the insignia.)

Ike's perks as the top executive included an extra $36,000 a year (adjusted for inflation) and his own plane, an unpressurized bomber— hardly the equivalent of a modern luxury jet. When Eisenhower visited his frontline people, he often drove himself. Recall that at Portsmouth, prior to Overlord, Ike turned down the comfort of a large English manor and decided to live in a trailer. And in an almost three-year span, he took one vacation, under orders, of about two weeks. Yet he insisted that his managers take leave to stay rested and refreshed.

Why did Eisenhower care so little for the comforts and luxuries to which he was entitled?

Because none of them helped him in his mission. That's an extreme course, but then D-Day Inc. was operating in the most extreme competition possible. The point is that Ike stayed focused on what he needed for success in the mission, even in his personal life. He wrote to his wife: "I cannot remember the time when I was free of these continuing problems involving staggering expense, destruction of lives and wealth, and fates of whole peoples."[24]

As successful as D-Day Inc. had been at the Battle of the Bulge, there was still a long way to go to complete the mission. At about the same time Ike wrote the above lines to his wife, he was formulating the final strategy to accomplish that very thing.

DEBRIEFING NOTES

STRATEGIES: DETERMINE YOUR MISSION; STAY FOCUSED; MOTIVATE AND MANAGE YOUR PEOPLE

- **Setbacks Are Opportunities**: Look hard and honestly at yourself, and take new actions. What have you got to lose?
- **Stay Calm**: It allows you to think.
- **Stay Optimistic**: It's contagious.
- **Know What You Need to Succeed**: It's crucial to separate what you need from what you want.
- **Get What You Need to Succeed**: Make sure you have whatever you *must* have to attain your company's goals.
- **Use What You Have**: Either build the workforce you need or adapt your strategies to fit the force you have.
- **Empower Your People**: Give them the room to fail, and encourage them to keep improvising.
- **You Commit First**: If you need commitment from your people—you should go first.

STRATEGIES: DETERMINE YOUR MISSION; STAY FOCUSED; COMMUNICATE

- **Learn from Your Mistakes**: If you try something again and again, isn't it time to realize you're making a mistake by doing so? Isn't it time to try something else?
- **You Are the Boss**: Don't forget that you're the boss, and your employees are not. If necessary, issue orders. Do you want to be responsible for results produced by someone who didn't follow your strategy?

NINE

COMPLETING THE MISSION

Maintaining Your Efforts to the Very End

"All during the Battle of the Bulge we continued to plan for the final offensive blows which, once started, we intended to maintain incessantly until final defeat of Germany," Eisenhower wrote.[1]

As intensely focused on winning the Bulge as Ike was, he never lost sight of the fact that D-Day Inc. still had to cross the Rhine and destroy Germany's ability to compete. Eisenhower was applying Strategy No. 3, "Stay Focused—Know and get what you need." He was all too aware that no matter how large a victory he won at the Bulge, D-Day Inc. had a lot of ground to cover in both the literal and metaphorical senses. He needed plans to implement his broad-front strategy for D-Day Inc. to proceed into Germany, and he needed coordination with the Soviet Union.

Until the Bulge, D-Day Inc. and the huge Red Army (almost a third again as big as all of D-Day Inc.'s forces in Europe) were separated by hundreds of miles of German and Polish territory. But within months, they would be closing that gap to the distance of a handshake. The meeting of the Soviet forces and D-Day Inc. was probably the largest "joint venture" in history, and the consequences if the meeting was pulled off incorrectly were horrific. When two gigantic forces are moving very fast to squeeze a third in between them, a solid understanding of both forces' operations and excellent communications between them are required. Eisenhower wanted to build that understanding and establish communications sooner rather than later.

In early January, as the Battle of the Bulge was still very much undecided, Ike sent his deputy, Sir Arthur Tedder, to Moscow to make the necessary arrangements. (Until Tedder set up direct communication, coordination would continue to be handled as it always had: by communication between the military members of D-Day Inc.'s board and the Soviet military establishment in Moscow.)

As Tedder was handling the coordination with the Soviets, Eisenhower and his executive team were laying out the plans to follow Ike's broad-front strategy:

- D-Day Inc.'s forces would go north and south of the Ruhr River.
- Monty would be in charge of the main thrust to the Rhine in the north. Bradley's generals, Hodges and Patton, would be in charge of secondary thrusts in the south.
- The two forces would encircle the Ruhr, choking off Germany's industrial core and badly damaging its ability to compete.
- From the Ruhr, D-Day Inc.'s forces would fan out all over Germany.

There were two keys to making this strategy successful: First, Eisenhower would use his reserves to exploit *any* opportunities that developed, whether in the north with Monty or the south with Bradley. And second, once D-Day Inc. was across the Rhine, Bradley would be the main man.

As General J. F. M. Whiteley (deputy chief of staff under Beetle Smith) put it, "the feeling was that if anything was to be done quickly, don't give it to Monty."[2] It seemed that Eisenhower had finally learned from bitter experience. It was the source of more trouble on Ike's executive team. George Marshall agreed with Eisenhower's strategy in giving the lead role to Bradley. But Monty thought his thrust wasn't getting the necessary priorities, of course. Bradley thought that—given recent history—Monty was receiving too high a priority. And Patton wanted and felt he had earned a larger role in the entire process.

With the final goal in sight, Ike was, at long last, done with debating and negotiating with his own executive team. Brooke wanted more forces committed to Monty, in effect creating a single-thrust strategy. And as if the issue hadn't been settled repeatedly, the idea of Eisenhower relinquishing direct control of the ground campaign was raised again. Ike wasn't interested in the slightest. He wrote, "I was determined to prevent any interference with the exact and rapid execution of those plans."[3] He remained committed to his strategy and ensured that it was followed. Beetle Smith said at an April 1945 press conference, a short time before the Germans finally surrendered: "Of all the campaigns I have known this one has followed most exactly the pattern of the commander who planned it. With but one small exception, it proceeded exactly as General Eisenhower worked it out."[4]

Simpson's Ninth Army crossed the Roer on February 23, 1945, about two weeks after the final traces of the Bulge had been eliminated from the American lines. By March 2, the Ninth Army had reached the Rhine and was preparing to cross. Eisenhower had believed that the Germans would mount the stiffest resistance possible on D-Day Inc.'s side of the Rhine, giving Ike's forces a chance to damage the competition severely. He was correct; the Ninth Army alone inflicted more than 36,000 casualties on its way to the Rhine. In total, approximately 250,000 Germans were captured, and at least as many were killed or wounded.

The success on the western side of the Rhine meant that Eisenhower's forces would face a much easier time once they crossed into Germany itself. Also deserving credit: the Allied air forces had bombed the Germans' fuel supply almost out of existence, immobilizing the defenders. North of Simpson, Monty's forces also reached the Rhine and got ready to move across. Hodges's First Army arrived at the Rhine on March 5; Patton's Third Army on March 8. Less than three months after the opening, disastrous phase of the Battle of the Bulge, D-Day Inc. was about to go head-to-head in German territory with a competitor that was literally on its last legs.

On March 7, Hodges's First Army captured a railroad bridge across the Rhine at Remagen. The terrain on the far side of the bridge was terrible for D-Day Inc.'s operations, and Remagen was not on the list of objectives for crossing the Rhine. Bradley wanted to push everything available over the bridge as soon as possible. He called Ike and asked if he should go ahead, even though Remagen wasn't part of the plan. Eisenhower replied, "Sure, go on, Brad, and I'll give you everything we got to hold that bridgehead. We'll make good use of it even if the terrain isn't too good."[5]

DETERMINE (AND REMEMBER) YOUR MISSION

- **If you're handed an opportunity, take it**. Be adaptable in your thinking, and always build some flexibility into your plans—you never know when something like the Remagen bridge will come into your hands, something that looked all wrong but turns out to be incredibly useful.

Remagen was exactly the kind of opportunity that Ike had been waiting for—he had the reserves ready to shift toward the city to exploit the situation to D-Day Inc.'s benefit, and he had the right executive in charge—Bradley. Eisenhower and Bradley knew there were risks—after all, Remagen had been left off the list of objectives for good reasons—but they believed in seizing an opportunity with all the speed and strength they could.

The Germans certainly understood how important the bridge

was—they did everything imaginable to destroy it, bombing it from the air and with heavy artillery fire, firing V-2 rockets at it, floating mines down the river toward it, even sending in frogmen to plant explosives. But by the time they finally succeeded and the bridge collapsed, D-Day Inc. had six pontoon bridges going across the Rhine at Remagen and a bridgehead that was twenty miles long and eight miles deep. "It constituted a threat to the entire German defense of the Rhine."[6]

While Hodges's First Army used its opening at Remagen to get across the Rhine, Patton's Third Army was tearing through the Saar-Palatinate, three thousand square miles of mountains, deep valleys, fortified positions, and the German First and Seventh Armies, who had been instructed that the area must be held. Attacking through the Saar-Palatinate should have been a nightmare; Patton went through the area in ten days. Bradley said that Patton had an "uncanny feel for the front." He proved Bradley absolutely and without equivocation right when "in the middle of the night, when no one was looking, where it was least expected, totally without the elaborate preparations Montgomery was making in the north, and two days ahead of him— Third Army crossed the Rhine."[7]

Late in March, Brooke met with Eisenhower on the banks of the Rhine to watch Monty's crossing of the river. By this time, the German armies on the western side (D-Day Inc.'s side) of the Rhine had been destroyed. Brooke had been the most significant internal foe of Ike's strategy. And now, as they watched their forces going into Germany, Eisenhower recalled that Brooke said, "Thank God, Ike, you stuck by your plan. You were completely right and I am sorry. . . . The German is now licked. It is merely a question of when he chooses to quit. Thank God you stuck by your guns."[8]

Brooke later claimed that Ike misquoted him. Even if Eisenhower quoted incorrectly, however, the thought was "spot on" as the British say—Ike had been completely right. After years of being swayed by internal opposition, Eisenhower had utilized the power of being

CEO and driven the organization in the direction he was convinced was correct. As a result, his forces were across the Rhine almost two months ahead of schedule. (Army engineers had predicted that spring flooding would be too intense to allow crossing before May. Ike had kept this informational tidbit to himself—he didn't want any of his managers using the prediction as an alibi for failing to perform.)

Once over the Rhine, Patton's Third Army was advancing more than thirty miles a day, and Hodges' First Army, operating on Patton's immediate left to the north, was moving almost as fast. They swept east and then north in a giant left hook to meet Simpson's Ninth Army on April 1. Only three days later, the Ruhr was surrounded, trapping more than 325,000 Germans and eliminating Germany's heavy industry from the competitive situation. With its manpower heavily depleted, its industry offline, its internal fuel and supply lines all but wiped out, and its current position right between D-Day Inc. and the Red Army, Germany was finished. In a month, there was nothing left but paperwork to shut down all German operations.

Early April was also significant for another reason: D-Day Inc. reached Ohrdruf-Nord, a subcamp of Buchenwald, the first concentration camp to be entered by Americans. Guards had slaughtered more than four thousand prisoners as the Germans retreated, and their bodies lay scattered throughout the camp. The guards had fled. Surviving prisoners were emaciated skeletons. Ike was shown the ditches filled with half-naked, rotting bodies. He turned pale as he visited Ohrdruf-Nord; Patton vomited.

Sixty-five years later, there are still idiots who deny the Holocaust happened. If some modern minds can only deal with the savagery of the Nazis by denying it ever occurred, imagine how devastating it was for the Americans confronting it on the spot. Eisenhower, able to look to the future even as he confronted a crisis in the moment, arranged for the press to enter the camps immediately. He also arranged for British ministers of parliament and American congressmen to see the camps. Ike wanted evidence of the atrocities "placed before the

British and American publics in a fashion that would leave no room for cynical doubt."[9]

Eisenhower wrote to George Marshall: "The visual evidence and the verbal testimony of starvation, cruelty, and bestiality were so overpowering as to leave me a bit sick. . . . I made the visit deliberately in order to be in a position to give *first-hand* evidence of these things if ever, in the future, there develops a tendency to charge these allegations merely to 'propaganda.'"[10]

★ ★ ★

On April 13, the daily, joint Army-Navy casualty list was headed by: ROOSEVELT, Franklin D., Commander in Chief.[11] Roosevelt, thirty-second president of the United States, had died the day before, on April 12, 1945. As commander in chief, he was Eisenhower's ultimate boss in the military. And he had functioned as D-Day Inc.'s chairman of the board. Thanks to the U.S. Constitution, succession planning for the United States of America is rock solid. Harry S. Truman became the thirty-third president. Although the Americans who formed the majority of D-Day Inc. were shocked and saddened, they continued to be fully committed to finishing their mission. FDR's death didn't slow down D-Day Inc.'s progress by a minute.

There was, however, one last political battle to be waged within D-Day Inc. Churchill had said, "There is only one thing worse than fighting with allies, and that is fighting without them." In this context, "with" means "alongside." In the history of D-Day Inc., however, "fighting with allies" frequently meant fighting "against" your own allies. Eisenhower had written to a colleague in the War Department in January 1943: "One of the constant sources of danger to us in this war is the temptation to regard as our first enemy the partner that must work with us in defeating the real enemy."[12] Despite Ike's recognition of the problem and his tireless work to solve it, there was a final intramural battle to be waged, and it was a doozy.

In a word: *Berlin*.

Eisenhower, like everybody else at D-Day Inc. from the board
to soldiers in the field, thought the final geographic objective was
Berlin. He had said to Montgomery several times, "Clearly Berlin
is the main prize."[13] As the realities on the ground changed, so did
Eisenhower's feeling about Berlin. By March 1945, this was the situation as he saw it:

- Capturing Berlin would not help him succeed at his
  mission. Destroying the Germans' military capability
  would—that meant eliminating their armies.
- At the Yalta Conference in February, FDR, Churchill,
  and Stalin—all on Ike's board—had agreed to occupation
  zones for Germany to be held by the United States,
  United Kingdom, and Soviet Union. Berlin was well
  inside the Soviet zone.
- The Soviets were about thirty-five miles east of Berlin.
  D-Day Inc. was about two hundred miles away in the west.
- The Soviets had 1,250,000 men and 22,000 heavy artillery
  pieces prepared for the final push to Berlin. D-Day Inc.
  couldn't devote those kinds of resources to Berlin and still
  accomplish the other items on its agenda.

Despite the strategic realities and the fact that the Soviets were
poised to take the city, the British desperately wanted to capture
Berlin, and so did most of the Americans who worked for Eisenhower.
Churchill understood the tangle of European politics better than any
man alive—he realized that as Germany waned, the Soviet Union was
already becoming the geopolitical competitor to the United States
and United Kingdom. The farther east D-Day Inc. could go, the
easier life would be in a postwar world.

Churchill also wanted Berlin for national pride. England had suffered long and hard at the Germans' hands. His country had stood

alone against the Nazis for two years, bloodied but refusing to give up. England deserved its victory in Berlin.

Monty, of course, had visions of riding in triumph into Berlin. It was only fitting that the man who first beat the Germans at El Alamein would be the man who rode into Berlin for their final defeat. American generals Patton, Hodges, and Simpson all thought that an American should lead the way into Berlin—according to their view, if not for American involvement, Monty would have lost the bloody war.

But Eisenhower just couldn't see the point of taking Berlin. He asked Bradley for an estimate of the "cost" of capturing the city. Bradley said 100,000 casualties. (He was wrong by a wide margin—the Soviets ended up absorbing more than 300,000 casualties.) Then Bradley added, "A pretty stiff price to pay for a prestige objective, especially when we've got to fall back and let the other fellow take over."[14] Bradley assumed that even if the Allies took Berlin, they would have to hand the city over to the Soviets since it fell within their zone. Ike agreed with him about everything: the price was too high, and the objective was prestigious, not strategic. Eisenhower didn't care about prestige. He wanted to beat the Germans at the lowest cost in lives possible.

When Ike looked at the map, the strategic objective was obvious: Dresden, not Berlin. Bradley's Twelfth Army Group was perfectly positioned to drive to that city, and it provided a logical link-up location with the Red Army. He acted decisively, wiring a message on March 28 to Stalin saying D-Day Inc. was directing its operations toward Dresden. Stalin quickly agreed that Dresden was the best rendezvous for the two forces. Monty, Brooke, and Churchill flew into a frenzy, attempting to have the decision overturned. George Marshall backed Eisenhower and was shocked at the British for not doing the same. After all the success Ike had directed the Allies to, Marshall was upset with the British attitude and informed them so. Churchill wrote a letter directly to Eisenhower, trying to rearrange the disposition of forces, but Ike refused to budge, and the British realized it was pointless to keep pushing. As a result, not a single item changed in Eisenhower's plans. D-Day Inc. would forgo the prestige of Berlin and instead pursue the elimination of the German forces.

AVOID PROJECT CREEP

- **Don't go astray.** You're not in business to collect trophies like Berlin. You're trying to beat the competition. This is the only time we've discussed this strategy, but it couldn't be more important. It applied to Operation Market-Garden as well as the taking of Berlin. Given the number of casualties in Market-Garden, and the huge number of lives saved by avoiding Berlin, you can see how important this is.

- **One project at a time.** Don't let "easy" success lull you into "while we're at it, let's tackle this objective too." One project at a time. Especially big, organization-wide projects.

Ike's past willingness to discuss strategy may well have caused delay and added deaths in the past. Now his decisiveness saved the Allies at least 300,000 casualties. Joe Stalin paid the price for Berlin. Stephen Ambrose wrote:

[Eisenhower] refused to race the Russians to Berlin. He was much criticized for this. It remains his most controversial decision of the war. . . . I have nothing to add to the debate, except this: in thirty years of interviewing GIs, reading their books and unpublished memoirs, corresponding with them, I have not yet heard one of them say that he wanted to charge into Berlin. For the GIs, what stood out about Eisenhower's decision was that he put them first.[15]

PRESTIGE OR PROFIT?

BANK OF AMERICA AND MERRILL LYNCH

On September 14, 2008, as the financial crisis was about to explode across markets and the collective consciousness of America, Bank of America announced it was purchasing Merrill Lynch for a bit more than $50 billion in stock. The combination of the largest consumer bank in the United States, Bank of America, with Merrill Lynch's wealth management business and $1.4 trillion in managed assets seemed perfect. Certainly preferable to Merrill Lynch going under, the way Bear Stearns and Lehman Brothers had a short time before the announcement.

Under CEO and chairman Kenneth Lewis, Bank of America had made a habit of making large, and somewhat daring acquisitions, such as mortgage lender Countrywide, the credit card lender MBNA, and FleetBoston Financial. But acquiring Merrill Lynch was the pinnacle.

In short order, however, Merrill Lynch lost $15.3 billion for the fourth quarter, and bonuses of $3.6 billion were paid out to Merrill employees. (When the Bank of America shareholders voted to approve the deal, they were unaware of the impending red ink.) The losses were so large that Bank of America found itself going back to the government for an additional $20 billion in bailout money.

According to a story in *Forbes*, although Lewis "was initially eager to snap up Merrill, he was given little choice by federal regulators when they urged him to move forward with the deal even when Merrill's losses turned out to be larger than first thought."[16] Even if Lewis felt he had little choice, does that excuse him? He wasn't responsible to the regulators; he was responsible to his shareholders. Eisenhower faced pressure from much of his board and several of his most important executives to take Berlin but realized that his ultimate responsibility to his shareholders (the American and British publics) required him to avoid incurring the immense losses necessary to capture Berlin.

By spring of 2009, Bank of America shareholders were so angry that they stripped Lewis of his chairmanship. In a surprise announcement at the beginning of October, approximately a year after Bank of America acquired Merrill, Lewis announced he was leaving as CEO.

MOTOROLA AND IRIDIUM

In November 1998, satellite-telephone provider Iridium opened its doors for business, backed by $6 billion from Motorola. Satellite phones are the ultimate, talk-to-anyone-from-anywhere device—the kind of phone that any rich, self-respecting playboy (or playboy wannabe) would need to stay in touch with his paramours around the world.

Nine months after launching, Iridium filed for Chapter 11 bankruptcy. According to *Forbes*, "Iridium's downfall: the rise of mobile phones and cellular networks. Absentee customer-service reps and annoying flaws in the company's Web site that made it difficult to apply for service didn't help, either."[17]

Before you put $6 billion into a company, wouldn't you make sure that its customer service experience was a good one? And while you're at it, a little crystal-ball gazing might have been in order—Motorola profited hugely from the very mobile phone market that helped knock off Iridium. The luster of having an out-of-this-world product was all shine and no substance, just as seizing Berlin only to turn it over to the Soviet Union would have been.

SUN MICROSYSTEMS AND STORAGETEK

Sun Microsystems, like Bank of America, had a history of making acquisitions, including splurging on a $4 billion deal to acquire tape storage company StorageTek in 2005. There was only one problem: "StorageTek's tape drives were aimed primarily at mainframes, a business that never connected with Sun's server or software sales."[18]

StorageTek is only one of a series of mistakes Sun made over the years, but it demonstrates the company's basic problem: no focus on what is necessary. It has fallen prey to dazzling ideas and acquisitions without defining what it needed for its success. Ike knew that Berlin was not necessary for

D-Day Inc. to succeed—beating the competition was. Sun seems to be without a clue.

   Forbes summed it up:

Like any star past its prime, Sun Microsystems is left with two choices: It can burn out, or it can fade away. If the struggling server vendor had signed away its independence to IBM in exchange for the tech giant's offer of $7 billion, the deal would have been a sad end for a Silicon Valley icon once worth more than $200 billion. . . . A better buyout offer isn't likely, given that Sun has been prostrating itself before potential acquirers that declined to bid on its thorny mix of servers, software and storage. . . . Potential saviors will be only more wary of making an offer. None is likely to spend more than IBM's fire-sale offer of $9.40 per share.[19]

The push toward Dresden—as well as southern Germany, Austria, and Czechoslovakia—was on, and in the last days of April, the Germans fell completely apart. "Their soldiers on the eastern front, rightfully fearing above all else capture by the Red Army, fought desperately. On the western front, they surrendered at the first sight of [Allied units]. German civilians tried to flee to the west so that they could be inside the Anglo-American lines when the end came."[20]

On April 30, the madman who started the war, Adolf Hitler, committed suicide, an appropriately pathetic ending. Hitler's successor, Admiral Karl Doenitz, attempted to negotiate a surrender to D-Day Inc., and only to D-Day Inc. Doenitz felt that his country would do much better at the hands of the Americans and British. President Truman, in an echo of FDR's policy, stated that only unconditional surrender of all German forces to the United States, the United Kingdom, France, *and* the Soviet Union was acceptable. Doenitz kept sending different emissaries to plead for a surrender to Ike's forces.

Eisenhower refused to meet face-to-face with any of the German emissaries until a surrender document was signed, a surrender to all of the Allies. His chief negotiator was Beetle Smith, whose abrupt, forceful personality came in handy. Smith insisted to each German negotiator that it was unconditional surrender to the Americans, British, French, and Soviets—or nothing. Eventually, the primary German negotiator accepted reality. He recommended to Doenitz that Germany surrender completely to all parties. Doenitz agreed.

At two o'clock in the morning of May 7, Smith and a delegation of British and French officers, along with a Soviet observer, accepted the signed surrender documents from the Germans. Ike waited in his office, pacing and smoking. At 2:41, Smith came into Eisenhower's office and announced that the war in Europe was over.

A team player to the end, Ike gathered the D-Day Inc. executives around for some photographs and then made a short newsreel and radio recording for the press. After the recordings were done, Smith suggested that a communiqué be written to inform the board of directors. The different executives all made an attempt to write the message. Smith said, "I tried one myself, and like all my associates, groped for resounding phrases as fitting accolade to the Great Crusade and indicative of our dedication to the great task just completed." Eisenhower listened to all the "resounding phrases," thanked everyone, and then dictated the message himself: "The mission of this Allied force was fulfilled at 0241 local time, May 7, 1945."[21]

A month later, Eisenhower was presented the Freedom of the City of London—an honor dating back to 1237. Ike gave a speech in Guildhall of London, with every major political and military personality in Great Britain in attendance. The appearance at the Guildhall was triumphal. In this moment of ultimate victory and praise, Ike said, "Humility must always be the portion of any man who receives acclaim earned in the blood of his followers and the sacrifices of his friends."[22]

DEBRIEFING NOTES

STRATEGIES: DETERMINE YOUR MISSION; STAY FOCUSED

- **If You're Handed an Opportunity, Take It**: Be adaptable in your thinking, build flexibility into your plans—you never know when something useful will come into your hands.

STRATEGY: AVOID PROJECT CREEP

- **Don't Go Astray**: You are not in business to achieve glamorous objectives. You are trying to beat the competition. If a project isn't going to do that, forget it.
- **One Project at a Time**: Don't let "easy" success lull you into "while we're at it, let's tackle this objective too." One project at a time. Especially big, organization-wide projects.

TEN

PERFORMANCE EVALUATION AND SUMMARY

Implementing Ike's Strategies

The short version of Eisenhower's performance evaluation: he succeeded at his job.

Eric Larrabee wrote that President Roosevelt's confidence in Ike "was justified many times over. To suggestions that the war in Europe should have been ended sooner, the proper answer is: *It was.* It had all been done in less than a year. It had been won by the time its planners had expected merely to have reached the German border, and none of the proposals for a quicker or easier victory are convincing."[1]

Ike succeeded at his job in magnificent fashion. He created the largest Allied military organization ever. He led the way as D-Day Inc. pulled off the three largest amphibious invasions ever: Torch (North Africa), Husky (Sicily), and Overlord (Normandy). No one before—or since—has ever tackled a project as complex, as large, or as daunting in its ramifications as Overlord.

Eisenhower failed to rein in Montgomery, and that led to the disaster of Operation Market-Garden.

But he succeeded by:

- committing utterly and completely to an Allied team,
- insisting on optimism and confidence at D-Day Inc.,
- demanding the Transportation Plan before Overlord,
- deploying the U.S. Airborne Divisions inland of Utah Beach,
- selecting Bradley over Patton as the U.S. ground commander,
- seeing the Battle of the Bulge as an opportunity,
- acting aggressively to seize that opportunity, and
- sticking to his broad-front, highly mobile strategy.

Nobody gets it all right, but Ike got it right when it counted. Stephen Ambrose summed up Eisenhower this way: "He was the most successful general of the greatest war ever fought."[2]

The Negative Side of the Ledger

Eisenhower was often a poor communicator, leaving people with conflicting interpretations of what he meant or expected. He tried too hard to be inclusive, to listen to every single point that anyone had to make—even if he had heard it all many times before. Ike often forgot that he wasn't a father figure or a psychologist; he was the boss. Because he wanted to leave his generals room to use their own initiative, his orders were not always clear. As the war progressed, however, his tolerance for listening to everything from everyone waned—he became more decisive and much more clear about the nature of his decisions. His American executives had no problem maintaining their own creativity while adhering to his orders.

Ike's biggest failing as a boss was losing focus. Fortunately this didn't happen often, and he never lost focus in a way that threatened the organization's survival or eventual success. But Operation

Market-Garden was a failure before it ever launched, because even if it had succeeded, it would not have gained D-Day Inc. the one objective it needed: a deepwater port for supplies. Eisenhower wanted to be aggressive and attack; he wanted to utilize the elite Airborne Army; he wanted Monty to move and move fast; *but* Ike lost track of what was really needed. He also ignored his subordinate's personality, forgetting that Monty *always* promised the moon and delivered considerably less.

The Positive Side of the Ledger

Eisenhower could have ordered his staff around. After all, he was Supreme Commander. But he emphasized teamwork—he was convinced that the only route to victory was through the alliance. He never played the part of the imperial CEO, even though he was better positioned to do so than most.

Despite his complete commitment to team, when the time came to make a decision, Ike was firm. He listened to every man in the room regarding the Go / No Go decision for Overlord, and then listened one more time when the bad weather forced him to make the decision all over again.

Eisenhower was responsible in the absolute sense of the word: he accepted *all* blame. Has anyone ever written a note like Eisenhower's on June 5, saying, "If any blame or fault attaches to the attempt it is mine alone"—accepting the entire blame for the potential catastrophe of the D-Day project?

He was optimistic at all times, at least publicly. In private he worried and lost his temper, but when dealing with most of his staff, with his board, and especially with the troops—he was calm, confident, and optimistic.

Ike kept his ego out of the process. He didn't bother preening for the press as Monty or Douglas MacArthur did. When D-Day

Inc. was successful, Eisenhower was quick to mention the men who'd made it happen: his Allied executive team.

One of the ways to measure a CEO's success is to track his or her career. After running one organization, did the CEO go on to success elsewhere? Bob Nardelli was forced out at Home Depot due to shareholder discontent, got the Chrysler top spot, and presided over the automaker's bankruptcy. Carly Fiorina was Hewlett-Packard's boss and tried to buy PricewaterhouseCoopers, decided against the acquisition, then fought a bruising battle with some of her board to acquire Compaq, and was dumped as CEO. She hasn't had another CEO job since.

Following his tenure as CEO of D-Day Inc., Eisenhower was named to the U.S. Army's top spot in November 1945, succeeding his World War II boss, George Marshall.

In 1948, Ike was named president of Columbia University in New York City.

In 1950, he was recalled to the army and was named commander in chief of NATO forces. He was the obvious choice as the "founding" CEO of NATO's *allied* military forces.

And, of course, in 1952, almost everyone was saying "I Like Ike," and he was elected president of the United States with 55 percent of the popular vote and an electoral college landslide. Americans still liked Ike in 1956, when he was reelected in a landslide with 57 percent of the popular vote, a more than 15-percentage-point margin over his opponent, and another lopsided result in the electoral college.

Eisenhower's record as CEO of the United States was substantial, despite his doing absolutely nothing about civil rights and next to nothing to stop Senator Joseph McCarthy's (R-WI) vicious anticommunist witch hunts. But Eisenhower disengaged the United States from the Korean War within five months of his inauguration. Five months. How astounding is that? Well, Harry Truman started the war, and two and a half years later, when his presidency ended, he seemed unable to halt the combat. John F. Kennedy and Lyndon Johnson escalated Vietnam without a hint that they knew how to stop the war. Gerry Ford, following Richard Nixon's policies, finally ended Vietnam after five years of the Nixon-Ford presidencies. George W. Bush never figured out how to get the country out of Afghanistan or Iraq. When you compare Eisenhower's five-month achievement to those of other presidents, it is miraculous.

Ike's presidency wasn't completely sure-footed in foreign affairs, but he managed to keep his countrymen calm during the early years of the Cold War, and he finished his presidency by deciding to not go into the anticommunist adventures of the Bay of Pigs and Vietnam. (Sometimes what you don't do is as important as what you do.)

Domestically, Ike had two major successes. Since FDR and the Great Depression, only two presidents have presided over balanced budgets: Dwight Eisenhower and Bill Clinton. And even more important than the balanced budget and much longer lasting in terms of its beneficial effect, Eisenhower championed the single largest and most successful public works program in the history of the United States: the Interstate Highway System. The initial build lasted thirty-five years, and with ongoing maintenance, refurbishing of existing roadways, and building new highways, the system is still an active public works program in the twenty-first century, creating employment and gigantic, beneficial ripple effects throughout the American economy.

Eisenhower's successes as president:

- Armistice in Korea in five months (Mission, Stay Focused)
- Championed the Interstate Highway System (Prioritize, Plan to Succeed, Plan to Implement)
- Balanced the budget (Plan to Implement)
- Avoided the Bay of Pigs (Stay Focused)
- Stayed out of Vietnam (Stay Focused)

An excellent record by any standard—one that most of his post-FDR colleagues would envy. These bullet points demonstrate the use of at least some of the Ten Business Strategies that Eisenhower used as CEO of D-Day Inc. Let's finish our examination of Ike as a business manager by reviewing his implementation of those strategies.

Strategy No. 1: Determine Your Mission

At least some of you reading this are thinking that a mission is not a strategy. Strategy is something you devise to fulfill your mission. Strategy exists to serve mission. Okay, that's probably all true. But defining and understanding your mission is a strategic exercise. Without a real knowledge of your mission, all the other strategic exercises, such as goal setting, planning, and communicating, are pointless. So maybe, strictly speaking, having a mission is not the same as having a strategy—but you can't have any strategy without having a mission. It is the Big Bang of all strategy, and therefore belongs in this conversation.

The other point to remember when discussing your organization's mission is that *the mission is not the same as the mission statement.* Jack Trout wrote in *Forbes,* "Fortunately, most companies put their mission statements in gold frames and hang them in their lobbies where top managers who have their own agendas ignore them."[3] Mission statements tend to be verbose, lumpy things that may or may not contain an organization's reason for being. Many contain hundreds of words in multiple sentences and still never manage to describe the company's ultimate purpose.

The chairman of D-Day Inc.'s board, President Franklin D. Roosevelt, declared the Allies were looking for "unconditional surrender" from their enemies. Applied specifically to D-Day Inc., unconditional surrender meant "beat the Germans with an Allied force."

There was no verbiage about increasing the value of the stock by X percent annually. Nothing about innovation or passion or fair treatment or employment or customer service. All of these values were implicit in the mission and did not require explicit statements. In seven words, the mission expressed the goal (beat the Germans) and the essential methodology (with an Allied force). Eisenhower and the executives at D-Day Inc. didn't need a lot of verbiage to remind them that their organization needed to continue growing in order to meet its challenges. They didn't need explicit statements about innovation; their competitive arena was filled with techno-logical innovation:

- The Germans built and launched the first missiles (V-2 rockets) and jet airplanes, and strove to build the first atomic bomb.
- The British created artificial harbors, invented radar, and broke German codes.
- The Americans designed all manner of landing craft, airplanes, and vehicles that hadn't existed on December 7, 1941, but were deployed—in mind-boggling numbers—two and a half years later on D-Day.

Ike didn't need to be told about having a "passion for excellence"—he was the one who called D-Day Inc.'s mission the "Great Crusade." He didn't need to be told about fair treatment or customer service. Ike made sure that whenever possible, French troops led the way in liberating each and every French town, including Paris. And the last thing he or any of his executives needed reminding about was how precious their employees were. Eisenhower didn't make a single deci-sion throughout the course of the war without weighing the potential cost in human life.

Let's take a look at a major, contemporary corporation and how it handles communicating its mission: Here is the Ford Motor Company mission[4] as expressed on their Web site in October 2009:

ONE FORD
One Team * One Plan * One Goal

ONE TEAM
People working together as a lean, global enterprise
for automotive leadership, as measured by:
*Customer, Employee, Dealer, Investor, Supplier, Union/Council,
and Community Satisfaction*

ONE PLAN
- Aggressively restructure to operate profitably at the current demand and changing model mix
- Accelerate development of new products our customers want and value
- Finance our plan and improve our balance sheet
- Work together effectively as one team

ONE GOAL
An exciting, viable Ford delivering profitable growth for all

First things first, remember that this is the only one of Detroit's Big Three that did not declare bankruptcy in 2009 and in January 2010 announced a profit—significant accomplishments. It's hard to imagine, however, that this mission is what kept them from Chapter 11. Ford's mission describes how the company will run and the kind of results they hope to achieve. This mission does not tell anyone what the company hopes to do to achieve success. It's not even specific as to what the company does, period. Yes, the word *automotive* appears under the "One Team" section, but that could refer to auto parts, insurance, financing, franchised mechanics or auto-body repair, or what Ford *actually* does, which is to design, build, sell, and maintain cars and trucks. If Ford gave me absolute power to redefine its mission, I'd come up with this:

To design, build, sell, and maintain the best cars and trucks in the world.

All the words in Ford's current mission would flow from that mission. But Ford put the lofty statements of purpose before the horseless carriage. This might explain why Ford is better off financially than its barely competent Detroit brethren but trails Toyota and Honda by a significant margin.

Forget about the verbiage. Your mission statement is not your mission. Figure out your mission in the most basic terms, ideally in words of one or two syllables, collected into one or two sentences. Then don't waste your time prettying up the language and putting the mission on your walls. If your mission is simple, it's easier to understand and easier to embrace. And more likely to succeed.

Strategy No. 2: Plan for Success

This kind of planning is really high-level decision making—committing to a path because that path offers the best (or only) chance of success. It's not the kind of planning that tells you how you are going to follow the path you've chosen; it's strictly about what needs to happen in the big picture. Not to sound negative, but at this stage of planning, the first risk assessment needs to happen. The risk assessment is still high level and can be as simple as "Can we survive if this goes wrong?" By the way, if the answer to that is no, you need to find another path. If there is no other path, you have to modify the only path to reduce your risk. A quick look at the 2008–2009 financial crisis shows that a lot of financial institutions didn't ask themselves this regarding credit-default swaps.

Before Eisenhower took the job as CEO of D-Day Inc., he had worked in war plans for George Marshall in Washington. His war-plans days convinced him that the only way to beat Germany was to compete head-to-head, and absolutely the only way to accomplish that was by coming into northern France via the English Channel. Marshall agreed with him wholeheartedly, as did Josef Stalin. Roosevelt also believed it was the most effective strategy, but was less forceful about it than the others. Could D-Day Inc. have survived if Overlord had failed? Yes. It would have been very ugly, but failure was survivable. The flipside risk question was "Can we afford continued operations if we don't take a chance on Overlord?" Ike and his board answered that question: No. Too many lives would be lost, in occupied territories, in the concentration camps, and on the battlefield as the war crawled on without Overlord.

The planning for success that led to Overlord is similar to BMW, Honda, Toyota, and other non-U.S. car companies deciding that if they were going to increase market share and profits in America, they needed to build manufacturing plants in the States. At the time, one of the advantages foreign-made cars had over American-made was better quality—the fear was that American-made Toyotas and Hondas would lower those companies' reputation for quality. That was a risk that couldn't be tolerated. The foreign manufacturers built their plants, trained their workers, and produced American-made cars of equal quality to their foreign-made counterparts.

By the same token, GM and Chrysler both failed to plan for success by not designing and building marketable, fuel-efficient cars. When oil prices soared and choked off the highly profitable SUV and pickup truck sales, those two companies didn't have an alternative that the driving public wanted. The proof of this particular pudding: According to the Department of Transportation, when the "Cash for Clunkers" program was launched during the summer of 2009, the top ten cars traded in were all from Chrysler, Ford, and GM. And none of the top ten cars purchased with the government rebate were from either Chrysler or GM. Ford managed to place two models in the "most purchased" category.

Amazon's decision to build itself as a purely virtual retailer was a similar piece of big picture planning for success. What made the Amazon idea take off was the utilization of Internet technology to eliminate the need for storefronts or printed catalogs or call centers. That allowed Amazon to drop prices—and its Web site allowed for a then-unique customer experience, where the site welcomes customers by name, allows them to track previous orders, and makes suggestions on what to buy based on previous purchases or by product searches on the site. All this from the comfort of the customer's own home, with no worries about finding a parking space or dealing with sales help that might or might not know what you want. No calling an 800 number (the reigning technology of its pre–Web sites day). The folks at Amazon thought big and created a whole new customer experience. Like Ike, Amazon went right for the heart of its competition and secured its future.

Plan for success. Answer the question: *How are we going to achieve our mission?*

Strategy No. 3: Stay Focused

Focus on what you need in order to succeed—and get it. When you focus a camera, you adjust the lens until the image you are looking at is sharp and clear. When you are focusing strategically, you make your adjustment by assessing need. Anything that does not fall under "need" should not be within your focus.

With Overlord, Eisenhower's first need was enough landing craft to bring the necessary forces ashore. D-Day's original date had been in May 1944, but Ike quickly realized that another month's production of landing craft would enable him to bring a critical mass ashore against his well-entrenched competition. He moved the date a month later to June.

Another item of need for Overlord was the supply situation. Overlord was going to land immense numbers of men and vehicles in France at a very swift pace. All of those men needed to be fed and clothed. And they all needed ammunition for their weapons. Their vehicles required fuel and spare parts. Supplying them became a greater challenge as time went on and their numbers increased.

Cherbourg was the closest major port to Overlord. Since a port was a necessity to handle the supply challenge, Eisenhower decided to place the westernmost tip of Overlord at Utah Beach—the closest beach to Cherbourg that was still suitable for Overlord. But Utah was far from ideal; the forces there were exposed to withering opposition due to the contours of the beach. The solution: Airborne drops would be made in support of Utah. This entire chain of decisions was within the mission focus, because each decision met a need. The forces needed supplies; supplies require a port for arrival; Utah Beach was a must to get near Cherbourg; Airborne landings were a must to secure Utah.

During the Battle of the Bulge, Eisenhower made a similar chain of needs-based decisions to enable D-Day Inc. to succeed: Bastogne and Stavelot had to be held, he dispatched the 101st and 82nd Airborne divisions to hold them; the 101st had to be relieved at Bastogne, Ike had Patton quit one battle and wheel north to rush to Bastogne; reserve forces had to be withheld until they could be utilized at just the right spot, and Eisenhower refused the multiple reinforcement requests he received so that he could take advantage of his reserve forces' power.

On the other hand, Eisenhower's biggest failure of the war, Operation Market-Garden, was caused by an appalling lack of focus on his part. The only objective Ike and D-Day Inc. absolutely had to have at that stage of the war (September 1944) was the port of Antwerp in working order. (The supply problem was continuing to rear its ugly head.) Instead of making his subordinate, Montgomery, free Antwerp, Ike approved Market-Garden. The approved plan, even if successful, would not produce the one objective D-Day Inc. needed—a deepwater port to relieve the supply problem. In the end, Eisenhower and Monty wasted thousands of lives and destroyed the usefulness of an elite force in a doomed operation.

Remember, we're talking about need here. Not something that might be wonderfully helpful or fantastically profitable—*need*.

Can't-live-without-it kind of stuff. Your company won't survive without it, or profits will drop sharply without it.

Did the guys at Enron need to create all those elaborate, phony businesses to eke out every last drop of profit? Enron was profitable before all the sleight of hand, and now the company is gone. Hard to see how phony businesses met the needs test. Speaking of Enron, how about their auditors at Arthur Andersen? Did they need Enron's business so much that they had to shield their eyes from the heart of darkness? Since Andersen is also kaput, it's impossible to believe that keeping one client, no matter how big, met the needs test.

More recently, Bear Stearns was a successful investment bank that allowed a relatively small number of its employees to expose it to gigantic, eventually lethal risks for the sake of *more* profits. Bear would have been profitable without taking those risks, but that didn't stop the folks there from indulging in risky business. That business ended up pushing Bear Stearns into selling itself in an insanely cheap fire sale. Did an intensely risky increase in profit meet the definition of need?

Strategy No. 4: Prioritize

Do what you need to do to succeed—nothing else, no matter how productive, matters. In the months before Overlord was launched, Eisenhower struggled with his board to gain control over all the Allied air forces operating out of the United Kingdom. D-Day Inc. had its own tactical air force to give its ground forces cover, but Eisenhower believed that Overlord *needed* more. He wanted to implement the "Transportation Plan"—the bombing of key railroad centers to largely immobilize the Germans and keep their reinforcements away from the Normandy beachhead.

The executives in charge of strategic bombing (attacks on oil refineries and depots, weapons factories, military bases within Germany) wanted to continue *their* mission, believing that the best action they could take to beat their German competitors was destruction of the

German industrial base and supply chain. Strategic bombing was extremely productive and fit into the Allies' strategies for completing their overall mission: beat the Germans.

The strategic bombing bosses had another urgent concern regarding the downside risk of the Transportation Plan. Bombing crucial railroad centers in France would likely kill many French civilians, the very people D-Day Inc. wanted to liberate.

Eisenhower made the Transportation Plan an absolute priority. For D-Day Inc. to succeed at its mission, the organization had to invade France over the beaches of Normandy. Once there, it had to stay there. If the Germans were able to knock D-Day Inc.'s forces back into the water, Overlord would fail. The best way to make sure that didn't happen was to implement the Transportation Plan and keep the Germans away from the beachhead. Ike understood the risk to French civilians but considered the Transportation Plan so essential for the success of Overlord (and the eventual liberation of the French people) that he insisted on having it. For the one and only time during the course of the war, Eisenhower used his trump card. He informed the British members of his board that if he didn't get control of the strategic air forces so that he could implement the Transportation Plan, he would be forced to resign. Ike won the contest over priorities and was given control of the strategic air forces. The Transportation Plan was implemented, and the Germans' movement behind their own lines was heavily restricted. D-Day Inc. secured its beachhead, and the rest, as they say, is history.

When Michael Dell began selling custom-built personal computers directly to customers, he was invading territory controlled by the likes of Compaq, IBM, Hewlett-Packard, and Apple—gigantic companies that built and sold PCs in standard models with some available options, the same way automobile companies manufacture cars. Dell's innovation was that he offered a number of different base models and a large array of options that could be mixed and matched at the customer's whim.

Because Dell sold directly to the customer, he was able to sell more computing bang for the buck. And he backed his product with risk-free returns and next-day, at-home service. It was a completely personalized customer experience unheard-of in the PC business at that time, and Dell made it happen several years before the advent of the Web. In 2009, twenty-five years after it started, Dell was the second largest manufacturer of PCs and No. 33 in the Fortune 100.[5] Michael Dell knew what his company's priorities had to be and went after them.

Strategy No. 5: Plan to Implement

Your plans for implementation will map out how you'll actually manage the project(s) to fulfill your mission.

In Eisenhower's case, the Plan for Success was the invasion of Normandy. The Plan to Implement was Overlord with its thousands of necessary details, minute-by-minute timing, and logistical chains stretching across the Atlantic Ocean and the continental United States.

Overlord included the basics of any implementation plan: the who, what, where, when, and how of the operation.

Who: Hundreds of thousands of men had to be trained in multiple disciplines—and to keep them sharp and ensure that their training applied to Overlord, there were training exercises and dress rehearsals until just a few weeks before Overlord launched.

What: Send five divisions, approximately 150,000 men, across five different beach areas that stretched across fifty miles of terrain. Carrying those men required a fleet of about five thousand ships (the largest armada of any kind in the history of the world), with each and every one of the ships loaded with exactly the right people and/or equipment and leaving at exactly the right time to arrive at exactly the right beach at exactly the right time.

Where: The coast of Normandy. Close enough to England to be manageable, but farther away than Calais so that D-Day Inc. might enjoy the element of surprise.

When: Dawn, June 5 or 6, 1944, when the proper combination of tides, weather, and moonlight gave D-Day Inc. its best chances of success.

How: The creation of an organization, D-Day Inc., capable of handling the who, what, where, and when. The "how" of any plan to implement is the forming and shaping of an organization capable of fulfilling the plan, and hopefully, the mission the plan serves. Success goes to the organizations that—through luck or design (preferably design)—are capable of fulfilling their own plans.

When Fred Smith created FedEx, he believed that the passenger routes flown by most airfreight shippers were economically unsound for the airfreight business. A system specifically for airfreight was needed, especially for the transport of time-sensitive shipments.

Smith started with an initial investment of $80 million. The who, what, where, and when of his plan to implement were, to a large degree, dictated by that $80 million limit. FedEx had to start small.

Who: The pilots and freight handlers.

What: Deliver small packages and documents on an overnight basis.

Where: Memphis International Airport. The company history says that Memphis was "selected for its geographical center to the original target market cities for small packages. In addition, the Memphis weather was excellent and rarely caused closures at Memphis International Airport. The airport was also willing to make the necessary improvements for the operation and had additional hangar space readily available."[6]

When: Operations began on April 17, 1973, with the launch of fourteen small aircraft from Memphis International. "On that night, Federal Express delivered 186 packages to 25 U.S. cities from Rochester, NY, to Miami, Fla."[7]

How: Creation of FedEx, an organization that handled airfreight in a completely new way. FedEx "was in the information business—that knowledge about origin, present whereabouts, destination, estimated time of arrival, price and shipment cost of cargo was as important as its prompt delivery. Another principle applied at FedEx was to make sure every employee felt they could share in the success of the company."[8]

Approximately two years after those 186 packages were delivered, FedEx almost went bankrupt. Smith refinanced and stuck to his plan. Today, according to the corporate Web site, FedEx has annual revenues of more than $35 billion, a workforce of more than 275,000 people around the world, and an average daily volume of more than 7.5 million shipments to more than 220 countries and territories. FedEx now has 658 aircraft, utilizing more than 375 airports worldwide, along with more than 80,000 motorized vehicles in its ground fleet. Smith's original Plan to Implement didn't deliver overnight success, but it got there eventually. The wait was worth it.

Strategy No. 6: Communicate

You have two primary audiences that you must communicate with: your people and your markets. If you can't communicate well with your people, you can't implement well. Success will become a tantalizing, unattainable dream.

If you can't communicate to your board, it's almost impossible to gain their support.

If you can't communicate with your executive team, they're going to be ineffective managers.

If you can't communicate with your workforce, you can't motivate. And an unmotivated workforce can be staggeringly unproductive. There's an old saying that you can't just talk the talk; you have to walk the walk. Most of the other strategies are about walking the walk. This one is all talk.

Ike was effective in communicating with his board. He was direct and honest about what he believed to be in the best interests of D-Day Inc. He was respectful, yet blunt, about not wanting to launch Torch (North Africa) because of the delay it caused in launching Overlord. The same was true when he needed to convince the board to give him control of the strategic air forces for the Transportation Plan. And again, when he wanted to avoid taking Berlin (and expending 300,000 casualties to do it). More often than not, Ike got what he needed—and wanted—from his board.

His communications with his management team were, for the most part, excellent. Eisenhower was open and direct and listened patiently to others, and as a result, they reciprocated in kind. As the planning for Overlord progressed, Ike's air boss, Leigh-Mallory, became more and more concerned with the planned airborne drops near Utah Beach and the casualty rate being projected for them. Those drops had been included at Ike's specific direction, but Leigh-Mallory was able to ask Eisenhower to cancel that part of the operation, which Ike denied. (And, afterward, when the operation was successful, Leigh-Mallory apologized for adding to Ike's large set of worries.)

Eisenhower also communicated well with most of his field executives. Not surprisingly, he found it easiest to deal with his fellow Americans, even George Patton. Ike had to correct Patton several times, but Patton got the message and performed brilliantly, especially as the executive in charge of the U.S. Third Army. Solid communications weren't limited to American execs at D-Day Inc. Eisenhower also had an excellent relationship with Sir Harold Alexander, his ground commander in Sicily. In fact, Ike and "Alex" got on so well, that Alex was the first choice for ground commander in Overlord. Unfortunately, Churchill nixed that idea, and Eisenhower was stuck with Montgomery, the one man in all of D-Day Inc. whom he never communicated with successfully.

Tons of ink have been spilled over Ike vs. Monty through the years by historians and journalists—I've spilled a little myself in this book. Part of the reason this tussle of personalities gets so much attention is the drama of the conflict. My particular reason for focusing on the conflict is that failures often illustrate a point as well as successes do.

The personal characteristics that worked so well with his other executives, the openness and patience, worked against Eisenhower when it came to Monty. The field marshal's arrogance was impenetrable. Ike's many attempts to work as a true team with Monty left him open to exploitation—Montgomery routinely redefined Eisenhower's directives to suit his purposes. And Ike compounded the problems by not taking a clear, hard line with Monty. Finally, during the Battle of the Bulge, after more than two years of ineffective action and bungled communications with Monty, Ike became forceful and direct. Lo and behold, the forceful approach worked. Ike followed up his hard-line success by ceasing to communicate with Monty unless it was absolutely necessary, and then his communications were to the point. His days of appealing to Montgomery as a teammate and colleague were over.

Eisenhower's mistake in communications with his executive colleagues was that he used a one-size-fits-all approach. His respectful, open style worked with 99 percent of his managers. But his personality meant that Ike took way too long to customize an approach that worked with Monty, the last 1 percent.

Ike was at his absolute best with his frontline forces. As often as he could, he visited them at their bases, at the airfields just prior to climbing into their planes, at the ports as they embarked on their ships, and in the hospitals after they had been wounded. His open, respectful style worked wonderfully with them; the magic ingredient was sincerity. Eisenhower never forgot the families who were home waiting for these young men or the futures that might be ahead of them. It was easy for him to be friendly with them—it was in his nature. It was easy to let them know his concern—it was in his heart.

Eisenhower also excelled in communicating on more public

stages, through the press and with the American and British people, his shareholders. He was forthright and sincere with the media and the public, and like his workforce, they loved him for it. The important thing to remember about this kind of communication with your frontline workforce, the press, your shareholders, and customers is: You can't fake sincerity. If you don't really believe your own people come first, don't say anything about it. People can spot a phony from a thousand miles away.

Lee Iacocca was the consummate communicator when he was in charge at Chrysler, starting in 1978. Only a year after Iacocca took over at Chrysler, the company was facing bankruptcy. Saving the company was a simple proposition: all Iacocca had to do was convince everyone to change everything. He persuaded the federal government to bail out the company by backing $1.5 billion in loans. Uncle Sam was no more eager to bail out an American corporation in 1979 than in the "Great Recession," but Iacocca persuaded them to do so.

He turned to the unions and said that Chrysler didn't have any $20-an-hour jobs anymore, but it had a fair supply of $15-an-hour jobs if anyone was interested. They were. He cut his own salary to $1 a year. The communication was symbolic—most people knew that Iacocca received stock in Chrysler and would become rich if the company rebounded, but they respected his putting his money where his mouth was. He and his executive team cut costs and introduced the fuel-efficient K-cars (an idea that had been rejected at Ford) and then went on to create the Soccer Mom market by launching the mini-van (another Ford reject), a product that was an auto sales leader for twenty-five years. Iacocca became identified with the new Chrysler; he was the brand consumers could trust. He looked television audiences in the eye and said, "If you can find a better car, buy it."

Chrysler turned around quickly and was able to pay off its federally backed loans seven years early. That's a pretty good return on the communications from a dollar-a-year CEO.

Strategy No. 7: Motivate Your People

Okay, when you get into the topic of motivating people, you're getting into the mushy stuff. What's the ROI on motivating people? How do you measure it? In tough times, shouldn't collecting a paycheck be motivation enough? I've had the dubious pleasure of working for organizations that had that attitude, and I can tell you from personal experience, it's not in the company's best interests to take that kind of position with its people. In companies that don't care about motivation, workers right on up through middle management routinely cut corners on the quality of jobs, provide poorer customer service, spend more time on personal phone calls and at longer lunches, and worst of all, escape from the dreariness of their jobs for hours at a time on the Internet. Believe me, no matter how closely you monitor people, there are plenty of avenues available to pass the time instead of working hard. And if you spend all your time monitoring your people to ensure they do their jobs, when are you going to have the time to do yours? To coin a phrase, an ounce of motivation is worth a pound of monitoring.

Issuing corporate communiqués that extol your people as your organization's No. 1 resource is not enough. You have to mean what you say right through to your bones. (See "sincerity" above in Strategy No. 6: Communicate.) Lots of companies say their people are important to them. Most of them don't act as if they believe their own verbiage—probably because they don't.

At one point in my life, many years ago, I worked for a very large professional services firm. The organization made a large number of claims about how well it treated its people. The compensation was pretty good, and the benefits weren't bad at all. But underneath the policies, the place always struck me as soulless. One of my neighbors was a partner at the company and we commuted together once in a while. One morning our conversation turned to this topic and he said something to the effect that all of this "people stuff" was pointless.

I looked at him long and hard and said, "If you could make money without having to have all these people, you would, wouldn't you?"

He didn't hesitate and replied, "Absolutely."

People were just overhead costs to him. No wonder I felt the firm had no soul.

Eisenhower, as we discussed in the Communicate strategy, honestly felt that D-Day Inc. had to be a people-first organization. He was asking for a level of sacrifice in job performance that, fortunately, has no equal outside the military or emergency responders such as the police and firefighters. But modern managers shouldn't dismiss Ike's example because of the life-or-death nature of his company's challenge. Corporations are faced with a lesser-but-still-intense challenge: good life or bad life. It would be great if corporations chose the good life for their people for altruistic reasons, but they can choose the good life and be sincere for commercial reasons. From my personal experience, I can say that workers who are treated better are more productive. Workers who are well treated are much more likely to rise to special challenges that require longer hours of work or demand the dazzling new idea for a product or service.

But don't listen to me; look at Eisenhower. He could have taken the attitude that his forces should do the best they could because it gave them a better chance of survival. Why the heck should he worry about their morale or waste time motivating them? But he did. He made sure that enlisted men got as much time on leave as officers. He sent his executives on leave before they burnt out from stress and fatigue. He worried about the little things, like making sure that enlisted men could get access to transportation for recreational activities as easily as officers, and that captured wine was distributed equally across the board. And he pressed his executives to be aggressive because he was convinced that aggressive action would save more of his people's lives in the end.

Henry Ford, the auto-manufacturing pioneer and inventor of the assembly line, was a major innovator in employee benefits. He wanted his assembly line workers paid enough that, over time, they could afford to buy one of the cars they made. He created his own consumer class—a real benefit for the workers since they could enjoy more pay and ride in a new Ford car, and a benefit for the company since it would sell more cars and have happier workers. (Ford later struggled bitterly with unions, but his early attitude on workers' compensation was truly enlightened.)

Ike also motivated people through example. In his earliest days as CEO of D-Day Inc., he told his executives that they were to present a cheerful, optimistic face to the world. That's exactly what he did throughout the war. In December 1944, at the battle conference during the Battle of the Bulge, Eisenhower told the executives present he didn't want to see any glum faces. In the final months of the war, Ike was in a great deal of pain. The knee he had injured while pushing a plane above the waterline ached constantly. He had a cyst on his back that required surgery. And, naturally enough for a man under such tremendous stress who was getting too little exercise, he was exhausted a great deal of the time. However, only Ike's inner circle was aware of his pain and fatigue. Whenever he was dealing with his board, his executive team at D-Day Inc., his workforce, or the press, he exuded energy and cheer. The minute he was alone, he slumped in his seat, depleted by the effort.

In April 1944, about two months before D-Day, Eisenhower wrote about the pressure involved in Overlord. "This time, because of the stakes involved, the atmosphere is probably more electric than ever before. . . . [A] sense of humor and a great faith, or else a complete lack of imagination are essential to sanity."[9]

The point: It's not enough to tell people to cheer up or have a good attitude—you have to have it yourself. And project it. Look at the enthusiasm of Wendy's founder, the late Dave Thomas. Or Ben & Jerry's Ice Cream founders, Ben Cohen and Jerry Greenfield, who tied their sense of fun to corporate good deeds and a quality product.

Strategy No. 8: Manage Your People

There's an old saying when economic times get tough, and executives have to take harsh action to save their companies: "It's not personal, it's business." Well, when it comes to managing people, it is personal *and* it is business. When it comes to talent, intelligence, attitude, and ambition, all people are not created equal. (Wouldn't it be boring if we were all Stepford employees and managers?) But the differences in those personal attributes can present a real challenge to a manager.

Eisenhower excelled at putting aside his personal feelings toward someone and working with him as a teammate. Several of the British executives who were originally assigned to his staff at D-Day Inc. were placed there by Winston Churchill and other board members in a deliberate attempt to make sure that the affable but supposedly nonstrategic Ike didn't mess up. Eisenhower was well aware of the reason for their assignments, but ignored the reason, and treated his British deputies respectfully as colleagues and often as friends. Men like Sir Arthur Tedder and Sir Harold Alexander quickly became fans and loyal lieutenants of Ike's.

Another area Eisenhower excelled in was spotting and promoting talent, regardless of seniority. He jumped Omar Bradley past other men who were Bradley's seniors and even assigned the difficult Patton to him. Bradley turned out to be the best field executive of the war and, in honor of his service, in 1950 became the fifth and last soldier to be given five-star rank, General of the Army. (George Marshall, the top executive of the U.S. Army, had done the same with Eisenhower, jumping him past senior men to the CEO spot at D-Day Inc.)

In 1984, Barry Diller resigned as chairman of Paramount Pictures. The powers that be at the studio passed over Michael Eisner, then president and CEO, for Diller's job at the top. The folks at the Walt Disney Company knew talent when they saw it, and gave the relatively young Eisner (forty-two) the position of CEO and chairman. Disney had been wandering in the Hollywood wilderness since the death of its founder, Walt Disney. There was an occasional hit movie, and the theme parks continued to bump along successfully if unimpressively. Eisner changed all that. He brought Jeffrey Katzenberg from Paramount, and they revitalized Disney animation with a string of huge hits: *The Little Mermaid, Beauty and the Beast* (the first animated film ever nominated for the Best Picture Oscar), *Aladdin,* and *The Lion King.*

A string of comedies and thrillers from the Touchstone and Hollywood Pictures brands reached adult audiences: *Down and Out in Beverly Hills, Ruthless People,* and *Stakeout* among them. The Disney Cruise Line was created, and the theme parks were expanded and improved. Merchandising, thanks in large part to the new animated successes, took off. By the time Eisner left the company twenty-one years later, its market capitalization had grown from about $3 billion to $60 billion. Kudos to the Disney board in 1984 for seeing the potential in a guy his previous employer had passed over.

In returning to Eisenhower's people management, it's impossible to avoid the two prima donnas, Patton and Monty. Both were difficult; both had substantial contributions to make. Ike treated them with a combination of patience, support, discipline, and threats. Ike's style worked with Patton, who from the time he took command of Third Army in France until he led it deep into Germany, performed superbly. Monty, on the other hand, never got Eisenhower's point, never changed in his behavior, and continued to under-deliver throughout the war. Ike couldn't just fire Monty the way he could Patton; his board had to approve it. Because firing the man was not in his power, when Eisenhower finally resorted to threats with Monty, he was indirect about them. Ike's mistake with Monty was in trying so hard for so long to make their relationship work. In early 1945, he froze Monty out, speaking to him as little as possible and as tersely as possible. The positive was that Eisenhower recognized the value that both men brought to the organization, put aside his own feelings, and did whatever he could to utilize their value.

In the late 1970s, I worked for Fairchild Publications, the publisher of *Women's Wear Daily*, among other publications. My boss
was the business manager of a group of trade newspapers, a woman
named Mary Zaccardo, known to one and all as "Mary Z." The fact
that Mary was the business manager of this approximately $5 million-
a-year group spoke to the fact that her boss had recognized talent
when he saw it and promoted it when he had the chance. Mary had a
commercial diploma from a New York City high school and no college degree. But she understood numbers and budgeting better than
many an Ivy League MBA, and she did a terrific job running the place
on a day-to-day basis.

When a new, niche publication was being created, the group was
in search of an editor. Mary lobbied for one of the women reporters on an existing publication in the group. The two women didn't
get along at all, an oil-and-water situation. They had been known to
argue with zest. But Mary believed the reporter was the right person
for the editor's job and pushed her for the position. The boss of the
group, as he usually did, took Mary's advice, and the reporter became
the editor of the new publication. She ran the magazine very well,
and it raked in additional advertising revenues for several years for
Fairchild. All because Mary's boss had recognized Mary's talent and
ignored her lack of a degree, and because Mary put aside her personal
feelings to push the right candidate for a job.

Strategy No. 9: Avoid Project Creep

Eisenhower's ultimate project—he had warm-ups in Africa and Sicily—
was to compete directly with the Germans in France, Belgium, Holland,
and Germany itself. His goal was to compete so successfully against his
opposition that the Germans became incapable of continuing. As has
been discussed previously, Ike and his American bosses felt the only
way to beat Germany was to go through Normandy. But his British
board members, with bitter past experience, wanted to try different

approaches. At different times pre-Overlord, Churchill wanted to go north through Italy and the Alps into Germany and/or launch a campaign in the Balkans and move northwest into Germany. Eisenhower was convinced that neither route would be effective and might well delay Overlord. With backing from Marshall and FDR, Ike's view prevailed—because neither of these ideas would get the job done.

After Overlord had been successful, after the Battle of the Bulge was won, and German forces were collapsing, Churchill and most of D-Day Inc.'s executives wanted to race for Berlin and sweep into the German capital. But Eisenhower's goal was to destroy the Germans' ability to compete, not to capture Berlin. Like the Italian and Balkan ideas, taking the German capital wasn't crucial to doing the job. Ike refused to add Berlin to his list of objectives, saved 300,000 casualties, and still eliminated his competition.

What's the difference between avoiding project creep and prioritizing (Strategy No. 4)? Prioritizing should be done as a project is coming together and being readied for launch. Avoiding creep occurs as the project is in process, and your people are coming up with all kinds of ideas—many of them really good—in reaction to what they see as the project is implemented. You want to harvest those ideas and plan to implement them—in the *next* project.

Any company that's launched a Web site is familiar with project creep. Especially since the technology is always changing and Web features that were only dreams become realities at an astonishing pace. Companies that need Web sites to sell product and process customers' orders may find their launch delayed because someone on the Web site team fell in love with social networking features and felt the company site needed to offer live chat with a company employee or blogging or online video or whatever. The problem is that all of these features, while wonderful, add to the cost and time of launching a new Web site. If they are not mission-critical, they have to be put aside for possible action later. (In version 2.0, as they say regarding software.)

Expectations for a project need to be set early and reinforced often. Succeeding at a project within the framework of deadlines and budget almost always comes down to some form of this question: *Is the wonderful new idea or feature that someone just thought of critical to the success of this project as it was defined and planned?*

Strategy No. 10: Be Honest

Let's face it: people struggle with honesty in all aspects of life. It's tough to be honest with yourself and face your strengths and weaknesses. It can be downright brutal to be honest with your colleagues, your workforce, and/or the press, especially about your core beliefs or your flaws. (Most of us are uncomfortable sharing our real values with other people—we're often afraid they won't agree with us and we'll lose their respect.) And finally, being honest enough to accept blame for a huge mistake when every instinct in you is screaming at you to run and hide is horribly difficult.

But without honesty, you can't be a truly great manager.

Eisenhower had the capacity to be honest, and that capacity made him a great manager.

He subjected himself to a rigorous self-assessment near the end of the North Africa campaign and realized he'd been too timid in his planning and in his dealings with his executive team. He showed immediate improvement after that.

When Patton slapped the soldier in Italy and created a potential public relations disaster, Ike leveled with the press, explaining his reasons for handling the situation as he did and informing them that Patton was a great commander and if they broke the story, D-Day Inc. would lose Patton's services. The media stayed quiet.

Ike was direct in his dealings with his board and his executives. He was clear about not wanting to go into North Africa because operations in Africa would delay Overlord. He never wavered in his commitment to the Transportation Plan despite executive and board opposition to the plan.

He didn't lie to himself or to anyone else, no matter how much easier it might have been to slip a harmless fib or two to his listeners. Eisenhower once said, "I know only one method of operation. To be as honest with others as I am with myself."[10] Even Monty appreciated this quality in Ike: "He merely has to smile at you, and you trust him at once. He is the very incarnation of sincerity."[11]

Bill Ford, great-grandson of Ford Motor Company founder Henry Ford, became Ford's chairman of the board in 1999. In 2001 he became CEO as well. Five years later, in 2006, Ford was in dire shape, having lost $12.6 billion—the worst year in its history. Bill Ford was capable of admitting to himself and the board that he wasn't the right man to hold the CEO's job. Most executives wouldn't have been able to do what Bill Ford did, giving the CEO's job to Alan Mulally. Although none of the American car companies are singing "Happy Days Are Here Again," only Ford avoided bankruptcy in 2009 and announced a profit in 2010, in large part because its boss (and company namesake, for crying out loud) was able to assess himself and the situation realistically and do what needed to be done.

"Be Honest" is not the last strategy by random chance. It's last because it's the hardest and toughest of all the strategies to do. When times are good, and one success follows another, it's easy to talk about all the wonderful things you and your company have truly achieved. In good times, most people can shrug their way through any needed apologies because success mitigates a multitude of sins. Sure, you made a mistake, but it didn't really cause much harm. And as they say in sports: no harm, no foul. But when times are tough, when the results of a mistake are magnified, it can be almost impossible to accept the blame for messing up. The more dire the consequences, the harder it is. And the more necessary it is.

In the morning hours of June 5, 1944, with the fate of D-Day Inc. and millions of lives hanging in the balance, Eisenhower proved his greatness as a manager and as a man by writing the note accepting the blame if Overlord turned out to be a disaster:

"Our landings . . . have failed . . . and I have withdrawn the troops. My decision to attack at this time and place was based upon the best information available. The troops, the air and the Navy did all that bravery and devotion to duty could do. If any blame or fault attaches to the attempt it is mine alone."

D-DAY INC.'S OWNERSHIP STRUCTURE, BOARD OF DIRECTORS, AND KEY PERSONNEL

Wholly owned subsidiary of the United States and United Kingdom's military services.

Board of Directors:

Franklin D. Roosevelt, president of the United States and
  chairman of the Board, D-Day Inc

Winston S. Churchill, prime minister of the United
  Kingdom, vice-chairman

Josef Stalin, general secretary of the Communist Party,
  leader of the Soviet Union

Henry "Hap" Arnold, general, CEO of U.S. Army Air Forces

Alan Brooke, field marshal, CEO of the British Army

Ernest J. King, admiral, CEO of U.S. Navy

George C. Marshall, general, CEO of the U.S. Army
  Other members of the board were Admiral William
  Leahy, chief of staff to President Roosevelt (the
  equivalent of the modern chairman of the joint chiefs),

and the senior British officers in charge of the Royal Navy and Royal Air Force.

Key Personnel:

General Sir Harold Alexander, Eisenhower's No. 2 in North Africa, Sicily, and Italy.

General Omar N. Bradley, commander of all U.S. land forces in France from June 1944 until the war's end in May 1945. Named five-star General of the Army in 1950.

Admiral Sir Andrew Cunningham, Ike's naval deputy from July 1942 until January 1944, when he became Britain's first sea lord.

General Courtney Hodges, commander of the U.S. First Army.

Air Chief Marshal Sir Trafford Leigh-Mallory, air forces deputy from January 1944 until war's end.

Field Marshal Sir Bernard Law Montgomery, commander of all British and Canadian forces in France from June 1944 until war's end. Became CEO of the British Army after the war.

General George C. Patton, commander of the U.S. Third Army.

Admiral Sir Bertram Ramsay, deputy naval forces from January 1944 until war's end.

General William H. Simpson, commander of the U.S. Ninth Army.

General Walter Bedell Smith, Ike's chief of staff at D-Day Inc.

Air Marshal Sir Arthur Tedder, Eisenhower's No. 2 from January 1944 until war's end, previously Ike's air forces deputy for North Africa, Sicily, and Italy.

GLOSSARY

Avalanche: Amphibious assault of Italy, September 9, 1943.

D-Day Beaches: From the west near Ste. Mère Église to the east near Caen along the north coast of Normandy—Utah and Omaha Beaches (both assaulted by U.S forces), and Gold, Juno, and Sword Beaches (assaulted by the British and Canadian forces).

Dunkirk: Site of miraculous evacuation of British forces in June 1940 by thousands of small craft, sailed by British civilians.

Gallipoli: Site of British amphibious assault in World War I in the Crimea—a disaster.

Husky: Amphibious assault of Sicily, July 10, 1943.

Market-Garden: Combined Airborne and Armored assault in Holland, September 17, 1944.

mulberries: Artificial harbors created by the filling of ship hulls with cement and then sinking the hulls. Used in the Normandy invasion.

Overlord: Amphibious assault of Normandy, June 6, 1944.

Sledgehammer: Planned "suicide" mission for September 1942 in northern France—to be used only in the event that the Soviet Union needed immediate relief.

Torch: Amphibious assault of North Africa (at Casablanca, Oran, and Algeirs), November 8, 1942.

U.S. ARMY STRUCTURE IN WORLD WAR II*

Squad: 9–10 men

Platoon: 3 or more squads, 16–44 men

Company: 3 or more platoons, 62–190 men

Battalion: 3 or more companies, 300–1,000 men

Brigade/Regiment: 3 or more battalions, 3,000–5,000 men

Division: 3 or more brigades, 10,000–15,000 men

Corps: 3 or more divisions, 20,000–45,000 men

Army: 3 or more corps, 50,000 or more men

Army Group: 3 or more armies, 100,000 or more men—
Bradley's Twelfth Army Group had more than a million
men in it by the end of the war.

---

* Source: Department of the Army

D-DAY INC. COMMAND STRUCTURE
(AS OF DECEMBER 1944)

BOARD OF DIRECTORS
CEO: Eisenhower

Twelfth Army Group: Bradley   Twenty-first Army Group: Montgomery

First Army: Hodges

Third Army: Patton

Ninth Army: Simpson

BIBLIOGRAPHY

Ambrose, Stephen E. *Band of Brothers: E Company, 506th Regiment, 101st Airborne from Normandy to Hitler's Eagles Nest*. New York: Touchstone, 1992.
——*Citizen Soldiers: The U.S. Army from the Nomandy Beaches to the Bulge to the Surrender of Germany*. New York: Simon & Schuster, 1997.
——*D-Day, June 6, 1944: The Climactic Battle of World War II*. New York: Touchstone, 1994.
——*Eisenhower: Soldier and President*. New York: Touchstone, 1990.
——*The Supreme Commander*. University Press of Mississippi, 1970.
Burns, James MacGregor. *Roosevelt: The Soldier of Freedom*. San Diego, New York, London: Harvest, 1970.
Churchill, Winston S. *Triumph and Tragedy*. New York: Bantam Books, 1953.
Cray, Ed. *General of the Army: George C. Marshall, Soldier and Statesman*. New York: Cooper Square Press, 1990.
Eisenhower, Dwight D. *Crusade in Europe*. Baltimore and London: The Johns Hopkins University Press, 1948.
Goodwin, Doris Kearns. *No Ordinary Time: Franklin and Eleanor Roosevelt: The Home Front in World War II*. New York: Simon and Schuster, 1994.
Korda, Michael. *IKE: An American Hero*. New York: HarperCollins, 2007.
Larrabee, Eric. *Commander in Chief: Franklin Delano Roosevelt, His Lieutenants, and Their War*. New York: Touchstone, 1987.
Meacham, Jon. *Franklin and Winston: An Intimate Portrait of an Epic Friendship*. New York: Random House, 2003.
Penrose, Jane, editor. *The D-Day Companion: Leading Historians Explore History's Greatest Amphibious Assault*. New Orleans: The National D-Day Museum, 2004.
Ryan, Cornelius. *A Bridge Too Far*. New York: Popular Library, 1974.
——*The Longest Day*. New York: Popular Library, 1959.

Web Sites

Academy of Achievement (http://www.achievement.org)

Arlington National Cemetery (http://www.arlingtoncemetery.net)

Bastogne Historical Center Web site (www.bastognehistoricalcenter.be)

The Conference Board (http://www.conference-board.org)

Dwight D. Eisenhower Centennial (http://www.history.army.mil/brochures/Ike/ike.htm)

Dwight D. Eisenhower Foundation (http://www.dwightdeisenhower.com)

Dwight D. Eisenhower Presidential Library and Museum (http://www.eisenhower.archives.gov)

FedEx Web site (http://about.fedex.designcdt.com)

Forbes (http://www.forbes.com)

Ford Motor Company (http://www.ford.com)

Franklin D. Roosevelt Presidential Library and Museum (http://www.fdrlibrary.marist.edu)

George Mason University's History News Network (http://hnn.us)

The *New York Times* (http://www.nytimes.com)

The Society of Corporate Secretaries and Governance Professionals (http://www.governanceprofessionals.org)

United States Holocaust Memorial Museum (http://www.ushmm.org)

Variety (http://www.variety.com/)

The *Wall Street Journal* (http://online.wsj.com)

NOTES

Introduction

1. Stephen E. Ambrose, *The Supreme Commander*, 418.

1: The Pressure Cooker—Start-up

1. Ambrose, *The Supreme Commander*, 55.
2. Eisenhower to Marshall, June 26, 1942, Eisenhower Papers (Ambrose, *The Supreme Commander*, 54).
3. Ambrose, *The Supreme Commander*, 56.
4. Ibid., 57.
5. Stephen E. Ambrose, *Eisenhower: Soldier and President*, 73.
6. Ibid., 77.
7. Cornelius Ryan, *The Longest Day*, 51.
8. Jon Meacham, *Franklin and Winston: An Intimate Portrait of an Epic Friendship*, 177.
9. The Franklin D. Roosevelt Presidential Library and Museum.
10. "Obama, F.D.R. and Taming the Press," *New York Times*, February 2, 2009.
11. Ambrose, *The Supreme Commander*, 73.

2: Lighting the "Torch"

1. Michael Korda, *IKE: An American Hero*, 303.
2. Ambrose, *The Supreme Commander*, 79.
3. Korda, *IKE: An American Hero*, 303.
4. Ambrose, *The Supreme Commander*, 84

5. Dwight D. Eisenhower, *Crusade in Europe*, 82.

6. Ibid., 83.

7. Ambrose, *The Supreme Commander*, 85.

8. Ibid., 93.

9. *Casablanca*, screenplay by Julius J. Epstein, Philip G. Epstein, and Howard Koch.

10. John Q. Barrett, "That One" & "That Man," George Mason University's History News Network, http://hnn.us/articles/55697.html.

11. Dwight D. Eisenhower, speech to the National Defense Executive Reserve Conference, Washington DC, November 14, 1957.

12. "Tylenol Posts an Apparent Recovery," *New York Times*, December 25, 1982.

13. "Company News; Ten Years Later, Coca-Cola Laughs at 'New Coke,'" *New York Times*, April 11, 1995.

14. "Succession Planning: How Everyone Does It Wrong," *Forbes.com*, July 7, 2009.

15. "Charles Bell, 44, Dies; Headed McDonald's," *New York Times*, January 17, 2005, and "No More Bench Strength," November 6, 2007.

16. "iPhone Owners Crying Foul over Price Cut," *New York Times*, September 7, 2007.

17. "Killing the Dream," *Forbes*, September 19, 2005; and "The Forgotten Promise," August 17, 2004.

18. "Afternoon Reading: Saturn Deal Could Be 'Smartest Automotive Move of the Decade,'" *Wall Street Journal*, June 8, 2009.

3: First Op

1. Eisenhower, *Crusade in Europe*, 95.

2. Ibid., 96.

3. Ibid., 103.

4. Ambrose, *The Supreme Commander*, 135.

5. Ambrose, *Eisenhower: Soldier and President*, 87.

6. Ibid., 87.

7. Korda, *IKE: An American Hero*, 353.

8. Eisenhower, *Crusade in Europe*, 115.

9. Ibid., 146.

10. Ibid., 148.

11. "Patton's Career a Brilliant One" (obituary), *New York Times*, December 22, 1945.

12. "Gen. Omar N. Bradley Dead at 88; Last of Army's Five-Star Generals" (obituary), *The New York Times*, April 9, 1981.

13. Eisenhower, *Crusade in Europe*, 215.

14. Ibid., 156.

15. United States Holocaust Memorial Museum, www.ushmm.org/wlc/article. php?lang=en&ModuleId=10007303.

4: Getting Husky

1. Eisenhower, *Crusade in Europe*, 160.

2. The Society of Corporate Secretaries & Governance Professionals, *Current Board Practices, 6th Study*.

3. Eisenhower, *Crusade in Europe*, 159–60.

4. Ibid., 214.

5. Ibid.

6. Ibid., 215.

7. The U.S. Department of Transportation—"Cash for Clunkers" program.

8. Ibid., 208.

9. Korda, *IKE: An American Hero*, 350–51.

10. Eric Larrabee, *Commander in Chief: Franklin Delano Roosevelt, His Lieutenants, and Their War*, 470–71.

11. Korda, *IKE: An American Hero*, 388.

12. Ambrose, *Eisenhower: Soldier and President*, 105.

13. Ibid.

14. Ibid., 106.

15. "Jeffrey Katzenberg, Biography," Variety.com.

16. "Ruling Upholds Disney's Payment in Firing of Ovitz," *New York Times*, August 10, 2005; "Disney 101," *Forbes.com*, August 11, 2005.

17. Eisenhower, *Crusade in Europe*, 176.

18. Ambrose, *Eisenhower: Soldier and President*, 107.

19. Ibid., 110.

20. Korda, *IKE: An American Hero*, 415.

5: Overlord—D-Day: Supreme Commander

1. Korda, *IKE: An American Hero*, 412.

2. Ambrose, *The Supreme Commander*, 303.

3. Ibid., 309.

4. Korda, *IKE: An American Hero*, 431, 434.

5. Ambrose, *The Supreme Commander*, 376.

6. Eisenhower, *Crusade in Europe*, 225.

7. Ambrose, *Eisenhower: Soldier and President*, 145.

8. Ibid.

9. Korda, *IKE: An American Hero*, 465.

10. Ibid., 462.

11. Ambrose, *The Supreme Commander*, 343, 342.

12. Ibid., 343.

13. Eisenhower, *Crusade in Europe*, 225.

14. Ambrose, *The Supreme Commander*, 404.

15. Ambrose, *Eisenhower: Soldier and President*, 128.

16. Ibid., 129.

17. Ambrose, *The Supreme Commander*, 347.

18. Korda, *IKE: An American Hero*, 460.

19. Ambrose, *The Supreme Commander*, 347.

20. "The Sinatra of Southwest Feels the Love," *New York Times*, May 24, 2008.

21. "Southwest Plans Buyouts After a Big Quarterly Loss," *New York Times*, April 16, 2009.

22. *New York Times* Web site: U.S. Markets—Airlines, as of September 16, 2009, http://markets.on.nytimes.com/research/markets/usmarkets/industry.asp?industryStartRow=21.

23. Ambrose, *The Supreme Commander*, 407.

24. Ryan, *The Longest Day*, 57–58.

25. Ambrose, *D-Day, June 6, 1944: The Climactic Battle of World War II*, 180.

26. Ryan, *The Longest Day*, 58.

27. Ambrose, *D-Day, June 6, 1944*, 189.

28. Ibid.

29. Ibid., 183.

30. Ryan, *The Longest Day*, 51.

31. Ambrose, *D-Day, June 6, 1944*, 187.

32. Ibid.

33. Ibid., 188.

34. Ibid., 189.

35. Ibid.

36. Associated Press, "AOL to End Support of Netscape Navigator," December 29, 2007.

37. "Netscape Moves to Raise Stakes in Browser War," *New York Times*, August 19, 1996.

38. Ibid.

39. Ibid.

40. "Netscape May Be Ready to Take on Microsoft Again," *Forbes.com*, April 6, 2000.

41. "State of the Art; Netscape 6 Browser: Mixed Bag," *New York Times*, November 30, 2000.

42. Ambrose, *The Supreme Commander*, 418.

43. Ambrose, *D-Day, June 6, 1944*, 193–94.

44. Ibid., 195.

45. Ibid.

6: Overlord: Actions and Results

1. Korda, *IKE: An American Hero*, 460.

2. Ibid., 479.

3. Ibid., 481.

4. Stephen E. Ambrose, *Citizen Soldiers: The U.S. Army from the Normandy Beaches to the Bulge to the Surrender of Germany*, 34–35.

5. Ambrose, *Eisenhower: Soldier and President*, 146.

6. Ibid., 149.

7. Ibid., 147.

8. Ibid., 148.

9. Ibid., 149.

10. Ibid., 154.

11. Eisenhower, *Crusade in Europe*, 280.

12. Korda, *IKE: An American Hero*, 516.

13. Ambrose, *Eisenhower: Soldier and President*, 158.

14. Ibid., 161.

15. Ibid., 163.

16. Ambrose, *The Supreme Commander*, 515.

17. Ibid.

18. Ibid., 516.

19. Ambrose, *Eisenhower: Soldier and President*, 159.

7: Losing Focus

1. Cornelius Ryan, *A Bridge Too Far*, 89.

2. Ibid., 599.

3. Ibid., 597.

4. Ibid.

5. Eisenhower, *Crusade in Europe*, 310, 312.

6. Ambrose, *The Supreme Commander*, 526.

7. Winston S. Churchill, *Triumph and Tragedy*, 172.

8. "Time Warner Turnaround in 2005?" *Forbes.com*, December 12, 2004.

9. "The Internet Grows Up," *Forbes.com*, January 1, 2000.

10. Ibid.

11. Ibid.

12. "Top Ten Business Blunders," *Forbes.com*, March 10, 2008.

13. "Time Warner's Digital Dilemma," *Forbes.com*, July 29, 2009.

14. Ambrose, *Eisenhower: Soldier and President*, 166–67.

15. Ambrose, *The Supreme Commander*, 534.

16. Ibid.

17. Ibid., 535.

18. Ibid.

19. Ibid.

20. Ibid., 536.

21. Ibid., 537.

22. Ibid.

23. Ibid.

24. Ibid., 538.

25. Korda, *IKE: An American Hero*, 522.

26. Ibid.

27. Ibid., 525.

28. Ambrose, *The Supreme Commander*, 547.

29. Ibid.

30. Korda, *IKE: An American Hero*, 532.

31. Ambrose, *The Supreme Commander*, 548.

32. Korda, *IKE: An American Hero*, 530.

33. Ibid.

34. Ambrose, *The Supreme Commander*, 551.

35. Korda, *IKE: An American Hero*, 533.

36. Eisenhower, speech to the National Defense Executive Reserve Conference.

8: "Nuts"

1. Eisenhower, *Crusade in Europe*, 340.

2. Ambrose, *The Supreme Commander*, 556.

3. Eisenhower, *Crusade in Europe*, 350.

4. Korda, *IKE: An American Hero*, 537.

5. Ibid., 539.

6. Academy of Achievement, http://www.achievement.org/.

7. Ambrose, *Citizen Soldiers*, 52.

8. Ibid., 224.

9. Headquarters, Third U.S. Army, General Orders No. 14 (January 14, 1945), http://www.arlingtoncemetery.net/amcauli.htm.

10. Bastogne Historical Center Web site (www.bastognehistoricalcenter.be).

11. Ambrose, *The Supreme Commander*, 562.

12. Ibid., 565–66.

13. Ambrose, *Eisenhower: Soldier and President*, 177.

14. Ibid.

15. Ibid., 178.

16. Ibid.

17. Ibid., 179.

18. Korda, *IKE: An American Hero*, 546.

19. Ambrose, *Eisenhower: Soldier and President*, 179.

20. Korda, *IKE: An American Hero*, 547.

21. Ambrose, *Eisenhower: Soldier and President*, 180.

22. Ibid.

23. Korda, *IKE: An American Hero*, 547.

24. Ibid., 549.

9: Completing the Mission

1. Eisenhower, *Crusade in Europe*, 366.

2. Ambrose, *Eisenhower: Soldier and President*, 182.

3. Eisenhower, *Crusade in Europe*, 371.

4. Ambrose, *Eisenhower: Soldier and President*, 183.

5. Ibid., 185.

6. Ibid., 186.

7. Eric Larrabee, *Commander in Chief: Franklin Delano Roosevelt, His Lieutenants, and Their War*, 492–93.

8. Eisenhower, *Crusade in Europe*, 372.

9. Korda, *IKE: An American Hero*, 574.

10. Ambrose, *The Supreme Commander*, 659.

11. Larrabee, *Commander in Chief*, 647.

12. Ibid., 501.

13. Ambrose, *Eisenhower: Soldier and President*, 192.

14. Ibid.

15. Ambrose, *Citizen Soldiers*, 457.

16. "Bank of America Chief to Depart at Year's End," *Forbes.com*, October 1, 2009.

17. "Top Ten Business Blunders," *Forbes.com*, March 10, 2008.

18. "Sun's Six Biggest Mistakes," *Forbes.com*, April 7, 2009.

19. Ibid.

20. Ambrose, *Eisenhower: Soldier and President*, 198.

21. Ambrose, *The Supreme Commander*, 667–68.

22. Korda, *IKE: An American Hero*, 586.

10: Performance Evaluation and Summary

1. Larrabee, *Commander in Chief*, 502.

2. Ambrose, *Eisenhower: Soldier and President*, 203.

3. "'Mission Statement' Words," *Forbes.com*, August 21, 2006.

4. Ford Motor Company Web site, http://www.ford.com/about-ford/company-information/one-ford.

5. Dell Web site, http://www.dell.com.

6. FedEx Web site, http://about.fedex.designcdt.com/our_company/company_information/fedex_history.

7. Ibid.

8. Academy of Achievement, http://www.achievement.org/.

9. Ambrose, *The Supreme Commander*, 348.

10. Ibid., 325.

11. Ibid.

ABOUT THE AUTHOR

Geoff Loftus has been gainfully employed in business journalism and corporate communications for more than a quarter century. Working both freelance and on staff, he has worked for Condé Nast, Deloitte Consulting, Fairchild Publications, and News Corp., as well as nonprofit organizations such as the Conference Board and the Society of Corporate Secretaries & Governance Professionals. Like many writers, he once dreamed of writing the great American novel but gave that up in an attempt to write the great American screenplay. The closest he came to that lofty achievement was writing *Hero in the Family* with John Drimmer for *The Wonderful World of Disney*. He has been a member of the Writers Guild of America, East, for more than twenty years. He lives in Scarsdale, New York, with his wife, Margy; son, Gregory; and the family's wonderful little dog, Heidi.

ACKNOWLEDGMENTS

I suspect that many authors have felt the way I do—that I should be thanking just about everyone I've ever met or ever read. Since that's utterly unfeasible, I'll stick to the few people I absolutely have to thank for their help.

First, thanks have to go to my sister Jill Quist, who recognized a good idea when she heard it, helped shape it into a book, and encouraged me every step of the way.

Alice Siempelkamp labored over multiple versions of this book, pushing me to do better. Thanks, Alice. Any failings herein are on me.

Thanks also to my agent, Coleen O'Shea. I am extraordinarily lucky to have her watching over me.

The same is true of my editor, Kristen Parrish, whose excitement for this project showed in every suggestion she made. *Lead Like Ike* is much better thanks to her.

I owe my parents many debts of gratitude but especially for a love of history that made this book possible.

Thanks to the Jesuits, who, to borrow from William Peter Blatty, taught me to think.

In no particular order, thanks to the many friends who have helped me get through writing this book and life itself: Lindy Sittenfeld, Erica Fross, Ted Canellas and Bob Roth, Greg Tobin, Sal Vitale, Gene O'Brien, and Ted West.

Finally and most important, thanks to my wife, Margy, and son, Greg. My life is unimaginable without them.